CW00499074

"I enjoy reading Phil Moore's b
the Christian life with pe

– Nicky

"In taking us straight to the heart of the text, Phil Moore has served us magnificently. We so need to get into the Scriptures and let the Scriptures get into us. The fact that Phil writes so relevantly and with such submission to biblical revelation means that we are genuinely helped to be shaped by the Bible's teaching."

– Terry Virgo

"Fresh. Solid. Simple. Really good stuff."

– R. T. Kendall

"Phil makes the deep truths of Scripture alive and accessible. If you want to grow in your understanding of each book of the Bible, then buy these books and let them change your life!"

***– P J Smyth**, GodFirst Church, Johannesburg, South Africa*

"Most commentaries are dull. These are alive.
*Most commentaries are for scholars. These are for **you**!"*

– Canon Michael Green

"These notes are amazingly good. Phil's insights are striking, original, and fresh, going straight to the heart of the text and the reader! Substantial yet succinct, they bristle with amazing insights and life applications, compelling us to read more. Bible reading will become enriched and informed with such a scintillating guide. Teachers and preachers will find nuggets of pure gold here!"

***– Greg Haslam**, Westminster Chapel, London, UK*

"The Bible is living and dangerous. The ones who teach it best are those who bear that in mind – and let the author do the talking. Phil has written these studies with a sharp mind and a combination of creative application and reverence."

***– Joel Virgo,** Leader of Newday Youth Festival*

"Phil Moore's new commentaries are outstanding: biblical and passionate, clear and well-illustrated, simple and profound. God's Word comes to life as you read them, and the wonder of God shines through every page."

– ***Andrew Wilson***, *Author of* Incomparable *and* If God Then What?

"Want to understand the Bible better? Don't have the time or energy to read complicated commentaries? The book you have in your hand could be the answer. Allow Phil Moore to explain and then apply God's message to your life. Think of this book as the Bible's message distilled for everyone."

– ***Adrian Warnock***, *Christian blogger*

"Phil Moore presents Scripture in a dynamic, accessible and relevant way. The bite-size chunks – set in context and grounded in contemporary life – really make the make the Word become flesh and dwell among us."

– ***Dr David Landrum***, *The Bible Society*

"Through a relevant, very readable, up to date storying approach, Phil Moore sets the big picture, relates God's Word to today and gives us fresh insights to increase our vision, deepen our worship, know our identity and fire our imagination. Highly recommended!"

– ***Geoff Knott***, *former CEO of Wycliffe Bible Translators UK*

"What an exciting project Phil has embarked upon! These accessible and insightful books will ignite the hearts of believers, inspire the minds of preachers and help shape a new generation of men and women who are seeking to learn from God's Word."

– ***David Stroud***, *Newfrontiers and ChristChurch London*

For more information about the Straight to the Heart series, please go to **www.philmoorebooks.com**.
You can also receive daily messages from Phil Moore on Twitter by following **@PhilMooreLondon**.

STRAIGHT TO THE HEART OF

I Thessalonians to Titus

60 BITE-SIZED INSIGHTS

Phil Moore

MONARCH BOOKS

Oxford, UK & Grand Rapids, Michigan, USA

Copyright © 2014 by Phil Moore.
This edition copyright © 2014 Lion Hudson.

The right of Phil Moore to be identified as author of this work has been asserted by him in accordance with the Copyright, Designs and Patents Act 1988.

All rights reserved. No part of this publication may be reproduced or transmitted in any form or by any means, electronic or mechanical, including photocopy, recording or any information storage and retrieval system, without permission in writing from the publisher.

Published by Monarch Books
an imprint of
Lion Hudson plc
Wilkinson House, Jordan Hill Road,
Oxford OX2 8DR, England
Email: monarch@lionhudson.com
www.lionhudson.com

ISBN 978 0 85721 548 2
e-ISBN 978 0 85721 549 9

First edition 2014

Acknowledgments
Scripture quotations taken from the *Holy Bible, New International Version* Anglicised. Copyright © 1979, 1984, 2011 Biblica, formerly International Bible Society. Used by permission of Hodder & Stoughton Ltd, an Hachette UK company. All rights reserved. "NIV" is a registered trademark of Biblica. UK trademark number 1448790. Both 1984 and 2011 versions are quoted in this commentary.
pp. 25–26: Extract from *Mere Christianity* by C. S. Lewis copyright © C. S. Lewis Pte. Ltd. 1942, 1943, 1944, 1952. Reprinted by permission of The C. S. Lewis Company
p. 36: Extract from interview with Billy Graham in *Christianity Today* © 1958 Billy Graham, used by permission, all rights reserved.
p. 40: Extract from *God Knows* by Minnie Louise Haskins. Copyright © Minnie Louise Haskins, 1908. Reproduced by permission of Sheil Land Associates Ltd.

A catalogue record for this book is available from the British Library.

Printed and bound in the UK, April 2014, LH26

This book is for the elders

of Everyday Church, London.

All of us, scrap metal that

God is turning into gold.

CONTENTS

LESSON THREE – TITUS: TRULY FRUITFUL

LESSON FOUR – 1 TIMOTHY: TRULY MATURE

LESSON FIVE – 2 TIMOTHY: TRULY READY

About the *Straight to the Heart* Series

On his eightieth birthday, Sir Winston Churchill dismissed the compliment that he was the "lion" who had defeated Nazi Germany in World War Two. He told the Houses of Parliament that *"It was a nation and race dwelling all around the globe that had the lion's heart. I had the luck to be called upon to give the roar."*

I hope that God speaks to you very powerfully through the "roar" of the books in the *Straight to the Heart* series. I hope they help you to understand the books of the Bible and the message which the Holy Spirit inspired their authors to write. I hope that they help you to hear God's voice challenging you, and that they provide you with a springboard for further journeys into each book of Scripture for yourself.

But when you hear my "roar", I want you to know that it comes from the heart of a much bigger "lion" than me. I have been shaped by a whole host of great Christian thinkers and preachers from around the world, and I want to give due credit to at least some of them here:

Terry Virgo, David Stroud, Dave Holden, John Hosier, Adrian Holloway, Greg Haslam, Lex Loizides and all those who lead the Newfrontiers family of churches. Friends and encouragers, such as Stef Liston, Joel Virgo, Stuart Gibbs, Scott Taylor, Nick Sharp, Nick Derbridge, Phil Whittall, and Kevin and Sarah Aires. Tony Collins, Jenny Ward and Simon Cox at Monarch Books. Malcolm Kayes and all the elders of The Coign Church, Woking.

My fellow elders and church members here at Everyday Church in Southwest London. My great friend Andrew Wilson – without your friendship, encouragement and example, this series would never have happened.

I would like to thank my parents, my brother Jonathan, and my in-laws, Clive and Sue Jackson. Dad – your example birthed in my heart the passion which brought this series into being. I didn't listen to all you said when I was a child, but I couldn't ignore the way you got up at five o' clock every morning to pray, read the Bible and worship, because of your radical love for God and for his Word. I'd like to thank my children – Isaac, Noah, Esther and Ethan – for keeping me sane when publishing deadlines were looming. But most of all, I'm grateful to my incredible wife, Ruth – my friend, encourager, corrector and helper.

You all have the lion's heart, and you have all developed the lion's heart in me. I count it an enormous privilege to be the one who was chosen to sound the lion's roar.

So welcome to the *Straight to the Heart* series. My prayer is that you will let this roar grip your own heart too – for the glory of the great Lion of the Tribe of Judah, the Lord Jesus Christ!

Introduction: God Turns Scrap Metal into Gold

You became imitators of us and of the Lord... so you became a model to all the believers.

(1 Thessalonians 1:6–7)

It has been the dream of every alchemist ever since the dawn of history. Men have searched in vain for a way of turning scrap metal into gold. For all their failed experiments with lead and copper, not one of them succeeded. The only person who knew how to turn scrap metal into gold was a carpenter from Galilee.

Jesus of Nazareth knew how to work with wood, but he preferred to use a different material. He loved to search for weak and unimpressive people on life's scrapheap and to transform the cheap metal of their lives into purest gold. An impulsive fisherman named Peter; a prostitute named Mary; a traitor named Matthew; a cynic named Thomas – the people he chose were of basest metal. Yet after three years with Jesus, they became the golden boys and girls who led a movement that went on to change the world.

The apostle Paul was the consummate example of how God turns scrap metal into gold. He was a Pharisee and a sworn enemy of the Church who did all he could to suffocate the Christian movement in its early days. He was such an unlikely candidate for God's mercy that he reminds Timothy that *"Christ Jesus came into the world to save sinners – of whom I am the worst."*[1] If we want God to turn the scrap metal of our own lives

[1] 1 Timothy 1:15. Paul wants to encourage each of us that our lives can be transformed into gold too.

into gold, Paul is the perfect person to show us how. Jesus took him and transformed him into the writer of the thirteen letters which form half the books of the New Testament.[2]

This commentary covers five of those thirteen letters, and I have not simply grouped them together because they appear together in the New Testament. I have grouped them together because they form a discipleship training school for anyone who wants God to transform their life and use them to save more people from the scrapheap. God inspired Paul to write these five letters so that you and I could be instructed in how to work with God in turning cheap and nasty metal into gold.

Paul never intended to write 1 and 2 Thessalonians. Whenever he planted a church in a city, he always stayed to take his converts through his basic discipleship training school in person. Had his enemies not chased him out of Thessalonica after only three weeks, Paul would have founded a training academy like the ones we read about, in Acts 18 and 19, at the house of Titius Justus in Corinth and at the lecture hall of Tyrannus in Ephesus. It is only because he was forced to flee the city so quickly that he wrote **1 Thessalonians** as the first lesson in his training school, teaching us how to be **true converts**. It is only because he was unable to return that he wrote **2 Thessalonians** as a second lesson, which teaches us how to be **true warriors** for Jesus.

The last three letters that Paul wrote were to individual graduates of the first two lessons in his discipleship training school. Paul stayed longer in Crete than he did at Thessalonica, so he was able to take his converts on the island through the first two lessons in person. He then left behind one of his graduates to take them through lesson three, so his letter to **Titus** lays out the syllabus that we need in order to be **truly fruitful**. Paul teaches Titus how to create churches full of Christians who

---

[2] Paul wrote 13 of the 27 books of the New Testament. We look at the other eight letters in *Straight to the Heart of Romans*, *Straight to the Heart of 1 and 2 Corinthians* and *Straight to the Heart of Galatians to Colossians*.

shine like gold in the sinful scrapyard of the world. If they learn lesson three, he promises in Titus 2:10 that *"in every way they will make the teaching about God our Saviour attractive."*

Paul wrote to another of his graduates a few months later and gave him the syllabus for lesson four in his discipleship training school. He had left Timothy behind at Ephesus, home to one of the largest and most influential churches, so **1 Timothy** explains how his young graduate can help the Ephesians to become **truly mature** in their faith.

Shortly after sending the letter, Paul was arrested and taken in chains to Rome. Before he was executed, he managed to write a final lesson, which completed his discipleship training school: **2 Timothy** acts as Paul's final will and testament in which he assures his converts that they are **truly ready** to continue the work after his death because God has turned the scrap metal of their lives into gold. The Emperor Nero could kill their teacher, but he could not stop a school full of students from going out into the world. Even today, almost 2,000 years after Paul's execution, God still invites us to study these five letters and to learn with the Thessalonians and with Titus and Timothy.

I love these five books of the Bible because they take us straight to the heart of Paul. The New Testament is unique among the holy scriptures of the world for the fact that much of its teaching takes the form of deeply personal letters. God wants to help us to think like Paul, to feel like Paul, to have faith like Paul, and ultimately to make the most of our lives like Paul. God wants to take our own lives from the scrapheap and to transform them into gold, just as he did the life of Paul.

I also love these five books of the Bible because they show us how to transform the lives of others. Acts 9:25 refers literally to Paul's converts as *"his disciples,"* even though they were first and foremost converts of Jesus. It's as if God wants to remind us that he uses people like us to effect his work of transformation. He wants to equip us and use us to create a mighty army of golden men and women who can, in turn, transform the world. Look around you. The world is in desperate need of such an army. For the sake of the hundreds of millions of people who are far from God and from his salvation, let's read these five letters and let's study them well.

The English poet John Milton urged his readers not to doubt that God can transform human lives, *"Of by fire of sooty coal th' empiric alchemist / Can turn, or holds it possible to turn / Metals of drossiest ore to perfect gold."*[3] Likewise, I also urge you not to doubt it as you read these five letters. God has given you a place in his discipleship training school. He has given it to you because he wants to transform your own life and to teach you to transform others.

He has done so because his desire has not changed in the past 2,000 years. He is still the God who loves to turn scrap metal into gold.

[3] John Milton wrote this in 1667 as part of his epic poem *Paradise Lost* (Book 5, lines 439–442).

Lesson One – 1 Thessalonians:

True Converts

God's Extras (1:1–3)

We remember before our God and Father your work produced by faith, your labour prompted by love, and your endurance inspired by hope in our Lord Jesus Christ.

(1 Thessalonians 1:3)

If anybody might have thought they knew how to turn scrap metal into gold, it was Paul. He was an expert in the Jewish Scriptures. He was an apostle and a successful church planter. In the two years before his arrival at Thessalonica in 50 AD, he had planted a dozen churches in Cyprus, Galatia and Philippi.

If anybody else might have thought they knew how to turn scrap metal into gold, it was Silas and Timothy. Silas was an apostle, a Roman citizen and an educated Greek speaker. He was a prophet and he had played a crucial role with Paul in planting the church at Philippi.[1] Timothy was young but he had already made some impressive sacrifices for the Gospel and to be part of Paul's church-planting team.[2]

Together, they had made a formidable team when they arrived at Thessalonica. The capital city of the Roman province of Macedonia boasted a population of over 200,000 people, which made it one of the largest cities in the world, but they were not daunted. By the time Paul and Silas were chased out

---

[1] Acts 15:32; 16:25–40; 1 Thessalonians 2:6. Silas was so good at Greek that he helped Peter write one of his letters (1 Peter 5:12). Silas was the Hebrew form of the Roman name *Silvanus*, which meant *Woody*.

[2] Acts 16:1–3. Circumcision was not just physically painful. It also meant associating with the Jewish race in a Roman Empire which was very anti-Semitic.

of the city three weeks later, they had made enough converts to plant a thriving church. By the time Timothy left a few weeks after that, the church was strong enough to stand on its own two feet without them.[3] If anybody might have thought that they knew how to take people off the pagan scrapheap and turn them into gold, it was Paul, Silas and Timothy.

That's why I find the start of 1 Thessalonians so surprising. The three men who wrote this letter from Corinth in 51 AD do not fool themselves that they played the leading role at Thessalonica. Paul and Silas do not introduce themselves as apostles.[4] They do not boast about their own credentials. They keep the focus on Jesus because Jesus alone played the leading role in the conversion of the Thessalonians. They worked hard with Jesus, but they never forgot that they were simply extras in the drama.

In 1:1, Paul places the focus firmly on Jesus.[5] He tells us that Jesus is distinct from God the Father, but that he is nevertheless the God of the Old Testament. Paul says he is the *Kurios*, the Greek word which is used throughout the Greek Old Testament to translate the Hebrew name *Yahweh*. Jesus is the Lord, the great *I AM* who spoke to Moses at the burning bush, who appeared to Isaiah in the Temple and who finally came to earth as a human being.[6] Paul does not use the word *Christ* as Jesus' surname. It is the Greek translation of the Hebrew word *Messiah*. Paul tells us that Jesus is the Lord and the Anointed One who always plays the leading role in true conversion. Anybody that he uses is simply one of his extras.

In 1:1, Paul also places the focus firmly on the Gospel. He

---

3 We can tell that Timothy stayed on at Thessalonica because he is mentioned in Acts 17:14 but not in 17:10.

4 This is particularly striking here because Paul introduces himself as an apostle in all his letters except for 1 and 2 Thessalonians, Philippians and Philemon.

5 Paul wrote 1 Thessalonians with Silas and Timothy but, as with his other co-authored letters, it is clear throughout that Paul is the main writer.

6 John 12:41 says this explicitly. Jesus was worshipped as Yahweh from the very start of Church history.

always begins his letters with the blessing *"grace and peace to you"* because this is the essence of his Gospel message.[7] Through Jesus' death and resurrection, God has reconciled us to himself and he has granted us a status we do not deserve. He has invited people who live in Thessalonica to make their new home *"in God the Father and the Lord Jesus Christ."* The Gospel makes us citizens of the heavenly city, living in two places at once, through faith in the one who turns scrap metal into gold.[8]

In 1:2–3, Paul places the focus firmly on God's activity. The reason he and his team were able to plant a church so quickly in Thessalonica was that God answered their prayers. Recognizing that they were God's extras had not made them lazy. It had inspired them to cry out to God *always* and *unceasingly*.[9] As a result, we read in 1:4 that God took the initiative, choosing to save many of the Thessalonians whom he loved. Luke tells us in Acts 17:4 that God *"allotted"* certain Thessalonians to the church, and Paul is not embarrassed to talk about God's sovereign right to choose.[10] He is delighted because he knows it means God's extras can never lose. If they pray for God to act, he will never fail to play the starring role in the world's salvation. The God who made the entire universe will hear our prayers and will transform scrap metal into precious gold.

In 1:3, Paul places the focus firmly on God's work in people's hearts. He does not feel the need to browbeat the Thessalonians into working hard, labouring diligently or enduring faithfully.

---

[7] 1 Thessalonians was Paul's second New Testament letter. Two years earlier, in 49 AD, he wrote this opening greeting in full to the Galatians: *"Grace and peace to you from God our Father and the Lord Jesus Christ."*

[8] Paul says this again in 2:14, reminding us that the churches *in* Judea are also *in* Christ Jesus. See also Ephesians 2:6–7 and Philippians 3:20.

[9] Paul returns to the theme of unceasing prayer in 2:13, 3:10 and 5:16–18. He saw no need to rush back to Thessalonica personally because he was so confident that God answers prayer.

[10] The Greek verb *prosklēroō* means *to add by lot* or *to assign by lot*. Acts 17:4 is therefore not just telling us that individuals joined the church, but that individuals were joined by God to the church.

He knows that all these things are simply the natural fruit of anybody who has God's Spirit at work on the inside.[11] Paul simply thanks God for answering his prayers by filling their hearts with the faith that always makes people work hard, with the love that always makes people labour diligently, and with the hope in Jesus that always makes people persevere under pressure.[12] Paul was delighted to see the fruit of his letting God be God and of his being content to act as one of God's extras.

Later on in 5:8, Paul will say more about the power of *faith, hope* and *love* to transform people from the inside out. He will also refer to it in 1 Corinthians 13:13. But these opening verses of 1 Thessalonians should be enough to make us stop and consider whether we truly believe that the Thessalonians were transformed by the grace of God or by the brilliance of Paul. Do we truly believe Paul when he tells us in Acts 14:15 that *"We too are only human, like you"*?

If we do, we will not place the first-century Christians in a different category from ourselves. If we believe that Paul and his team were God's extras, we will expect the same power to be at work in our own lives. We will expect to see as many converts as Paul and to see their lives transformed by God just as rapidly as the lives of the Thessalonians. Are you willing to be one of God's extras and to place the spotlight on his power instead of on yourself? If you are, you are ready to see what God alone can do in a person's life when they let him play the starring role.

---

[11] Paul reinforces this in 1:6 and 4:9 by saying that their joy is *"joy given by the Holy Spirit"* and that they love one another because they *"have been taught by God to love each other."*

[12] The Greek word for *hope* is *elpis*, which means *confident expectation* rather than wishful thinking. Knowing what is stored up for us in heaven (Colossians 1:5) acts as an anchor for our souls (Hebrews 6:18–19).

Chain Reaction (1:4–10)

The Lord's message rang out from you not only in Macedonia and Achaia – your faith in God has become known everywhere.

(1 Thessalonians 1:8)

Jesus didn't tell his followers to plant churches. He didn't tell them to change communities or to lobby governments. He simply told them to go and make disciples. If they made true converts, churches would naturally be planted; if churches were planted, communities would be changed; if communities were changed, governments would listen. True converts always unleash a Gospel chain reaction on the world.

When Paul was converted in 33 AD, it did not look much like an event that was going to change the world. His Pharisee friends were so appalled that they tried to kill him, and many Christians found it hard to accept that *"The man who formerly persecuted us is now preaching the faith he once tried to destroy."*[1] Isolated by his conversion, Paul was catapulted into fourteen years of obscurity in which he studied the Scriptures in Arabia, Syria and Cilicia. At the end of those fourteen years, he looked no different on the outside, but there is nothing more powerful than a person who is truly converted on the inside. His example challenged Silas and Timothy to leave everything to work with him, and together they made radical converts like themselves in Thessalonica. They tell their converts in 1:5–6 that *"You know*

[1] Galatians 1:23. Paul describes the years immediately after his conversion in Galatians 1–2.

how we lived among you for your sake. You became imitators of us and of the Lord."

Many church leaders complain that their congregations do not follow them, but Paul tells us that people always follow their leaders. They may not copy what their leaders say but they never fail to copy what their leaders do. That's the principle of the Gospel chain reaction. What is embodied by church leaders is replicated throughout the church body, and what is embodied by a church is replicated in those around them. If we want to see communities and cities transformed by the Gospel, we need no other plan than the one that Jesus has already given us: Go and make disciples.

Paul and his teammates became radical disciples, so they are able to remind the Thessalonians that they commended the Gospel to them *"not simply with words but also with power, with the Holy Spirit and deep conviction."*[2] Although Paul performed miracles of healing, he is talking here about the miracle of true conversion. He is telling us that when the Thessalonians saw what the Holy Spirit had done in his own heart, it convicted them deeply and made them want to be part of God's Gospel chain reaction too. That's why he and his team refer to *our* Gospel and not just *Jesus'* Gospel.[3] When the Thessalonians saw how completely Paul and his team had embraced the Gospel, they could not resist their call to *"Follow my example, as I follow the example of Christ."*[4]

When the Thessalonians believed the Gospel, they launched the next step in the Gospel chain reaction. Paul knew that they were truly converted because he saw straightaway

[2] Paul is not devaluing the preaching of God's Word, as we will see in 2:13–16. He is simply pointing out that true faith in God's Word is always marked by deep changes to a person's lifestyle.

[3] Paul knows that the Gospel belongs primarily to God the Father (2:2, 8, 9) and to Jesus the Son (3:2). He simply wants to emphasize that we make it our own when we take part in the Gospel chain reaction.

[4] 1 Corinthians 11:1 echoes 1 Thessalonians 1:6. We make disciples by becoming true disciples ourselves.

such obvious fruit in their lives. They were as convicted of sin and as open to the transforming work of the Holy Spirit as he was. They allowed the Gospel to reshape completely their pagan way of thinking, and they let the Lord start turning the scrap metal of their lives into precious gold.[5] When their friends rejected and persecuted them, just as Paul's had, they responded with the same joy that made Paul and Silas sing in their prison cell at Philippi. We cannot work up this kind of joy ourselves; it can only be worked out through the Holy Spirit, which is why it made the non-Christians around them sit up and take the new church's message seriously. Paul and Silas were not alarmed when they were forced to flee the city after only three weeks. They could see from the Thessalonians' joy in the face of suffering that they were truly converted. They had plainly become *"imitators of us and of the Lord."*

The Gospel chain reaction continued. Paul and his team are writing from Corinth, the capital city of the Roman province of Achaia, and they can see the shockwaves of what has happened at Thessalonica all around them 350 miles away. When they planted churches in Berea and Corinth, they were helped by the fact that all of Macedonia and Greece were talking about the changes in Thessalonica.[6] Paul modelled true conversion to the Thessalonians; they modelled true conversion to their city; this resulted in more converts who made the church a model to their entire region. When Paul tells the Thessalonians in 1:8 that *"The Lord's message rang out from you,"* he uses the Greek word *exēcheomai*, which means *to echo forth* like a cry in a dark

[5] The Greek phrase which is translated *deep conviction* in 1:5 is *plērophoria pollē*. It means literally *a great amount of full confidence* that Paul's message was true.

[6] Achaia was the name of the Roman province which comprised the Peloponnese, or southern Greece. *"Macedonia and Achaia"* is therefore roughly equivalent to the whole of modern Greece.

cave, because true conversion fills every corner and crevice of this dark world with the sound of life.[7]

Paul hasn't finished. He tells the Thessalonians that *"your faith in God has become known everywhere."* Paul came to Thessalonica because it commanded the east–west trade route from the Adriatic to the Black Sea and the north–south trade route from the Aegean to Illyricum in modern-day Croatia. Paul has met Illyrian sailors at the port city of Corinth who convince him that the Gospel chain reaction is working fast. Seven years later, Paul could tell the Romans that *"There is no more place for me to work in these regions"* because *"from Jerusalem all the way round to Illyricum, I have fully proclaimed the gospel of Christ."*[8] He had started a chain reaction of true conversion – first in himself, then in his team, then in the Thessalonians, and then across the entire eastern empire.

An anonymous monk lamented in his old age in around 1100 AD that

> *When I was a young man, I wanted to change the world. I found it was too difficult to change the world, so I tried to change my nation. When I found I couldn't change the nation, I began to focus on my town. I couldn't change the town and as an older man, I tried to change my family. Now, as an old man, I realise the only thing I can change is myself, and suddenly I realise that if long ago I had changed myself, I could have made an impact on my family. My family and I could have made an impact on our town. Their impact could have changed the nation and I could indeed have changed the world.*

[7] Paul does not measure the health of a church based on the number of seats filled on Sunday but on how much the Word of God echoes forth from it from Monday through to Sunday.

[8] Paul wrote this in 57 AD in Romans 15:19 and 23.

You are not an old monk so you still have time to learn the principle of the Gospel chain reaction. Paul and his team made radical converts in Thessalonica because they were radical converts themselves. Surrender your life completely to Jesus today and watch him set off a chain reaction in you. Watch him start convicting people around you to change until you can say with Paul and his team: *"You know how we lived among you for your sake. You became imitators of us and of the Lord."*

Turn and Wait (1:9–10)

They tell how you turned to God from idols to serve the living and true God, and to wait for his Son from heaven.

(1 Thessalonians 1:9–10)

One of my sons would be dead had it not been for a quick-witted midwife who spotted a complication during his birth. Sadly, one of my friends has a son who was not so fortunate. He was starved of oxygen at birth and he is still brain-damaged to this day. How a person is born affects their entire life, and Paul tells us that the same is true of being born again. How we are converted affects what type of Christian we become.

C. S. Lewis gave a famous radio broadcast in which he asked *"Is Christianity hard or easy?"* He pointed out the seeming contradiction between Jesus' command that his followers must take up their cross and die, and his promise that following him is an easy yoke and a light burden. He argued that there is no contradiction. If we surrender everything to Jesus at conversion, the Christian life is easy, but if we only surrender conditionally, the Christian life is a daily nightmare.

> *Cutting the grass may keep it short: but I shall still produce grass and no wheat. If I want to produce wheat, the change must go deeper than the surface. I must be ploughed up and re-sown... It is hard; but the sort of compromise we are all hankering after is harder – in fact, it is impossible. It may be hard for an egg to turn*

into a bird: it would be a jolly sight harder for it to learn to fly while remaining an egg.[1]

Paul understood this. That's why he preached the Gospel in a way that forced people to follow Jesus fully or not at all. Thessalonica was a major world trade centre, since it boasted one of the greatest natural harbours in the Aegean Sea and controlled the Egnatian Way, which carried freight by land from the Adriatic to the Black Sea, so it had attracted a large community of Jewish merchants. Acts 17 tells us that Paul went to this Jewish community first, showing them that their Old Testament Scriptures prophesied that the Messiah would be crucified and raised from the dead. Then he offended their Jewish sensibilities by telling them that the murderers in the prophecies were the members of their own Sanhedrin. Only a minority of Jews could stomach this message, but Paul was not concerned. The Church's biggest danger has never been too few converts but too many false ones. Paul wanted people to turn from their old way of living and to the Lord, or he didn't want them to pretend to believe at all.

Even as Paul's teaching offended many Jews in the city, it attracted pagans in even greater number. Acts tells us that there were many *"God-fearing Greeks"* in the city – in other words, uncircumcised pagans who believed in Yahweh but who had not converted to Judaism – and Paul's message helped them to put their finger on what was lacking in first-century Judaism. Paul offended them as much as he had done the Jews by telling them that following Jesus meant confessing that their Greek idols were lifeless and that the pagan worldview of Socrates and Plato was in fact folly.[2] He told them that they could not follow Jesus unless they sacrificed all they held most dear. It was a

---

[1] Broadcast in 1943, C. S. Lewis published it as a chapter in his book *Mere Christianity* in 1952.

[2] Acts 14:15, 17:29–30 and 19:26 show that this was Paul's consistent message whenever he preached to pagans.

price that many of them were willing to pay, so Paul celebrates in 1:9–10 that *"you turned to God from idols to serve the living and true God."* Christian conversion means turning *from* serving false gods and turning *to* serve the true God instead.

Imagine a speedboat without an engine. That's what it's like when we confess sin but do not turn *to* Jesus as Lord. Paul describes our relationship to God by using the Greek word *douleuō*, which means *to serve as a slave*, because he wants us to grasp that Christian freedom means deciding to become a slave of God. If we point our hearts towards obedience, God will fill us with his Holy Spirit and empower us to cut through the waves of life and to experience the thrill of full-throttle Christianity. If we swing between obedience and disobedience, however, God loves us far too much to entrust us with heaven's power. One of the ways in which he convicts us that our conversion is false is by making our lives feel like a speedboat without an engine.

Now imagine that same speedboat with a powerful engine but still tethered to its moorings. That's what it's like when we turn *to* God but fail to turn *from* our former idols. Even sins that have been forgiven will hold us back from enjoying life as God intends unless we renounce them and allow Jesus to free us from them (John 8:34–36). Turning to Jesus while clinging on to our pre-conversion thinking is like powering up the engine on a speedboat but leaving it tethered to the bank – we may sound noisy and impressive but we will never go anywhere. We need to turn to God and *from* false idols. Then we become like an untied speedboat zooming forward at full throttle.

Acts 17 tells us that the Jews chased Paul and his team out of Thessalonica because they were jealous of what was happening among the pagans. They were furious that Greeks were receiving the power of God without tethering themselves to the Jewish idols of circumcision and Law-keeping.[3] Paul and

[3] Paul explains in Ephesians 5:5 that things do not need to look like Greek gods to be idols. Any false priority that gets in the way of complete surrender to Jesus, however good, is in fact a detestable idol.

Silas left quickly to stop their new converts from getting caught up in a wave of bitter persecution, but by the time they wrote from Corinth they had heard the news that their converts were being persecuted all the same. That's why they end this chapter by reminding them that true Christian conversion is about waiting as well as turning.

Paul's letters to the Thessalonians are sometimes referred to as the "eschatological epistles" because he fills these letters with encouragements to fix our eyes on how world history is going to end. This hope strengthened us in 1:3 and it strengthens us again here in 1:10. God calls us to *"wait for his Son from heaven, whom he raised from the dead – Jesus, who rescues us from the coming wrath."* True surrender to Jesus means living for the Day when he will return to judge the world. It will be a day of vindication for true converts and a day of shame and exposure for those who have merely playacted as Christians. Paul ends each of the five chapters of 1 Thessalonians with a reminder that this Day is coming. True conversion is costly at the outset but thereafter it is easy. False conversion is easy at the outset but thereafter it is painful, right up until the moment of intense pain and horror when Jesus returns to expose every lie.

C. S. Lewis concludes that turning from our old priorities and waiting for Jesus to return is not a purer kind of Christianity, but the only kind: *"What I want to make clear is that this is not one among many jobs a Christian has to do; and it is not a sort of special exercise for the top class. It is the whole of Christianity. Christianity offers nothing else at all."*

Big Stakes (2:1–12)

We speak as those approved by God to be entrusted with the gospel. We are not trying to please people but God, who tests our hearts.

(1 Thessalonians 2:4)

Last weekend I went for a walk through the park with my youngest son. We played a game in which we tried to push over some massive trees which were over fifty years old. Of course they did not budge, but it would have been very different if we had gone there when they were little saplings. Unless the park keeper had tied them to a big stake, even my young son would have been able to topple them to the ground.

Paul spent the first chapter of 1 Thessalonians describing true conversion and the power it unleashes in a Gospel chain reaction. Christians often forget this but the Devil doesn't, which is why Paul spends the second and third chapters of 1 Thessalonians exposing five ruses by which the Devil tries to neutralize God's work in the hearts of believers. Put more positively, if we are wise to these five tricks, even the Devil knows he cannot stop us from growing up strong and fruitful. He can no more thwart God's work in our lives than a little boy can topple a massive tree.

Paul warns us against the first of the Devil's ruses in 2:1–12. New Christians are very vulnerable to the winds of false teaching, of disappointments, of doubts and of emotional highs and lows, so they need to be supported by strong Christian leaders in the same way that saplings are supported by big stakes in the ground.[1] We can tell that the Devil had tried this ruse on the Thessalonians because Paul launches into an impassioned defence of his ministry. One of the downsides of the city's democratic system of government was that most Thessalonians had little respect for their elected leaders. The Devil had used this to promote cynicism towards Paul and his team, using their individualism to make them claim to be slaves of Jesus who did not owe allegiance to any human leader. Paul acts quickly because he knows that, detached from his strong support, his converts in Thessalonica will be toppled very quickly.

Paul addresses their doubts about his leadership by reminding them of *his love towards them.* Children become strong adults under the care of loving parents, and converts become strong Christians under the care of loving leaders. Paul and his teammates remind the Thessalonians in 2:1 and 2:9 that they are all *"brothers and sisters."* They remind the Thessalonians in 2:7 that they cared for them tenderly like *"a nursing mother,"* and in 2:11–12 that *"we dealt with each of you as a father deals with his own children, encouraging, comforting and urging you."*[2] If you are ever tempted to think you do not need to become a member of a particular church under the care of particular leaders, these verses are for you. This family talk reminds us that no Christian becomes strong in their faith without being staked to spiritual brothers and sisters and fathers and mothers. We need to resist the Devil's ruse if we are to become the mighty oaks of righteousness which Isaiah 61:3 says that Jesus' followers ought to be.

Paul also addresses their doubts about his leadership by reminding them of *his commitment to the truth.* He and his

[1] Paul uses the Greek word *antechomai* in 5:14 to describe strong Christians *supporting* weak Christians. This was a word used by ancient Greek gardeners to describe the stakes that supported sapling trees.

[2] Note the perfect balance between a mother's love and a father's toughness. Love without toughness indulges sin. Toughness without love provokes rebellion. Healthy Christians need to receive both.

teammates had arrived at Thessalonica after being beaten and imprisoned at Philippi, the other leading city of Macedonia. They had encountered fierce opposition from the Jews at Thessalonica but they had refused to stop preaching the Gospel because they cared more for what God thought about them than for public opinion. Paul reminds the Thessalonians in 2:9 that he and his team worked harder for the Lord than any earthly slave works for his master. Theirs was a merchant city, but he poured out his money, time and energy to preach the truth for free.[3] He and his teammates are the perfect stake to which the Thessalonians ought to bind themselves because they have proved themselves to be strong and straight preachers of the truth.

Paul also addresses their doubts about his leadership by reminding them of his *lifestyle while he was among them*. His enemies might accuse him of trying to trick people like a fisherman baiting his hook, but God knows that Paul and his teammates never used flattery or hid behind masks while they were among them.[4] They behaved with such integrity that the Thessalonians must confess with God *"how holy, righteous and blameless we were among you who believed."* His enemies might accuse him of acting like a dictator, but the Thessalonians know that he refused to assert his authority as an apostle, preferring instead to win them over willingly by teaching them as gently as a child.[5] His enemies might accuse him of being greedy for their

[3] It appears that Paul worked by night as a tentmaker in Thessalonica in order to fund his church-planting ministry during the day (Acts 18:3; 2 Thessalonians 3:7–10).

[4] Paul uses a similar word to the one he uses in 2:4 when he tells Timothy to act as an approved workman in 2 Timothy 2:15. Paul is giving us a general example here for every Christian leader to follow.

[5] Some people argue that the Greek word *apostoloi* should be translated *missionaries* in 2:6–7, but there is no reason to do so unless it is to deny Ephesians 4:11 by restricting apostleship to Paul and the Twelve. Although Timothy appears not to have been an apostle (2 Corinthians 1:1; Colossians 1:1), it appears that Silas was, just like Barnabas (Acts 14:14) and James (Galatians 1:19).

money, but the Thessalonians know how hard he and his team worked to avoid placing any burden on their converts.[6]

The Devil loves to slander faithful leaders because he is the father of lies and because he knows it drives a wedge between sapling Christians and the mature leaders they need to help them to grow up straight and strong.[7] He loves to estrange children from their parents and Christians from their leaders. We must not let him do so.

The Devil failed to detach the Thessalonians from Paul. He is able to urge them at the end of these twelve verses *"to live lives worthy of God."* He is not telling them to try to earn God's approval through their lifestyle, since he uses this same Greek word *axios* in 2 Thessalonians 1:3 to mean *"rightly so."* He is simply urging them to grow up straight and strong and in keeping with the calling that they have received to rule with Christ. The Thessalonians realized that everything was staked upon their being staked to Paul.[8] We need to be equally wise to the Devil's ruse. Hold onto the church leaders God has given you and trust God to use them to grow you into Christian maturity.

[6] Paul says literally in 2:6 that *we could have been weighty* – either in using their authority or in placing demands on their converts. They refused to burden them like the idlers in 5:14 and 2 Thessalonians 3:6–12.

[7] Jesus tells us in John 8:44 that the Devil speaks his native language whenever he lies and slanders.

[8] Paul also uses the word *axios* to say something similar in 2 Thessalonians 1:11, Ephesians 4:1, Philippians 1:27 and Colossians 1:10. Our lifestyle should be in keeping with the grace that God has lavished upon us.

Soil (2:8–12)

We cared for you. Because we loved you so much, we were delighted to share with you not only the gospel of God but our lives as well.

(1 Thessalonians 2:8)

Paul didn't have to tell his converts at Thessalonica to commit themselves to a single local church. There was only one church in the city and every Christian chose to be part of it. Instead, he had to warn them to make sure that they were more than just nominal members. Trees cannot grow strong without being deeply rooted in soil, and Christians cannot grow strong without sharing their lives deeply with one another.

Jesus had modelled this with his twelve disciples. Mark 3:14 tells us that he called them *"that they might be with him"*, dropping other priorities in order to spend time with one another. It was only after three years of sharing life together that he sent them out into the world. That's what discipleship means. It's how God turns the scrap metal of our lives into gold.

If anybody might have thought that he could transform lives through the Gospel alone without planting people in the soil of a local church, it was Paul. Much of our understanding of the Gospel comes from his letters, so it is hard to think of anyone in Church history who has understood the Gospel better than Paul. Nevertheless, he warns us in 2:8–12 that the Devil's second ruse is to draw Christians out onto the margins of the church in which God has planted them. In Western cities, this is particularly easy because there are so many good churches and so many great sermons to download remotely from church websites all around the world. It is easy to shop around for Christian fellowship in the same way as we look for bargains in different grocery stores. We need to listen to Paul's statement in 2:8 that people get discipled best in the context of community: *"We cared for you. Because we loved you so much, we were delighted to share with you not only the gospel of God but our lives as well."*

One of the earliest Christian revivals in Europe was led by Benedict of Nursia. He grew disillusioned with the way that many Christians took advantage of the many churches in their cities to avoid accountability to one another. If a believer was challenged over their walk with God, they avoided the challenge by simply switching to a different church. Benedict of Nursia spearheaded a reaction to this, which became known as monasticism. In his *Rule of Saint Benedict*, which was written in around 530 AD and which has been used as a handbook for monasteries ever since, he commanded monks to take a vow of *"stability"* with one another.[1] Stability means being rooted. This was a sixth-century way of recognizing that an essential aspect of our growth as Christians is a commitment to share our lives with one another. Churches act as the soil in which we can grow strong through our interactions with one another. The Church historian Mark Noll argues that this recommitment to deep Christian community resulted in the greatest revival of the Middle Ages.[2]

If every Christian needs to guard against the Devil's second ruse to make us self-sufficient islands, cut off from the mainland of God's People, church leaders face a particular challenge. They face a subtle temptation to cut themselves off from the people God has tasked them with strengthening. When I first became a church leader I was told by an elderly vicar that he had strenuously avoided making deep friendships with anyone

[1] *The Rule of St Benedict* (chapter 58).

[2] Mark Noll in *Turning Points: Decisive Moments in the History of Christianity* (1997).

in his congregation during fifty years of ministry. Familiarity breeds contempt, he warned me, sounding like an aloof colonel in some far-flung corner of the British Empire. He warned me that friendships with people in the congregation would inevitably undermine the authority of a leader. He could hardly have sounded more different from Paul and his teammates: *"Because we loved you so much, we were delighted to share with you not only the gospel of God but our lives as well."*

Robert Coleman writes:

> *The church obviously has failed at this point, and failed tragically. There is a lot of talk in the church about evangelism and Christian nurture, but little concern for personal association when it becomes evident that such work involves the sacrifice of personal indulgence... Unless new Christians, if indeed they are saved, have parents and friends who will fill the gap in a real way, they are left entirely on their own to find the solutions to innumerable practical problems confronting their lives, any one of which could mean disaster to their new faith. With such haphazard follow-up of believers, it is no wonder that about half of those who make professions and join the church eventually fall away or lose the glow of a Christian experience, and fewer still grow in sufficient knowledge and grace to be of any real service to the Kingdom. If Sunday services and membership training classes are all that a church has to develop young converts into mature disciples, then they are defeating their own purpose...*
>
> *There is simply no substitute for getting with people, and it is ridiculous to imagine that anything less, short of a miracle, can develop strong Christian leadership. After all, if Jesus, the Son of God, found it necessary to stay almost constantly with his few disciples for three years,*

and even one of them was lost, how can a church expect to do this job on an assembly line basis a few days out of the year?[3]

Billy Graham, one of the greatest evangelists of the twentieth century, agrees. In the early days of his ministry, before anybody knew how much impact his life would have on the world, he was asked how he would go about trying to change a large city. He replied that

> *I think one of the first things I would do would be to get a small group of eight or ten or twelve men around me that would meet a few hours a week and pay the price! It would cost them something in time and effort. I would share with them everything I have, over a period of a couple of years. Then I would actually have twelve ministers among the laymen who in turn could take eight or ten or twelve more and teach them. I know one or two churches that are doing that, and it is revolutionizing the church. Christ, I think, set the pattern.*[4]

Mothers and fathers share their lives with their children. As a result, their children grow. Church leaders need to be able to say with Paul in 2:9–10: *"Surely you remember... You are witnesses... of how holy, righteous and blameless we were among you who believed."*

Every Christian needs to find such leaders and to make whatever promise of stability best reflects the teaching of Benedict of Nursia today. Roving believers do not grow into mature disciples. We all need to be rooted in a specific patch of soil. We need to find spiritual parents and brothers and sisters with whom we can share our Christian lives.

---

[3] Robert Coleman in *The Master Plan of Evangelism* (1963).

[4] Billy Graham speaking in an interview in the October 1958 edition of *Christianity Today* magazine.

Light (2:13–16)

When you received the word of God, which you heard from us, you accepted it not as the word of men, but as it actually is, the word of God.

(1 Thessalonians 2:13)

Shortly after I started working for a church, I went rabbit hunting on my father-in-law's farm. Don't get offended if you are a vegetarian. I didn't manage to kill a single rabbit with my air rifle. All I did was learn about the third ruse that Paul tells us the Devil uses to stop Christians from growing into mature believers.

I had been praying and fasting that God would use me to make an impact on my community. In my naivety, I assumed that the way that this would happen was by God giving me a download of power from the Holy Spirit without my needing to do anything myself. The onus was entirely on him. All I needed was for him to give me the same ammunition that he gave to Paul in Thessalonica. After several hours of shooting at rabbits to no effect, I hit one so squarely that there was no doubt I had hit it. The rabbit sprang back in surprise, looked at me accusingly, then carried on eating the contents of my father-in-law's field. I suddenly realized that I had been hitting rabbits all morning but my air rifle was too small a calibre to do anything more than annoy them.

At the very moment that I was trying to kill one of his creatures, I felt God speak to me. It marked a complete turning point in my life and ministry. I suddenly realized that I was asking God for ammunition when the barrel of my life was too small for me to handle any more power than he had already given me. The following morning I woke up two hours before my children and started studying the Bible in order to increase the size of the bullets I could handle. I did the same thing almost every day for the next five years, teaching myself Greek and Hebrew along the way, and one of the results is the *Straight to the Heart* series of Bible commentaries. As I pored over the Scriptures, I discovered what Paul means when he tells us in 2:13 that the Thessalonians grew as Christians because they accepted *"the word of God... not as the word of men, but as it actually is, the word of God."* The Devil is not afraid of passive prayers for ammunition, but he is petrified of believers who study the Bible and increase the size of the ammunition that God can give them.

The churches in Judea understood this. The Jewish Christians had been drilled from a young age in the importance of learning the Old Testament Scriptures. Jesus had warned the teachers of the Law that *"You study the Scriptures diligently because you think that in them you have eternal life. These are the very Scriptures that testify about me, yet you refuse to come to me to have life"*[1] – but when Jews converted to Christ they studied the Scriptures more instead of less. They didn't throw out spiritual discipline along with their dry academia. They redeemed it by developing such a high calibre of understanding about God's character and ways that God used them to fire Gospel bullets that reached as far as Macedonia.

Paul was a Jewish believer, and he spent the first nine years after his conversion studying the Scriptures in Arabia and Tarsus.[2] He tells us in Romans 16:25–26 that his understanding

[1] John 5:39–40. Jesus was not telling them to stop studying the Scriptures. Far from it. He also warned in Matthew 22:29 that *"You are in error because you do not know the Scriptures or the power of God."*

[2] We are told a little about these nine years of obscurity in Galatians 1:17–18 and Acts 9:30 and 11:25. In Paul's letters, we benefit from the astonishing insights that he gleaned from the Old Testament Scriptures.

of the Gospel and his passion to share it with the pagans stemmed from the things that the Holy Spirit revealed to him as he read the Old Testament prophets. He tells us in Romans 15:20–22 that he received clarity while reading Isaiah 52:15 that he was to pour out his life preaching the Gospel to the unreached cities of the world. It is easy to assume that Paul was so effective because he received a sudden download of God's power quite by chance, but the New Testament insists that if we want God to entrust us with bigger bullets, we need to increase the calibre of our understanding. Trees need light to grow strong and tall. In the same way, Christians need to be enlightened by studying the Bible and by treating it as the Word of God. If we do so, we will be able to handle the heavenly firepower that God longs to give us.

Timothy also grew strong by exposing his heart and mind to the light of God's Word. Paul did not include him in his team because of his courage or his talents. He chose him because his Jewish mother and grandmother had instilled in him such a passion for God's Word that Paul saw *"from infancy you have known the Holy Scriptures, which are able to make you wise for salvation through faith in Christ Jesus."*[3]

Paul praises the Thessalonians for imitating the example of the Jewish Christians, as they saw it in the lives of Paul and Timothy.[4] They understood that their pagan background meant they needed to study the Jewish Scriptures in earnest, which is why Paul rejoices in 1:6 that *"You became imitators of us and of the Lord, for you welcomed the message."*[5] Unlike their Jewish neighbours who drove out Paul without checking against God's

[3] Acts 16:1; 2 Timothy 1:5; 3:15.

[4] When church leaders treat the Bible as the very words of God, others follow their lead. If preachers want people to take the Word of God seriously, they must not apologize for it themselves!

[5] Since the Greek word *logos* in 1:6 and 2:13 simply means the *word* or *message*, it could refer to the Gospel rather than to the Old Testament Scriptures. However, Paul makes it clear in 4:8 that he expects the Thessalonians to accept the whole of his teaching as the very words of God.

Word what he said, these pagan converts resisted the third ruse of the Devil.[6] They grew tall and strong through the daily enlightenment that comes from God's Word.[7] The calibre of their understanding grew so large that God was able to use them to fire Gospel bullets into many unreached regions of the pagan world.

On the eve of World War One, the British foreign secretary Sir Edward Grey remarked that *"The lamps are going out all over Europe, we shall not see them lit again in our lifetime."*[8] The Devil is performing the same trick today in the hearts of many believers. A recent British survey suggests that only a third of Christians read the Bible every day and that less than two-thirds read the Bible in any given week. Sixty per cent of those who read the Bible confess that they understand so little that it does not change their lives.[9]

But on the eve of World War Two, another British statesman told a very different story. King George VI told his subjects that *"I said to the man who stood at the Gate of the Year, 'Give me light that I may tread safely into the unknown.' And he replied, 'Go out into the darkness and put your hand into the hand of God. That shall be better to you than light, and safer than a known way.'"*[10] If we treat the Bible as the Word of God and put our hand into his hand by reading it every day, we will grow strong like trees in sunlight. We will avoid the Devil's third trick to stop the scrap metal of our lives being turned into gold.

---

[6] Acts 17:11 says that the Berean Jews were unlike the Thessalonian Jews because *"they received the message with great eagerness and examined the Scriptures every day to see if what Paul said was true."* Paul warns that God will judge the Thessalonian Jews for trying to block out from the pagans the light of God's Word.

[7] Paul tells us in 2:13 that the Word of God is as active in our hearts as sunlight is in the leaves of a tree. He tells us that it *"is at work in you who believe."*

[8] He recorded this in his memoirs, entitled *Twenty-Five Years 1892–1916*.

[9] All of this data is taken from a UK survey by the Bible Society in 2008 entitled *Taking the Pulse*.

[10] King George VI said this in his Christmas Day broadcast in 1939. He was quoting from a poem by Minnie Haskins entitled *God Knows*.

Warmth (2:17–3:10)

Brothers and sisters, when we were orphaned by being separated from you… out of our intense longing we made every effort to see you.

(1 Thessalonians 2:17)

Every gardener knows that young saplings need to be kept warm if they are to survive and thrive. It therefore isn't particularly surprising that Paul tells us the same is also true of Christians. What is surprising, however, is the forcefulness with which he pleads with us not to fall for this fourth ruse of the Devil. Having already warned us to commit ourselves to a local church and to its leaders, he now emphasizes the importance of deep Christian friendship within the church. He uses the warmth of his own friendships to urge any believer who does not have similar friendships to come in from the cold.

In 2:17, Paul surprises us by the intensity of his desire for close Christian friendship. Having likened the Thessalonian believers to his children earlier in the chapter, he mixes his metaphors by telling them that being separated from them in Corinth feels as painful as being orphaned.[1] His enemies might tell them that he sent Timothy to see them because his heart had moved on to other projects, but Paul assures them that nothing could be further from the truth. *"Out of our intense longing we made every effort to see you"*, he tells them. Paul was not a spiritual loner and nor must we be. The warmth of his

---

[1] The Greek word *aporphanizō* was only used for children losing their parents, never the other way around.

language ought to challenge us to pursue deeper friendships with other Christians.

In 2:18, Paul surprises us by treating Christian friendship as a spiritual battle. We might have expected him to tell the Thessalonians that he could not return to their city because it would mean his friends losing the money they had posted for him as bail.[2] We might have expected him to tell them that he could not return because he was too busy planting churches in Berea, Athens and Corinth. But instead he tells them that *"Satan blocked our way,"* because the Devil sees the importance of deep Christian friendships, even if we do not. If he cannot keep us from church and from listening to the preaching of church leaders, he will try to cool our friendships with other believers. We are warned in 1 Peter 5:8 that *"Your enemy the devil prowls around like a roaring lion looking for someone to devour,"* and this is one of the main ways in which he tries to pick off sheep from the edge of the flock. Make no mistake about it. The Devil is trying hard to rob you of friendships with other Christians in order to hinder God's work in your life.

In 2:19–20, Paul surprises us by treating Christian friendship as something glorious, which will last forever. He does not see his relationships with the Thessalonians as incidental details in his life. He sees them as something that will affect his experience of eternity. He tells the Thessalonians that when Jesus returns, they will be his victory crown (the Greek word *stephanos* in 2:20 was used for the laurel crowns that were won by victors in the Olympic Games), because the Thessalonians are a key part of the hope, joy and glory that he will experience on that Day.[3] We will not be faceless nobodies throughout eternity.

---

2 If the bail paid by the Christian leaders at Thessalonica in Acts 17:9 included a restraining order against spending time with Paul and Silas, it would explain why only Timothy stayed on in the city.

3 Paul uses the Greek word *parousia* to refer to the sudden *arrival* of Jesus in 2:19, 3:13, 4:15 and 5:23 and in 2 Thessalonians 2:1 and 2:8. This was the word that was used to refer to a state visit by the emperor.

We will be aware of our friendships on earth. Being too busy to invest in warm friendships with Christians now means we are too busy with this world to invest in one of the few things that will last forever.[4]

In 3:1–5, Paul surprises us by telling us that the Devil works hard to tempt us to neglect warm friendships with other Christians. He calls the Devil *"the tempter"* in 3:5 and says that he preferred to work in Athens without Timothy rather than risk allowing the Devil to drive a wedge into his friendships with the Thessalonians.[5] *"We could stand it no longer... I could stand it no longer... I was afraid"*, he writes without any attempt to hide his feelings. He does not see Christian fellowship as a quick cup of tea after a church service. He sees it as the only thing strong enough to enable us to survive the persecution that is coming.[6] The Roman legions were only able to repulse the barbarian hordes because they were trained to stand strong together. In the same way, Christians can only withstand persecution if they stand shoulder-to-shoulder as dear friends.

In 3:6–10, Paul surprises us by the amount that he believes warm Christian friendships help us to grow. It isn't surprising that he believes that his being with the Thessalonians will encourage them, telling them in 3:10 that *"Night and day we pray most earnestly that we may see you again and supply what is lacking in your faith."* But what is surprising is how much he believes that they will also encourage him, despite the fact that they are new believers and he is an apostle. He tells them that simply hearing news from them via Timothy has so encouraged him, has brought him such joy and has made him so thankful

---

[4] Just like all the other chapters in 1 Thessalonians, chapter 2 ends with a reference to Jesus' second coming. Whatever else we teach new converts, we must teach them to live for Jesus' return and for the age to come.

[5] Paul left Silas and Timothy in Berea while he preached in Athens (Acts 17:14), and when they arrived he sent Timothy back to Thessalonica (Acts 18:5).

[6] Unless we prepare new Christians for persecution and trials, they will quickly fall away from their newfound faith (Matthew 13:20–21; Mark 13:13). The apostles therefore did so in Acts 14:22 and 1 Peter 4:12.

that he feels as though *"now we really live."*[7] If even Paul needed to be strengthened in his faith through his warm friendships with other Christians, we are crazy to expect that we can ever grow strong as believers on our own.

This is the thinking that made Paul consider it the gravest punishment for a troublemaker to be excluded from his friendships with people in the church. It is why he describes such action as *handing a person over to Satan* in 1 Corinthians 5:5 and 1 Timothy 1:20. So let's not allow foolishness or laziness or shyness to rob us of the thing that Paul prized so highly as a source of great growth for his converts. Let's not fool ourselves that church meetings and great Bible teaching can replace what is found in Christian small groups or in deep Christian friendships. God didn't send us a message; he sent us a Messiah. He didn't invite us to join a programme, but a person. He didn't give us a form to fill in, but a family to call our own.

Trees cannot grow strong without warmth and nor can we grow strong without warm and loving friendships with other believers. If you do not have relationships like those Paul describes in these verses, he urges you to come in from the cold.

[7] Paul uses the Greek word *euangelizō* in its normal secular sense in 3:6 when he says that Timothy has *brought good news* from the Thessalonians. This reminds us that the Gospel gladdens people by telling them as much about the great things Jesus saves us *for* as it does the horrific fate he saves us *from*.

Roots (3:10–13)

May the Lord make your love increase and overflow for each other and for everyone else, just as ours does for you.

(1 Thessalonians 3:12)

Nobody ever sees a tree drinking water. That's because it does so through its roots deep underground. We cannot see it drinking but we know that it has done so from the way in which the water, rich in minerals, makes it strong on the inside. The fifth ruse of the Devil targets the secret devotional life of Christians. Paul reminds us that we need to ensure we are strengthened by God as he works beneath the surface in our hearts.

In 3:10, Paul and his team remind us for the third time in as many chapters that all of their public successes in Thessalonica were due to private prayer. They told their converts in 1:2 that *"We always thank God for all of you and continually mention you in our prayers."* They told them in 2:13 that *"We also thank God continually because... the word of God... is indeed at work in you who believe."* Now they tell them in 3:10 that *"Night and day we pray most earnestly that we may see you again and supply what is lacking in your faith."* It is easy to admire Paul's success at making disciples, yet he doesn't want us to admire him; he wants us to copy him. If we want to be as fruitful as Paul in public, we need to learn to pray like him in private.

It is easy to make Christians feel guilty that they don't pray enough, but that is not what Paul is trying to do. He is simply imitating the way that Jesus spent a sleepless night in prayer in Luke 6:12 before choosing his twelve disciples. He is simply reminding us that Jesus was only confident that the Church would succeed in its first weeks and months because he could tell Peter in Luke 22:32 that *"I have prayed for you, Simon, that your faith may not fail."* Paul is simply inviting us to grasp what the disciples did when they concluded in Luke 11:1 that their biggest request of Jesus should be *"Lord, teach us to pray."* If Jesus had to draw strength from his Father in private prayer to sustain his public ministry, so must we.

Paul is encouraging us to follow the example of the first Christians. The Greek word he uses in 3:10 for God *supplying* what is lacking in our faith is *katartizō*, which means literally *to mend* or *to repair*. It is the same word that is used in Matthew 4:21 and Mark 1:19 to describe the disciples mending their fishing nets before Jesus called them to be his disciples. Every fisherman knew that mending nets was essential to catching fish. If a fisherman neglected this unglamorous work behind the scenes, he would catch few fish and even the ones he caught would quickly swim away. Paul wants us to grasp what Peter and John grasped instinctively. Our effectiveness in public for Jesus will only be as great as our willingness to let Jesus strengthen us in private.[1]

In 3:12, Paul reminds us that we can only be strong if we are deeply rooted in Jesus. Only he can make our hearts overflow with love for one another and for the unsaved world.[2] Our biggest need is not better worship songs to help us love God more, or better church programmes to help us love one another more, or better outreach strategies to help us love the lost more. Our biggest need is for God to pour out his love into our hearts

---

[1] We are told about Paul's public ministry in Acts, but we are told about his prayers behind the scenes in each of his New Testament letters. We need to imitate both aspects of Paul's ministry.

[2] Paul uses the phrase *"for each other and for everyone else"* in 3:12 and 5:15 to refer to Christians and non-Christians. Since Jesus was called a friend of sinners in Luke 7:34, his followers should be too.

through his Holy Spirit as the result of fervent prayer.[3] It is encouraging to see that Paul's prayers were quickly answered. He is overjoyed in 2 Thessalonians 1:3 that *"the love all of you have for one another is increasing."*

Some of Paul's language deliberately echoes the words of Jesus to the Samaritan woman in John 4. Jesus told her that *"Whoever drinks the water I give them will never thirst. Indeed, the water I give them will become in them a spring of water welling up to eternal life."* He was talking about the work of the Holy Spirit beneath the surface in our hearts, as he states more clearly in John 7:37–39: *"Let anyone who is thirsty come to me and drink. Whoever believes in me, as Scripture has said, rivers of living water will flow from within them."* Paul is not satisfied that the Thessalonians have had an initial experience of the Holy Spirit at conversion. He prays that they may go on being filled with the Holy Spirit in ever-increasing measure until they overflow with love for God, for one another and for unbelievers right across their region.

In 3:13, Paul emphasizes one last time that only the Holy Spirit can truly strengthen us from the inside out. Young saplings receive rich minerals from the soil as their roots suck up rainwater, and Christians grow strong as the Holy Spirit works deep inside them to put strength into their weak hearts. Paul's hope that the Thessalonians will become increasingly blameless and holy is not based on a list of rules that he has given them or on an accountability programme that he has started. It is based on the inner work of the Triune God. He expects the Holy Spirit to strengthen their hearts to prepare them to stand in the presence of God the Father when Jesus the Son returns in glory.[4] Paul was only with the Thessalonians for three weeks,

---

[3] Romans 5:5 tells us that this is precisely what God wants to do. Prayer is not a chore. It is laying hold of the willingness of God to work in our lives.

[4] As in every other chapter in 1 Thessalonians, Paul ends chapter 3 with a reference to Jesus' second coming. Jesus will return with his holy angels (Mark 8:38) to be joined by his holy followers (1 Thessalonians 4:17).

but the Holy Spirit is with them always. Paul believes his prayers for them in Corinth are just as effective as they would be if he were praying for them in Thessalonica.

James Fraser, the British missionary to the Lisu people of China, discovered the importance of praying for believers to be strengthened on the inside by the Holy Spirit. Heavy snowfall prevented him from visiting his converts in the mountain villages for eight months of the year. Distressed, he was convicted that he should spend the time he would have spent travelling back and forth praying for them instead. The results of his experiment were astounding. The converts in the mountain villages grew much faster than his converts in the lowlands despite the fact that he was with them all year round. He told his friends back in England that he had made a very encouraging discovery:

> *Christians at home can do as much for foreign missions as those actually on the field. I believe it will only be known on the Last Day how much has been accomplished in missionary work by the prayers of earnest believers at home... Solid, lasting missionary work is done on our knees. What I covet more than anything else is earnest, believing prayer.*[5]

The fifth ruse of the Devil is to stop us praying in private for the Holy Spirit to strengthen us and those around us in the unseen reaches of our hearts. Let's not be too busy to pray for God to fill us with the Holy Spirit. What Paul covets more than anything else for us is that we be rooted in Jesus through earnest, believing prayer.

---

[5] Quoted by Geraldine Taylor in *Behind the Ranges: The Life-Changing Story of J.O. Fraser* (1944).

Contagious Lifestyle (4:1–12)

We instructed you how to live in order to please God, as in fact you are living. Now we ask you and urge you in the Lord Jesus to do this more and more.

(1 Thessalonians 4:1)

It must have been very exciting to take part in Paul's discipleship training school in Corinth or Ephesus. It isn't hard to see why thousands of new believers flocked to hear his teaching about how God could turn the scrap metal of their lives into gold. But I am very glad that he never had the chance to set up a similar training school in Thessalonica. He was forced to summarize his teaching in a letter, so we have the privilege of sitting in on his training school too.

In chapter 1, Paul taught us the difference between true and false conversion, telling us that one of the marks of a genuine believer is that they become part of a Gospel chain reaction. In chapters 2 and 3, he taught us about five ways in which the Devil tries to stop that chain reaction. If we stake ourselves to leaders and build warm relationships with one another, and if we devote ourselves to church life and to Bible study and to private prayer, nothing can prevent us from being fruitful. Chapters 4 and 5 provide the conclusion to the first lesson in Paul's discipleship training school. He shows us how to make our faith in Jesus so contagious that people all around us will want to follow Jesus too.

Paul starts in 4:1–12 with some very practical teaching about contagious Christian lifestyle. He does not need to give the Thessalonians the same detailed teaching about the substance of the Gospel that we find in Romans or Ephesians because he gave it to them during the three weeks he spent in Thessalonica.[1] Instead he focuses on the practical outworking of our faith in the Gospel as we walk out our salvation every day.[2] It is clear from 4:1–2 that he taught about this while he was with them, but now he urges us *"in the Lord Jesus"* and warns us *"by the authority of the Lord Jesus"* that if we do not walk out our Christian faith, we may not have true Christian faith at all.[3]

True converts instinctively want to discover what God's will is for their lives. Paul gives us the answer in 4:3, and it's very simple: God's basic will is for us to live holy lives. In time he may reveal to us a more specific calling, but first we must simply copy the lifestyle of Jesus.[4] Those who are truly justified through the Gospel (*declared* holy in God's courtroom) always want to be sanctified through the same Gospel (*made* holy in their daily lives). Since we cannot be forgiven for sins about which we are not repentant, it follows that the truth of our repentance is proved by our willingness to leave those sins behind.

Paul focuses on sexual purity in 4:3–8, not because sexual sins are more deadly than others but because they are more obvious. Greek culture was most at odds with the teaching of Jesus in its attitude towards promiscuity, adultery and homosexuality. Paul therefore tells us that the genuineness

---

[1] Paul knows that they grasp the Gospel well enough not to think he is telling them to earn God's pleasure in 4:1. Having been *declared* holy in Jesus, we please God by letting him *make* us holy through Jesus too.

[2] Although most modern English translations of 4:1 and 4:12 talk three times about how we should *live*, Paul actually uses the Greek word *peripateō* to tell us how we must *walk* out our Christian faith in our daily lives.

[3] Paul tells us that true converts always want to embrace a holy lifestyle, adding in 4:8 that to reject this instruction is to reject God the Father and his Holy Spirit.

[4] Paul also tells us in 5:18 that God's general will for us is that we be thankful in all circumstances. Holiness and thankfulness are the gateway through which we must all pass to discover his specific will for our lives.

of our conversion to Christ can be seen by whether or not we reject the sexual lusts and practices of the pagans. The Gospel enables us to "take possession of our own vessel," controlling ourselves to find sexual enjoyment in its only proper place within marriage.[5] Whenever a person starts treating sex as a holy gift from God, it is obvious that the Gospel has begun to change their sinful heart.[6]

Paul knows that repenting of sexual sin is a big challenge for new believers. That's why he gives us four reasons why we should take these instructions very seriously. First, he uses the Greek word *pleonekteō* in 4:6 to warn us that sex outside marriage means *defrauding* a person's marriage partner out of the sexual purity that they ought to be given. Second, he tells us in 4:6 that there is no such thing as safe sex outside marriage because the Lord will avenge the sexual wrongs that we commit against our neighbours. Third, Paul tells us in 4:7 that sexual sin is a denial of our new identity as Christians, since *"God did not call us to be impure, but to live a holy life."* Fourth, he warns us in 4:8 that to reject this teaching is to reject God the Father and his Holy Spirit. We need to be radical about sexual sin because it is sin against one another, against the Lord, against ourselves and against the Spirit who makes us holy.[7]

Paul teaches us in 4:9–12 that instead of indulging in sexual sin we should devote ourselves to *agapē*, the *selfless love* that God wants to work in our hearts. Paul tells the Thessalonians in 4:9 that they already have this love as a result of his prayers

---

[5] The Greek word *skeuos*, or *vessel*, in 4:4 can refer either to our *body* or to our *marriage partner* (as it does in 1 Peter 3:7). The Greek verb *ktaomai* can mean either *to possess* or *to acquire*, so these instructions are equally relevant to married people and to single people who are looking for a marriage partner.

[6] Paul has no time for the view that sex is dirty. He tells us that sex within marriage is *"holy and honourable."*

[7] The Holy Spirit fills us in order to make us holy. The clue is in the name. Paul uses a Greek present participle in 4:8 to tell us literally that the Lord wants to *go on giving* us his Holy Spirit every day.

in 3:12, since they *"have been taught by God to love each other."*[8] He does not see this answered prayer as a substitute for further teaching, but encourages them to cooperate with the Holy Spirit in order to love one another all the more. Instead of using their hands to sin, they should use their hands to work hard and to attract the pagans in their city to Jesus through the beauty of their daily lives.[9]

This is the major theme of this final section of 1 Thessalonians. Paul tells us that a holy lifestyle is not simply pleasing to God and the proof of our conversion. It is also the thing that God uses to set off his Gospel chain reaction. A repentant lifestyle is very costly but it is also very contagious. When pagans see a community of people who love one another instead of sleeping with one another, and who use their hands to help instead of swindling one another, they sit up and take notice. When the Gospel is demonstrated as well as declared to unbelievers, it spreads like wildfire. True converts make true changes to their lives, which in turn attracts many more people to Jesus.[10]

Paul's instructions are offensive to our sex-crazed culture but we are even crazier if we fail to listen to what he is telling us here.[11] Paul tells us that our lifestyle is the proof of our conversion and that God will use it to make those around us sit up and listen to the Gospel. Paul wants you to develop a contagious lifestyle *"so that your daily life may win the respect of outsiders."*

---

[8] The word *theodidaktoi*, or *taught by God*, is yet another expression of Paul's conviction that only God can change a person from the inside out. God alone can turn scrap metal into gold.

[9] Paul uses the word *ambition* in 4:11 because selfishly ambitious unbelievers are attracted by the sight of people whose ambition is for holiness and for the honour of God instead. See also Romans 15:20.

[10] Paul argues this even more strongly in Titus 2 as part of the third lesson in his discipleship training school.

[11] In July 2013 a man was arrested for preaching from these 12 verses outside the church I lead in London. The lifestyle that Paul describes is attractive and offensive in equal measure to our pagan culture.

Contagious Hope (4:13–5:11)

We do not want you to be uninformed about those who sleep in death, so that you do not grieve like the rest of mankind, who have no hope.

(1 Thessalonians 4:13)

Ancient Greek culture was very pessimistic about what happens to us after we die. In the poems of Homer, the closest thing the Greeks had to sacred scripture, the great hero Achilles laments in the Underworld that *"I would rather be a paid servant in a poor man's house above ground than be king of kings here among the dead."*[1] If even their heroes found nothing but misery beyond the grave, the pagans in Thessalonica had very little to hope for. That's why Paul tells his converts to expect their Christian hope to be highly contagious in their city.

Timothy had just arrived in Corinth with news from Thessalonica. Although he brought a good report, one fly in the ointment was the news that many of Paul's converts were still pessimistic about what would happen to them when they died. They were still affected by the words of the Greek philosopher Epicurus, which were carved on many gravestones in the city: *"I was not; I was; I am not; I do not care."*[2] They still lived as if the Greek poet Theocritus was right when he wrote that *"There is hope for the living but there is no hope for the dead."*[3] Some

[1] Homer in his *Odyssey* (11.488–491).

[2] Epicurus taught in Athens in around 300 BC. Paul met many Epicureans in Athens in Acts 17:18.

[3] Theocritus wrote this in the third century BC in his *Idyll 4* (line 42).

of them had started to despair when the first church members died, thinking that they had somehow missed out on the second coming of Jesus. Paul therefore describes in patient detail for us what will happen when Jesus returns. He wants us to see that we have an eternal hope that is so contagious that it will help us to spread the Gospel all across the world.

In 4:13–18, Paul assures the Thessalonians that those who die will not be short-changed out of enjoying the return of Jesus in triumphant glory. Paul reminds them that Jesus said that believers who die are only "sleeping"[4] until they are awoken by the sounding of a great alarm clock on the Final Day.[5] Believers grieve when their loved ones die (Jesus wept in John 11:35 and the early Christians mourned in Acts 8:2) but our grief is for our own loss and not because we believe our dead friends have missed out on a share in Jesus' glory. Unlike the pagans who weep because they have no hope, we know that those who die first will be the first to be raised to life when Jesus reappears.[6] They will be caught up into the clouds and will meet Jesus in the air like the friends of a victorious general who join him outside the city to take part in his triumphal entry. The believers who are still alive will then join them in order to come down to earth together and to enjoy the same contagious hope: a share in the Messiah's eternal glory.[7]

---

[4] Jesus says dead people are *sleeping* in Matthew 9:24, Mark 5:39, Luke 8:52 and John 11:11–13. Paul uses the same metaphor in 1 Corinthians 11:30, 15:6, 15:18 and 20, and Luke uses it in Acts 7:60 and 13:36.

[5] Jehovah's Witnesses try to argue from 4:16 that Jesus is an archangel rather than God because he returns *"with the voice of the archangel."* However, triumphant kings always returned with heralds who proclaimed their victory. Paul is saying that the archangel Michael will herald the arrival of the Son of God (Jude 9).

[6] Paul tells us in Philippians 1:23 and 1 Corinthians 15:52 that Christians who die go to be with Jesus immediately in heaven. They will not receive their resurrection bodies, however, until God sounds the final trumpet on the Last Day. See the chapter "The Trumpet" in *Straight to the Heart of 1 and 2 Corinthians*.

[7] Paul is not talking about a "rapture" in 4:17, much less our being whisked away to heaven. Revelation 21–22 tells us that we will come back down to

The letters to the Thessalonians are known as the "eschatological letters" because they teach us a lot about what will happen at the end of world history. Since they are lessons one and two in Paul's discipleship training school, this is important. Paul clearly believes that, for us to become mature Christian disciples, we need to receive instruction in the Christian hope of what will happen at the end of time. We must not obsess about the detail, becoming so focused on the future that we neglect our opportunity to become contagious Christians in the present, but neither must we allow ourselves to be uninformed about how the drama of world history is going to end. A fifth of 1 Thessalonians and a third of 2 Thessalonians are devoted to eschatological teaching, and each of the five chapters of 1 Thessalonians ends with a reminder that Jesus is going to return. We need this hope to keep us smiling through the waves of persecution and setbacks which punctuate Church history. This hope is contagious. Whenever it is visible, it attracts mortal men and women to place their hope in the Gospel.

In 5:1–10, Paul tells the Thessalonians that they have misunderstood Jesus' teaching about his second coming. When Jesus said he would return suddenly, like *"labour pains"* and like *"a thief in the night,"*[8] he was not saying that he would keep believers in the dark about what is going to happen at his appearing. We are not children of the darkness but children of the day! Jesus will not surprise us like a burglar because we are not the ones who will suffer his wrath on Judgment Day.[9] We are waiting expectantly, clothing ourselves with the faith and

---

earth with Jesus to enjoy his perfect re-creation of the world.

[8] The reference to labour pains in 4:3 links back to Jesus' words in Matthew 24:8 and Mark 13:8. It speaks of the unexpected rebirth of creation when Jesus suddenly returns. See Matthew 19:28 and Romans 8:19–23.

[9] Paul uses a different Greek word for *sleeping* in 5:6–10 from the one he used in 4:13–15, perhaps in order to contrast the peaceful sleep of Christian death with the perilous sleep of spiritual complacency.

hope and love that Paul commended in 1:3.[10] Jesus has rescued us from the coming wrath, as Paul promised in 1:10, and so our lifestyle proclaims that we belong to the holy age to come and not to the sinful age which is passing away.[11] We proclaim hope beyond the grave to a world that believes, in the words of the Greek playwright Aeschylus, that *"When a man dies and the thirsty earth sucks up his blood, there is no resurrection."*[12] No wonder unbelievers find this Christian hope contagious. It is the news that every mortal man and woman secretly longs to hear.

In 4:18 and 5:11, Paul tells the Thessalonians to encourage and build one another up in these amazing truths. He knows that a proper understanding of what will happen when Jesus returns changes absolutely everything: how we live, how we die and how we grieve for those who die before we do. I discovered this personally when some tragic circumstances led to my attending two funerals on consecutive days. The first funeral was of an unbeliever. It was stark and bleak and, even though the relatives tried hard, it was devoid of any shred of hope or explanation. The second funeral was of a Christian and, even though the congregation cried, it was so full of hope and celebration that it felt more like a wedding.

Unless Jesus returns in our lifetime, every single one of us is going to die. Unbelievers know this too, which is why they find our Christian hope so attractive. When pagans see people staring death in the face and laughing because they know it does not have the final word, it starts a Gospel chain reaction. Put your hope in the Risen Saviour who is coming back soon. You will find that your hope is contagious.

---

[10] Paul is picking up on the imagery of Isaiah 59:17. He does so again in Romans 13:12 and Ephesians 6:13–18.

[11] Paul tells the Thessalonians in 5:9 that God *appointed* them to receive salvation, just as he told them in 1:4 that God *chose* them for salvation. He expects his teaching about election to encourage both them and us.

[12] Aeschylus writes this in his play *The Eumenides* (lines 647–648).

Contagious Community (5:12–18)

Live in peace with each other... Always strive to do what is good for each other and for everyone else.

(1 Thessalonians 5:13, 15)

When Paul and his teammates arrived in Thessalonica, they found a group of people who believed that they were the community of God. There had been so few Jews at Philippi that there was no synagogue in the city, but Thessalonica was different. Paul did much of his preaching in the synagogue that belonged to the city's thriving Jewish community. It soon became clear why the God-fearing pagans had decided not to become part of the synagogue.[1] For all its bluster, it was not the community of God at all.

The early Christians found that this was true in every city. When James 2:2 refers to the church in Jerusalem, it refers to it in Greek as an alternative Christian *synagogue*. When Paul was rejected by the Jewish synagogue in Corinth, Acts 18:7 tells us that he *"left the synagogue and went next door to the house of Titius Justus."* He deliberately set up a rival Christian synagogue as an authentic community of God, which is one of the reasons why Acts 17:5 tells us that the Thessalonian Jews were so jealous of Paul's work in their city. Paul and the other apostles set out to

[1] Greeks who converted to Judaism were seen as Jews, so when Luke tells us in Acts 17:4 that *"a large number of God-fearing Greeks"* were in the synagogue, he is telling us that they knew that something was not right about the Jewish community. They remained interested but they refused to convert to Judaism.

do what the Jewish synagogues had tried to accomplish but had failed. They established a contagious community of believers at the heart of every city, knowing that this was the best way to attract cities to follow Jesus.

In 5:12–13, Paul tells us that the church will be a contagious community if its members honour their leaders. Thessalonica was one of the most democratic cities in the Roman Empire, ruled by a council of elected officials known as politarchs.[2] Since they had the power to elect and to turf out these politicians, the Thessalonians respected their leaders about as much as most Westerners respect their own politicians today. The Jewish synagogues had adopted the idea of democracy wholesale and they amazed their neighbours by respecting their leaders even less than the pagans. When the synagogue ruler at Corinth made a foolish miscalculation, Acts 18:17 tells us that his congregation physically assaulted him in the street.[3] That's why Paul tells his converts that they need to love and respect their leaders. If they do so, they will send a powerful message right across their city: there is a refreshingly different community, which believes its leaders have been appointed by God.[4]

In 5:13–14, Paul tells us that the church will be a contagious community if its members honour one another. We can tell from Acts 17 that Thessalonica was as full of strife and jealousy and racism as any other Roman city. Arguments and riots flared up easily, so Paul says that people will take notice if his converts

---

[2] Historians used to think that Luke got it wrong when he called the rulers of Thessalonica *politarchs* in Acts 17:6 and 8. They were forced to confess their arrogance when archaeologists unearthed several inscriptions that confirmed that Luke was right and they were wrong. We can always trust the Bible.

[3] 1 Corinthians 1:1 suggests that, as a result of this ill treatment, the synagogue ruler Sosthenes devoted himself to helping Paul to create his better community of God next door.

[4] We can tell how much our culture needs this message from the way that the 2011 NIV subtly mistranslates *"those who are over you in the Lord"* so that it reads *"those who care for you in the Lord."* Paul tells Christian leaders not to apologize for their God-given authority.

simply *"live in peace with each other."* He is not telling us to pretend that we get on better with one another than we do. He is telling us to be loving and patient towards people that we do not get on with at all! We are to warn the idle and unruly, to comfort the fainthearted and to help the weak in a way which demonstrates that we love them all.[5] Real friends care enough for one another to dispense with the polite façade, to speak the truth in love and to listen to candid feedback from one another. Unbelievers are longing for an authentic community in which they can be honest and yet accepted. If our churches become that place, we will start a Gospel chain reaction. Our churches will become contagious communities.

In 5:15, Paul tells us that the church will be a contagious community if its members love those who are not yet believers. It is not enough for Christians to forgive and help one another. They are also to strive to do good to those who are not yet part of their community.[6] The church is not like a Freemasons' Lodge or an old boys' club where members do good turns for one another to the detriment of outsiders. Their attractiveness comes from their willingness to love and serve people who are not part of their tribe. They imitate their Saviour by laying down their lives for their enemies and striving *"to do what is good for each other* ***and for everyone else."*** When churches only help their own members, outsiders see through their self-centred agenda, but when they love unbelievers in the way that Jesus first loved them, outsiders find it very attractive.

In 5:16–18, Paul tells us that the church will be a contagious community if it is always joyful and grateful towards God. Instead of being known for wagging an accusing finger at their sinful city, churches should be known for raising their

---

[5] Paul sees pastoral care as a "one another" task rather than as a task exclusively for church leaders. The challenge is to discern which people are idle and unruly, which are fainthearted and which are weak.

[6] Paul also stresses our duty to love unbelievers in 3:12 and in Galatians 6:9–10.

hands towards the Lord in constant worship for all he has done for them. When times are hardest, such churches become even more contagious because only the Gospel can make a person thankful in every circumstance.[7] Paul tells us that this is God's will for every church, not least because it is the way in which the Gospel catches the attention of an unbelieving world. When people with a contagious lifestyle and a contagious hope gather together in contagious community, the gates of hell cannot resist the Gospel they proclaim.

The missiologist Roland Allen notes the importance of contagious community to Paul's strategy for making disciples all across the world:

> *Many missionaries in later days have received a larger number of converts than St. Paul; many have preached over a wider area than he; but none have so established churches. We have long forgotten that such things could be... Men have wandered over the world, "preaching the Word," laying no solid foundations, establishing nothing permanent, leaving no really instructed society behind them, and have claimed St. Paul's authority for their absurdities... St. Paul's theory of evangelising a province was not to preach in every place in it himself, but to establish centres of Christian life in two or three important places from which the knowledge might spread into the country round...*
>
> *He came as an Apostle of the Church of God, and he did not simply seek to gather out individual souls from amongst the heathen, he gathered them into the society of which he was a member... The apostle who preached to them was a member of it, and he preached as a member of it, and as a member of it he invited them to enter*

---

7 When Paul urges us to pray *continually* in 5:17, he uses the same Greek word which he used to describe his own prayer life in 1:2–3 and 2:13.

it, to share its privileges and its burdens, its glory and its shame... St. Paul's preaching ever appealed to and demanded the exercise of the two highest and deepest convictions of men, their sense of individual responsibility and their sense of social communion with their fellows.[8]

[8] The British missionary Roland Allen in his seminal book *Missionary Methods: St Paul's or Ours?* (1912).

How to Hunt Your Enemies (5:15)

Make sure that nobody pays back wrong for wrong, but always strive to do what is good for each other and for everyone else.

(1 Thessalonians 5:15)

Thessalonica was a city whose name proclaimed that it did not look kindly upon its enemies. Its name meant "Victory in Thessaly" and it commemorated the bloodiest battle in the whole of ancient history.[1] After defeating his enemies at the Battle of Crocus Field in Thessaly in 352 BC, King Philip of Macedon crucified the defeated general and drowned all of the soldiers who surrendered. Thessalonica was therefore a city whose name warned that anyone who attacked it would be hunted down and killed.

Paul and his friends knew what it was like to be on the receiving end of Thessalonian hostility. The normal Greek word which the New Testament uses for unbelievers *persecuting* Christians is *diōkō*, which literally means *to pursue* or *to hunt down*. Paul and Silas knew what it felt like to be pursued and hunted down by the Thessalonians. Acts 17 tells us that a violent mob attacked the house where they were staying and dragged their host and several other leading Christians before the rulers of the city. *"These men who have caused trouble all over the world have now come here"*, they told the politarchs, playing on their

[1] Philip's daughter was born on the day of the battle so he named her Thessalonica, or *"Victory in Thessaly"*. Her husband founded the city in 315 BC and gave it his wife's name.

inherent distrust of outsiders. *"They are all defying Caesar's decrees, saying that there is another king, one called Jesus",* they added in order to arouse the hostility of those who ruled for the unforgiving Emperor Claudius. Paul and Silas fled the city under cover of darkness as soon as night fell. They knew that it was safer to be pursued and hunted by a hungry lion than by Thessalonians with a grudge.

This background is important if we want to understand what Paul is saying in 5:15. He ends his teaching about how to be a contagious community by telling us that there is something specific that we can do to captivate the world's attention. We are to look for the places where our culture is most entrenched in sin and we are to model the opposite attitude. In a sex-crazed city we are to be sexually pure. In an intellectually arrogant nation we are to be fools for Christ. In a dog-eat-dog world we are to look out for one another's needs and not just for our own. And in Thessalonica, that most unforgiving of cities, Paul's converts were to return good for evil and love for hatred until their enemies were so attracted to the Gospel that they surrendered their lives to Jesus too.

Most English translations fail to capture what Paul is saying when he tells us to *"Make sure that nobody pays back wrong for wrong, but always strive to do what is good for each other and for everyone else."* The word he uses for striving is *diōkō*, the very same word that was used for non-Christians hunting and pursuing and persecuting followers of Jesus. Paul tells his converts at Thessalonica that whenever their enemies hunt them down to do them harm, they must respond by hunting them down just as doggedly in order to do them good.

This was not what the Thessalonian Christians wanted to hear, but it is what it always means to follow Jesus. When he was mocked and spat on and beaten and crucified, Jesus cried out, *"Father, forgive them, for they do not know what they are doing."* His loving kindness hunted down the souls of his enemies so tenderly that the gospel writers tell us the squad of soldiers who crucified him were converted as he died.[2] When he was mocked and deserted by his half-brother James and his leading disciple Peter, Jesus hunted them down with such forgiveness that they both became key leaders in the Early Church and wrote parts of the New Testament. Pursuing people with love instead of vengeance is far from easy, but we are never more like Jesus than when we do.

Paul had been on the receiving end of such forgiveness from the contagious Christian community in Jerusalem. He had looked after the coats of the men who martyred Stephen, nodding his approval. He had been shocked when Stephen used his dying breaths to pray, *"Lord do not hold this sin against them."* Although many people assume that his Damascus Road conversion was sudden, it seems to have started when Stephen hunted him down with love and forgiveness as he died. Jesus told him on the Damascus Road that *"It is hard for you to kick against the goads."* A goad is the sharp stick with which a farmer pursues a stubborn cow or donkey. Stephen's dying words of love had evidently plagued Paul's thoughts and pursued his soul. He assures us that we will see those who hate us converted if we hunt them down with love and forgiveness in the same way too.[3]

Few Christian commands are more difficult to follow than the command to forgive our enemies. That is why it is so powerfully attractive. We live in a culture that is more like Philip of Macedon than Jesus of Nazareth. Sean Connery sums it up in the movie *The Untouchables* when he describes his tactics for imprisoning Al Capone: *"You wanna get Capone? Here's how you get him. He pulls a knife, you pull a gun. He sends one of yours to the hospital, you send one of his to the morgue! That's the Chicago*

---

[2] Luke 23:34, 47; Matthew 27:54. John 19:34–35 suggests that one of the soldiers was still alive and in the church at the time of writing.

[3] Acts 7:54–8:3; 26:14.

Way, and that's how you get Capone."[4] When we refuse to take the Chicago Way or the Thessalonica Way, we attract the world's attention. They know deep down that *"to err is human, to forgive divine."*[5]

The people of Thessalonica worshipped a group of goddesses known as the Furies, who pursued wrongdoers with terrifying vengeance. They saw it as an act of worship to the Furies whenever they pursued vendettas against one another. The historian John Griffiths tells us that *"Embedded in the Greek morality of retaliation is the right of vendetta... Vendetta is a war, just as war is an indefinite series of vendettas; and such acts of vengeance are sanctioned by the gods."*[6] Paul tells us that we also need to pursue vendettas if we want to be a contagious community. But our vendettas always have to be vendettas of love.

In 380 AD, the Emperor Theodosius issued the Edict of Thessalonica. It marked a major turning point in history because it ended persecution against the Christians by declaring that henceforth the Christian Gospel was the official faith of the Roman Empire. It is no coincidence that the edict was proclaimed from Thessalonica. It was the fulfilment of Paul's promise to his converts in the city three centuries earlier. If we pursue our persecutors with love and hunt down our enemies with forgiveness, God promises to make our churches contagious communities. The God who turns scrap metal into gold promises that he will turn our fiercest enemies into our closest friends.

---

4 Sean Connery plays Jim Malone in *The Untouchables* (Paramount Pictures, 1987).

5 The English poet Alexander Pope says this in his *Essay on Criticism* (1711).

6 John Gwyn Griffiths in *Divine Verdict: A Study of Divine Judgement in the Ancient Religions* (1991).

How Paul Said Goodbye (5:19–28)

The one who calls you is faithful, and he will do it.

(1 Thessalonians 5:24)

Letting go of your children is never easy. If you have ever waved a son off to university or walked a daughter down the aisle, you know that only too well. One of the hardest aspects of parenting is knowing how to let go and to allow our children to stand on their own two feet.

Paul told us in chapter 2 that he discipled his converts in Thessalonica like a mother or a father. Signing off this letter to his spiritual children must have been extremely difficult for him. They were still immature and persecution was coming. Paul was over 350 miles away in Corinth. But in these final verses of 1 Thessalonians Paul gives six reasons why he is able to say goodbye. You should find them helpful if you are a parent who needs to learn to let go of your children or if you are a church leader who needs to learn to trust God with the Christians in your care.

Paul is able to say goodbye to his converts in 5:19 because *he knows they have the Holy Spirit*. Even though he gives them the first lesson in his discipleship training school in this letter, he has not forgotten that he is merely God's extra and that Jesus is the one who always plays the starring role. He told them in 4:9 that they were *theodidaktoi*, or *taught by God*, and he continues to trust God to carry on teaching them after he signs off his letter. All they need to do is ensure they do not quench the Holy Spirit's work deep in their hearts. The fact that the Greek word for *quench* in 5:19 is the root of our own word "asbestos" reminds us that God will empower any believer to stand firm as long as they do not allow unconfessed sin to insulate them from the fire of the Holy Spirit.[1]

Paul is able to say goodbye to his converts in 5:20–22 because *he knows God has not finished speaking to them*. He is not a "Bible deist" who believes that God spoke the Bible into being and then promptly lost his voice. He urges them to listen to the words of prophecy, which the Holy Spirit gives them to build up and strengthen one another in God.[2] Yes, the pagans of Thessalonica were heavily influenced by demonic prophecies at the oracle of Delphi, but that was no reason for them to despise the genuine prophecies that the Holy Spirit inspires people to bring.[3] If we test prophecy, we will be able to distinguish what is real from what is false, remembering that prophecy is just as much despised when we allow human thoughts to masquerade as God-given utterances as it is when we forbid prophecy altogether.[4] Paul let go of his spiritual children because he trusted God to keep on speaking words of comfort and guidance to them. We can have that same confidence with our own children and with the Christians in our care.

Paul is able to say goodbye to his converts in 5:23 because *he knows God always finishes what he starts*. Since God has justified them, declaring them righteous through the Gospel,

---

[1] Paul tells us in 2 Timothy 1:6 that, far from insulating ourselves from the fire of the Holy Spirit, we ought to feed the fire with the oxygen of faith so that it bursts into an ever brighter flame.

[2] 1 Corinthians 14:1–5, 39–40. The phrase "Bible deist" was coined by Jack Deere in chapter 17 of his book *Surprised by the Voice of God* (1996). The cost price of the book is worth it even for that one chapter alone.

[3] The Greek text is ambiguous in 5:22. Is Paul telling us to reject *every kind* of evil or *every appearance* of evil? Both. We must reject false prophecy and anything that brings genuine prophecy into disrepute.

[4] The Greek word that Paul uses for *despising* in 5:20 means literally *setting at nothing*. Churches that talk a lot about prophecy can still despise it by deflating people's practical expectations of its power.

Paul has no doubt that he will also sanctify them, making them righteous in their day-to-day lives through the same Gospel. Since God has filled them with his Holy Spirit to change them from the inside out, Paul has no doubt that he will keep on doing so until they are blameless. Paul deliberately matches the three aspects of what it means to be human to the three persons of the Godhead. We can trust God the Father, God the Son and God the Holy Spirit to work together in order to sanctify our spirit, soul and body fully, working from the inside out.[5]

Paul is able to say goodbye to his converts in 5:24 because *he knows they need God far more than they need him*. This may sound obvious but it is surprisingly easy to forget. Too many church leaders suffocate the people that they lead by trying to play the primary role in their discipleship. Paul never forgot that the only way he could take people from the scrapheap and turn them into gold was by remembering that *"The one who calls you is faithful, and he will do it."* Even though he knew that the Thessalonians wanted him to visit them instead of Timothy, he addresses their overdependence upon him by writing as *"we"* and *"us"* throughout this letter. Then he addresses their overdependence upon his team as a whole by switching the focus onto the God who is able to supply their every need. If you are a parent who needs to let go of a child or a church leader who needs to let go of a Christian, you should find this very helpful. We can say goodbye because discipleship, from beginning to end, is always about God and not us.

Paul is able to say goodbye to his converts in 5:25–27 because *he knows they will not fall for the five ruses of the Devil* which he outlined in chapters 2 and 3. He knows they are committed to private prayer (5:25), to honouring their leaders

---

[5] Note the order here. God always changes people from the inside out and never from the outside in. This verse goes alongside 2 Thessalonians 2:13, Ezekiel 36:26–27, Acts 26:18 and Galatians 3:3.

(5:25), to warm friendships with one another (5:26),[6] to the reading of Scripture (5:27)[7] and to gathering together as a local church (5:27).[8] Paul can sign off his letter gladly because he is sure in these three verses that they have heeded his warnings in chapters 2 and 3.

Finally, Paul is able to say goodbye to his converts in 5:28 because *he believes in the grace of God*. Paul preached grace (Acts 14:3; 20:24), enjoyed grace personally (Acts 14:26; 15:40) and committed all of his converts to that same grace too (Acts 13:43; 20:32). Our failure to trust God with those we disciple through the Gospel is often a sign that we do not yet believe the Gospel entirely ourselves. We need to learn to say to people with Paul in Acts 20:32: *"I commit you to God and to the word of his grace, which can build you up and give you an inheritance among all those who are sanctified."*

Paul has said goodbye. He has finished the first lesson in his discipleship training school. He has taught us what true conversion means and he has prepared us to take part in the Gospel chain reaction which is spreading all across the world. If we turn from false idols to serve the true and living God, if we resist the tricks of the Devil and if we allow the Holy Spirit to make us contagious Christians, Paul assures us that our lives will begin to be transformed by God's amazing power. We will discover that God is able to take the scrap metal of our lives and turn it into pure and precious gold.

[6] Greek and Roman families would greet each other with a kiss to express their warm love for one another. See also Romans 16:16, 1 Corinthians 16:20, 2 Corinthians 13:12 and 1 Peter 5:14.

[7] 2 Peter 3:15–16 makes it clear that the Early Church regarded Paul's letters as being part of Holy Scripture.

[8] In 5:23, Paul sees the Church as such a united body that he refers to them having one body, one soul and one spirit together. He does the same in 1 Corinthians 6:19, Galatians 6:18, Philippians 4:23 and Philemon 25.

Lesson Two – 2 Thessalonians:

True Warriors

Things Change, God Doesn't (1:1–12)

Paul, Silas and Timothy, to the church of the Thessalonians in God our Father and the Lord Jesus Christ.

(2 Thessalonians 1:1)

Paul had hoped that if he stayed away from Thessalonica, the Christians in the city would be protected from excessive persecution. His hopes had failed. At the start of 52 AD, about six months after he wrote his first letter, he received terrible news.[1] Paul's enemies in Thessalonica had turned on the church he left behind, and they were doing all they could to eradicate the Christian faith from their city.

On one level, this news meant that everything had changed. The Jewish opponents of Christianity were no longer waiting for Paul to come back to Thessalonica; they had changed their tactics and were trying to wipe out the young church before he returned. The first Roman persecution against the Christians took place twelve years after Paul wrote 2 Thessalonians, so all of the persecution which we read about in this letter came from the jealous Jews who opposed him in Acts 17. Paul needed to act quickly so he wrote them the letter that forms the second lesson in his discipleship training school. Having taught the Thessalonians how to be true converts, he now equips them to be true warriors in the suffering army of Jesus Christ the King.

[1] It appears Paul wrote these two letters from Corinth, and we know from Acts 18:12 that he was at Corinth while Gallio was proconsul there. An inscription at Delphi tells us that Gallio was proconsul from 51 to 52 AD.

Lots of things had changed at Thessalonica, but God had not. There is no sense of panic in Paul's tone as he writes this second letter to the city. His opening words in 1:1–2 are almost identical to the opening words of his first letter. He is still writing with his teammates Silas and Timothy. He is still assured that his converts live in two places at once: both in Thessalonica and in God the Father and the Lord Jesus Christ. Paul still greets them with the same blessing, *"Grace and peace to you from God the Father and the Lord Jesus Christ."*[2] However much things had changed, God was every bit as sovereign and faithful as before. Things change, but God doesn't. Christians need to know that in their heart of hearts if they are to become true warriors.

One of the reasons why Paul begins this second letter in the same way as his first one was that his Jewish enemies had started playing dirty. He tells us in chapter 2 that they had tried to unsettle his converts by sending them a forged letter in his name. They knew enough about the Old Testament Scriptures to recognize that Paul's eschatological teaching in his first letter would galvanize the church to remain strong against persecution, so they sent a second letter in his name in order to infect the church with false ideas about how world history would end. Paul tells us in chapter 3 that the contents of this false letter had so discouraged the Christians that many of them reacted by becoming lazy and disruptive. Paul opens this letter in the same way as his first one so that his converts will know for sure that it really has come from him.[3]

Paul continues to emphasize in 1:3–4 that nothing has changed. He tells the Thessalonians that he and his teammates still continue to pray for them. Although he talks about *endurance* this time rather than *hope* because he needs to train his converts

---

[2] This is a more complete version of the blessing that Paul and his teammates abbreviated at the start of 1 Thessalonians. Paul uses a version of this blessing to start all of his New Testament letters.

[3] Paul's words in 2 Thessalonians 3:17 are also a reaction to the false letter which he tells us about in 2:1–3.

to be warriors, he is still focused on the same three Christian virtues that he mentioned at the start of his first letter: faith, hope and love.[4] He uses the same Greek word that he used in 1 Thessalonians 3:12 and 4:10 to tell his converts that their love for one another is *increasing* in response to his prayers and teaching. Although their troubles are increasing, so is their faith in God's power to bring them through.[5] They are not merely holding their ground. They are becoming true warriors who keep on marching forward in the right direction.

Paul describes their persecution in 1:5–10 in a way that emphasizes that nothing has changed since he wrote his first letter to them. When he tells them that God will *count them worthy* of his Kingdom, he uses a similar Greek word to the one he used in 1 Thessalonians 2:12.[6] Having devoted a fifth of 1 Thessalonians to eschatological teaching, he continues by devoting a third of 2 Thessalonians to yet more teaching about what will happen at the end of time. If there is any change, it is simply that Paul gets even more excited as he describes our hope for the future. He told us in 1 Thessalonians 2:12 and 3:13 that Jesus will come back with his holy angels to give us a share in his glorious Kingdom, but here he tells us that Jesus will come back to reveal us as his holy People and to be glorified by giving us his Kingdom![7] We will not simply be spectators of Jesus' glory when he returns. We can persevere under any shameful trial today because we know that on that Day we will be participators in his glory.

---

[4] Paul highlighted these three virtues in 1 Thessalonians 1:3 and 5:8. See also 1 Corinthians 13:13.

[5] Faith is not just to be guarded. It is to be grown, and this is the sign of a healthy Christian. The longer we walk with God, the more we should learn to trust him. Faith that doesn't grow actually grows stagnant.

[6] The Greek verb *kataxioō* in 1:5 is a compound form of the adverb *axiōs* in 1 Thessalonians 2:12. We can tell from Paul's use of the adjective *axios* in 1:3 that by *worthy* he means *in keeping with* our calling. See also 1:11.

[7] The angels were Jesus' *holy ones* in 1 Thessalonians 3:13, but we are his *holy ones* in 2 Thessalonians 1:10.

Paul continues to emphasize in 1:11–12 that nothing has changed. He repeats his promise that he is constantly praying for the Thessalonians, and he repeats the charge he gave them in 1 Thessalonians 2:12 to live lives worthy of their divine calling. He repeats his confidence that God alone will play the starring role in transforming their scrappy lives into gold. God is at work in their hearts to give them good desires and the faith to follow through on those desires. Paul ends this first chapter by repeating the gracious Gospel promise that Jesus dwells in us and that we dwell in Jesus.

A lot had changed in Thessalonica in six months but God had not changed, so those things meant nothing at all. Whatever changes are happening in your own life, this should comfort you today. In the midst of life's ever-changing winds and storms, God never changes. A. W. Pink puts it this way:

> *God has neither evolved, grown, nor improved. All that he is today, he has ever been, and ever will be... Herein is solid comfort. Human nature cannot be relied upon; but God can! However unstable I may be, however fickle my friends may prove, God changes not... All praise to his glorious name, he is ever the same. His purpose is fixed, his will is stable, his word is sure. Here then is a rock on which we may fix our feet, while the mighty torrent is sweeping away everything around us.*[8]

[8] A. W. Pink in *The Attributes of God* (1930). This comes from his chapter on "The Immutability of God".

The Glory and the Horror (1:5–10)

He will punish those who do not know God and do not obey the gospel of our Lord Jesus.

(2 Thessalonians 1:8)

Jesus is polite but that doesn't mean that he says please. I can't find a single occasion in the gospels when Jesus ever felt the need to say please to anyone. He is the King of heaven and he did not come to earth in order to ask us to do him a favour. His brand of politeness is to stand before two doors, to hold one open, and to tell us we can choose which one of the two doorways we wish to use.

There are times when it is right to present the Gospel as a heavenly request to men and women. Paul writes in 2 Corinthians 5:20 that *"We implore you on Christ's behalf: be reconciled to God."* Nevertheless, we must not forget that in the same verse Paul says we are Christ's ambassadors and speak the very words of God. When Paul preached in Athens, he warned his hearers in Acts 17:30 that *"God commands all people everywhere to repent."* Now he tells us something similar in 2 Thessalonians 1:8. The Gospel is not simply a request to be considered. It is a divine order to be obeyed.

Paul did not spend much time in 1 Thessalonians describing the substance of the Gospel, preferring to focus on its practical outworking instead. He certainly makes up for it now. He tells us that the Gospel is a choice between two eternal destinies. Jesus has opened the door of salvation and now he beckons us to follow him through the door. The Gospel is not so much an invitation to allow God through the door of our own hearts as it is a command to walk through the right doorway ourselves.[1]

Paul describes these two doorways in glorious and horrific detail. The first door leads to a place of such torment and despair that C. S. Lewis confessed, *"There is no doctrine which I would more willingly remove from Christianity than this, if it lay in my power. But it has the full support of Scripture."*[2] What Paul says about hell is shocking but it is not unfair. It is God's considered judgment (1:6) upon those who have chosen to do evil (1:6), to reject God (1:8a) and to disobey his Gospel (1:8b). It is the destiny of all those who refuse to worship God with their lives and who say that they would rather live their lives without him. They refuse to pass through the doorway that Jesus has opened through his blood because they would rather die than be part of a world where God is recognized as God and they are not. In the end they get what they want.

Paul's description of the second doorway is as glorious as the first one is horrific. It takes us into a new world where God reigns as undisputed King and where those who suffer for his Kingdom in this world receive their reward (1:5). Jesus will usher in this world when he returns to earth from heaven in all his glory to reveal that he was Lord of the universe all along – he was simply giving people a bit more time to choose (1:7). Nobody will be able to resist his powerful angel army and nothing will be able to prevent him from destroying this earth with fire (1:7). Like a farmer burning the stubble in his field so that he can plant a fresh harvest, Jesus will remake the heavens and the earth as they were always meant to be. He will not whisk us away to heaven, but will bring heaven down to earth and

---

[1] When Jesus says that he is knocking on the door of our hearts in Revelation 3:20, he is talking to Christians. His offer to fill our hearts only comes after we have obeyed his Gospel command.

[2] C. S. Lewis in *The Problem of Pain* (1940).

dwell with us forever.[3] He will glorify himself by transforming us into the perfect people we were always born to be and by allowing us to marvel and worship him in this new world which will never come to an end (1:10).

The Thessalonians were suffering in the short term, but this hope would turn them into unflinching warriors. They were marching on a one-way journey to a new home which would make all their sufferings worthwhile.

Our hearts have become so infected by the sinful world in which we live that some of us view these verses as bad news rather than good news. Instead of rejoicing that a day is coming when God's justice will be vindicated in the eyes of the entire world, it is easy to join with the wicked in blaming him for overreacting towards sin. Rob Bell is not the only one who thinks it would be better news if we were able to say that *"History is not tragic, hell is not forever, and love, in the end, wins."*[4] But Paul is insistent. The good news of the Gospel is that, along with God's love, his glory and justice and righteousness also prevail. God loves people so much that he lets them take whichever doorway they choose: an eternity of joyful obedience to him or an eternity of reaping the reward of trying to act like little gods ourselves.

Paul tells us that the Gospel is a message to be obeyed. Those who rebel against it will be punished with *olethros aiōnios*, or *eternal destruction*. They will be *"shut out from the presence of the Lord"* in a place devoid of any good, and they will be *"shut out from... the glory of his might"* in a place devoid of any second chances.[5]

Paul takes us back to his teaching in 1 Thessalonians 5:15

---

[3] We can read more about this in 2 Peter 3:7–13 and Revelation 21–22.

[4] Rob Bell in *Love Wins* (2011). His book was popular because it tried to explain away Paul's horrific words.

[5] Revelation 14:10 clarifies that Paul is not saying Jesus will be unable to see people in hell. He is simply saying that they will have missed their chance to respond to Jesus' offer of salvation.

when he tells us in 1:9 that God will take *ekdikēsis*, or *revenge*, on those who persecute his People.[6] This link tells us how we should respond to the glory and the horror presented by these two doorways. We must not pretend that hell is less real than it is. We must endure hardship with such hope that those who persecute us become convinced that the Gospel must be true. We must hunt them down with love, pursuing them like warriors whose endurance proves that a Day of Judgment is coming which will end their spiteful judgments against us.

Jesus is not saying please. He has opened a doorway through his blood to forgiveness and eternal life. He is commanding us to obey the Gospel by stepping through the door, and to proclaim this Gospel command to all creation. The Gospel is not to be debated, dissected, doubted or despised. It is to be obeyed and to be proclaimed as a command to everyone. Mark Dever reminds us that

> *To evangelise is to declare on the authority of God what he has done to save sinners, to warn men of their lost condition, to direct them to repent, and to believe in the Lord Jesus Christ... We don't fail in our evangelism if we faithfully tell the gospel to someone who is not converted; we fail only if we don't faithfully tell the gospel at all.*[7]

---

[6] Although some English translations talk about God *punishing* rebels in 1:9, the word *ekdikēsis* means literally *vengeance* or *revenge*. Hell is a punishment that fits the crime.

[7] Mark Dever in *The Gospel and Personal Evangelism* (2007).

Greeks Bearing Gifts (2:1–2)

We ask you, brothers, not to become easily unsettled or alarmed by some prophecy, report or letter supposed to have come from us.

(2 Thessalonians 2:1–2)

The Ancient Greeks were masters at the art of military deception. Paul's enemies at Thessalonica were no exception. They had sent a false letter in his name, and he warns the Christians not to treat it as a one-off ploy. It was simply a skirmish in the war of deception which the Devil wages against God's People.

The most famous example of Greek military deception was the Wooden Horse of Troy. The Trojans woke up one morning to discover that overnight the Greeks had abandoned their ten-year-long siege and disappeared. All that remained of their campsite was a giant wooden horse, which they had dedicated to the gods in return for a safe voyage home. The excited Trojans dragged the horse into the city to take centre stage in their victory celebrations. Only their high priest Laocoön was suspicious, telling them that *"I fear the Greeks, even when they are bearing gifts."*[1] Sure enough, the horse was filled with Greek soldiers who crept out and slaughtered the drunken Trojans while they slept. The Greeks conquered Troy through deception where force of arms had failed.

Paul's enemies at Thessalonica had realized that their persecution was making the Christians more united and more confident that Jesus was in control (1:3–4). They had noticed with dismay that unbelievers were beginning to take the

[1] Virgil tells us this in his epic poem *The Aeneid* (2.49).

Christians' resilience as evidence that their Gospel might be true (1:5). They therefore created their own equivalent of the Wooden Horse of Troy. They forged a letter from Paul and his teammates, which carried a very different message from that of 1 Thessalonians. It undermined the Gospel promise that Jesus is coming back to end world history and usher in his new creation. It told them that they had misunderstood Paul: the second coming was simply a clever metaphor. It had already happened when the Holy Spirit came on the Day of Pentecost or when they believed in Jesus and welcomed him into their hearts. This forged letter had unsettled, alarmed, discouraged and confused the Christians. Paul pleads with them like Laocoön of Troy not to fall for the enemy's lies.

The Devil still loves to twist and misrepresent the teaching in Paul's letters. When Charles Russell founded the Jehovah's Witness sect, he twisted 1 Thessalonians 4:16 to argue that Paul saw Jesus as a powerful archangel rather than as God. He went on to teach that Jesus would return in 1874, and when this failed to happen he revised the date to 1914. When this second date also failed to result in Jesus' appearing, he informed his followers that Jesus had come back – he had simply done so invisibly. But let's look to our own house before we laugh at the way that sects and cults fulfil Paul's warnings in 2 Thessalonians 2. As we saw in the last chapter, many mainstream theologians perform contortions to explain away Paul's teaching about hell. Christian bookshops are full of groundless speculations about Paul's eschatology. While Paul was still alive, he could tell the Thessalonians in 3:17 that they should not trust any letter from him unless it had his signature at the bottom.[2] But nowadays it is far easier to misquote him because dead men are unable to reply.

When the Ancient Greeks failed in one ruse, it did not

[2] Examples of this signature of authenticity can be found in 1 Corinthians 16:21 and Colossians 4:18.

stop them. Their persistent creativity was legendary. When the Athenian general Pericles fought a battle near a shrine dedicated to the god Pluto, he disguised one of his officers as the god in purple robes and in a chariot drawn by gleaming white horses. When Pluto rode out at the start of the battle and shouted to Pericles that the gods of Olympus were on his side, his enemies turned and fled before a single arrow was fired.[3]

Paul therefore warns the Thessalonians not to see this forged letter as an isolated incident. He tells them to be wise to the Devil's attempts to deceive them through false prophecy as well.[4] A few years ago, my wife and I counselled a girl in her twenties who had been a very joyful Christian convert but who plunged into depression after following Jesus for a year. As we asked her questions to determine what might have robbed her of her initial joy, she revealed that a man at work had shared with her that God had told him she was the woman he was going to marry. She was immature enough in her faith to believe him – how could she defy the voice of God? – but she was losing sleep and weight and sanity because she was not attracted to the man at all. When we exposed the prophecy as a lie, the relief on her face was enormous. Her joy quickly returned as she was released from the clutches of a modern-day Pericles.

For every incident like this one, I can point to dozens more when the genuine gift of prophecy has led to breakthrough. Paul warns us in 1 Thessalonians 5:20–22 that we must not respond to the Devil's lies by despising prophecy, but by testing it. One of the ways we do this is by resisting the Devil's five basic ruses, which Paul described in 1 Thessalonians 2 and 3. If we stake ourselves to trusted leaders and root ourselves in a local church, pursuing deep relationships with one another

---

[3] The Roman writer Frontinus records this deception in his *Stratagems* (1.11.10).

[4] Paul does not actually refer to *false prophecies* in 2:2. He warns us not to be unsettled *dia pneumatos* – either *through a spirit* or *through the Spirit* – because misapplied prophecies are just as dangerous as false ones.

and devoting ourselves to Bible study and to private prayer, we will be spared many griefs. Paul is training us to become true warriors for Jesus, and warriors are strongest when they are standing shoulder-to-shoulder together behind their leaders.

The Greeks used another famous deception to defeat the Romans in a sea battle. King Antiochus III pretended that his ships were slower than they were so that his men were able to throw jars filled with vipers onto the decks of the Roman ships when they came alongside. The jars smashed and the vipers started biting the Romans, distracting them so much from the battle that the Greek fleet was able to win.[5] That's a good picture of what Paul warns against in 2:2 when he tells the Thessalonians not to believe every *report* or, as some English translations put it, not to believe *word of mouth*. The Devil loves to hurl jars full of venomous gossip onto the decks of the Church through a blog or a tweet or a rumour or a false accusation – anything that will distract us from the real battle which rages for the salvation of the world.

So let's not fall for the Devil's tricks. Let's remember that by the time of Paul the whole of Greece had been conquered by the smart and savvy soldiers of Rome. The Devil fights dirty because he knows he has to. He knows that we are on the winning side. Let's be wise to his many deceptions as true warriors for Jesus Christ the King.

5 Frontinus tells us this in *Stratagems* (4.7.10). This naval engagement took place in 190 BC.

Game, Set and Match (2:3–12)

Then the lawless one will be revealed, whom the Lord Jesus will overthrow with the breath of his mouth and destroy by the splendour of his coming.

(2 Thessalonians 2:8)

I like to watch a lot of tennis with my children. We live in Wimbledon, so it was always likely. Since tennis matches can go on for four or five hours, I often send my children to bed halfway through a match and record the rest so that we can watch it together the following day. By then, our viewing experience is very different. My children sit on the edge of their seats, agonizing over each point and worrying that their favourite player is going to lose the match. I am relaxed because I already know the final score. I already know that the player we are supporting will turn the match around in its closing moments and will go home with the trophy.

The letters to the Thessalonians are known as the "eschatological epistles" because Paul says so much about what is going to happen at the end of world history. When the Thessalonians believed the false letter, they started acting as if it were game, set and match to the Devil already. Paul writes the second chapter of 2 Thessalonians to inform them that they are still in the first set of world history. They can trust God that at the end of the match they will be on the winning team.

First, Paul tells us to expect it to look as though God is losing at many points in history. He tells us in 2:3 that we should expect *apostasia*, a Greek word that means more than just the rebellion of unbelievers against God. Apostasy refers to people who were once devout believers turning their backs on the Lord. Paul tells us not to be surprised when people who looked like great church members and great church leaders throw it all away by rejecting the truth and refusing to carry on submitting their lives to the Lord. It is possible that Paul is referring particularly to the Jews rejecting Jesus as Messiah throughout most of history, since the only other place in the New Testament where the word *apostasia* is used is to refer to Jews abandoning the faith of their fathers (Acts 21:21), but a quick survey of Church history suggests that Paul also means something more. There has never been a period when people who look like believers have not chosen to compromise and throw away their faith in Christ. Paul tells us not to despair or doubt God's plan when we see this on the scoreboard. He tells us to be true warriors who are unshaken because Jesus predicted all along that this would happen.[1]

Second, Paul tells us to expect the rise of an individual known as "the man of lawlessness". This is where Paul's teaching gets a little complicated, but pay attention, because Paul says that it is vital. He only spent three weeks in Thessalonica but it is evident from 2:5 that "the man of lawlessness" formed part of his initial teaching.[2] He told his converts about Jesus' warning in Matthew 24 that the prophecy in Daniel 7 had only been partly fulfilled. It had been fulfilled in the short term when King Antiochus IV replaced the Lord's altar in the Temple at Jerusalem with a rival altar to the Greek god Zeus in around 169 BC, prompting the Maccabean rebellion.[3] But it would also be

---

[1] For example, Jesus predicts this in Matthew 24:12 and throughout much of Revelation.

[2] Whatever else we teach new converts, it is vital that we give them similar eschatological teaching.

[3] This altar to Zeus is called *"the abomination that causes desolation"* in Daniel 9:27, 11:31 and 12:11. Jesus tells us that it prefigured an even worse abomination (Matthew 24:15; Mark 13:14).

fulfilled in the long term by a person infiltrating the Church and trying to shift its focus away from the cross of Jesus and on to his own pet idols instead.[4]

Third, Paul tells us that this struggle will take place throughout the whole of AD history. A particular individual will be the ultimate Man of Lawlessness towards the end, but there will be many little men and women of lawlessness in every generation. Paul tells us that their power is already at work in the world but that God's grace is holding back the great Man of Lawlessness until the very end of time. John says something similar when he tells us that *"the Antichrist is coming, even now many antichrists have come."*[5] Paul does not want us to be surprised when the match looks increasingly hopeless in its final stages, because many people believe this false gospel and these false miracles which are inspired and empowered by the Devil. As true warriors, we must not panic as the battle reaches its final crescendo. When we see these things, it simply shows us that God's game plan is unfolding exactly as he said it would.

Fourth, Paul tells us to expect frequent waves of persecution against Christians. Just as King Antiochus killed many Jews to occupy their Temple, these men and women of lawlessness will mistreat Christians in their lust to infiltrate the Church and to divert its worship away from Jesus. Sometimes this persecution will be obvious: abuse, imprisonment and death. At other times it will be more subtle: laughter, exclusion and hatred. Whatever it looks like, we must stand firm in our faith. It will never be game, set and match to the Devil.[6]

---

[4] The Greek word for *lawlessness* is *anomia*, which means *rejecting the Law*. We can therefore expect such individuals to deny the moral absolutes of Scripture and to call people to worship false freedom instead.

[5] 1 John 2:18, 22; 4:3; 2 John 7. In English the prefix *anti-* means *"opposed to"* but in Greek it means *"instead of"*. The man of lawlessness therefore does not simply oppose Jesus. He wants to supplant him.

[6] 1 John 4:3 refers to *"the spirit of the antichrist,"* which reminds us that this struggle is not with human beings (Ephesians 6:12). A powerful demon is at work through each of these men and women of lawlessness.

Fifth and most important of all, Paul tells us that we can expect an amazing turnaround in the final stages of world history. In 2:3, he gives the "man of lawlessness" a second name. He also calls him "the man doomed to destruction."[7] He is the one *"whom the Lord Jesus will overthrow with the breath of his mouth and destroy by the splendour of his coming."*[8] He may win some important points and start acting as if he has already been crowned champion, but he cannot stand before the mighty serve of the Risen Lord Jesus. One little blow and Jesus will topple his man-made kingdom like a house of cards. When Jesus returns, the brightness of his glory will be more than enough to sweep the reign of darkness away.[9]

This chapter is very detailed but in some ways it is not detailed enough. Who is the great Man of Lawlessness? Who holds him back until the proper time? Paul does not tell us because he thinks this is enough information to turn us into true warriors.[10] We need not panic when it looks like it is game, set and match to the Devil, because we know that Jesus will emerge as victor in the end. He is coming back to earth and we will praise him for his game plan throughout eternity.

---

[7] The Greek phrase means literally *the Son of Destruction*. It is the same phrase that Jesus uses to describe Judas Iscariot in John 17:12.

[8] Paul uses the Greek word *parousia* to describe Jesus' *arrival* back on earth in 2:1 and 2:8, just as he did in 1 Thessalonians 2:19, 3:13, 4:15 and 5:23. The man of lawlessness also has his own fake *parousia* in 2:9.

[9] It is foolish to imagine that God will save all people at the end, even if they have not repented of their sin. Jesus' holiness will be so splendid on that Day that anything sinful will inevitably be destroyed.

[10] Paul calls these events a *mustērion* in 2:7, which means *a secret only revealed by God*. All we know is that in Daniel 10:12–13 the man of lawlessness is hindered by a struggle between powerful angels and demons.

Push and Pull (2:9–12)

They perish because they refused to love the truth and so be saved.

(2 Thessalonians 2:10)

You have probably heard the joke about the man who tried to get his sofa down the stairs of his apartment block. One of his neighbours saw him sweating and took pity on him but, if anything, it felt harder with his neighbour's help. Eventually, he gave up in exhaustion and told his neighbour that he didn't think they would ever manage to get the sofa down the stairs. *"Down the stairs?!"* asked his surprised neighbour. *"I thought we were trying to get the sofa* ***up*** *the stairs!"*

If you feel unfruitful in your attempts to share the Gospel and win people to Christ, it is possible that this is your problem. If we fail to understand what the Holy Spirit is doing in people's hearts, we can find ourselves working against him. Paul expects his teaching about the end of world history to make us want to share the Gospel urgently with others. He therefore finishes his teaching about the man of lawlessness with two important insights which help us work together with the Holy Spirit.

First, Paul warns us not to treat the Gospel as God's message to *the unhappy pagan*. Think about it. Most contemporary Gospel preaching assumes that unbelievers are dissatisfied with their lives and that they will respond to Jesus if we show them he is the answer to their unmet needs. If they are lonely, Jesus will be their friend. If they are afraid, he will be their shelter. If they feel guilty, he will be their forgiveness. If they feel empty, he will give their life meaning. The problem with this message is not that it is untrue – the Bible tells us that Jesus really is the answer to all these needs. The problem is that this is only part of the truth. Most unbelievers are not unhappy at all. Paul tells us in 2:12 that they *delight in wickedness.*

If we share the Gospel as nothing more than God's promise to help unhappy unbelievers, we will find ourselves working against the Holy Spirit. Non-Christians will notice our assumption that faith in Jesus is only for weak people and they will therefore resist whatever else he is doing in their hearts. Christians will stop sharing the Gospel when their friends tell them that they are content with things other than Jesus filling each of these needs. Even if they persist in sharing, their friends will simply point out that many professing Christians seem lonelier and emptier and unhappier than they are. The truth is that people refuse to delight in the Gospel because they are already finding their delight in a life of sin and rebellion against God.

On 15th April 1912, the *Titanic* sank during its maiden voyage. Three-quarters of its passengers died in the icy water, even though its lifeboats were half-empty. Most of the passengers refused to believe there was a problem, so the earliest lifeboats left the ship less than a third full.[1] Now imagine that you are on the *Titanic* and have a chance to warn the passengers. Would you try to tell them that lifeboats are more comfortable than cruise liners? Would you tell them that you have a fantastic lifeboat testimony and that they will enjoy their voyage so much more if they have a lifeboat testimony too? Of course not. They would simply point out that the lifeboats look colder and much less inviting than the comforts of their cabin. Instead, you would tell them the complete truth: that the ship is sinking and that the lifeboats, uncomfortable as they are, offer the only hope of salvation. The Holy Spirit will not work with us if we peddle

[1] "Lifeboat 1" saved only 12 people, despite having capacity for 40. Only five of those 12 were passengers.

a false Gospel to those around us. He is waiting for us to tell them that they are like the happiest passenger on the *Titanic*. However delightful their life is without Jesus, they need to repent and receive him as Lord before it is too late.

Second, Paul warns us not to treat the Gospel as God's answer to *the confused pagan*. Unbelievers do not reject the truth because they cannot understand it. They reject it because they choose to misunderstand it. Paul tells us in 2:10 that, because they delight in wickedness, *they refuse to love the truth*. They perish because they do not want the Gospel message to be true. We need to reason with people to show them that the Christian faith is reasonable and true, but we must not pander to their egos by pretending that they are honest seekers who simply lack information.[2] Paul reasons with people throughout the book of Acts by showing them that they have wilfully chosen to believe a lie and can only be saved if they repent and embrace the truth of the Gospel.[3]

Professor Thomas Nagel of New York University shares very honestly about his own atheistic worldview:

> *I want atheism to be true and am made uneasy by the fact that some of the most intelligent and well-informed people I know are religious believers. It isn't just that I don't believe in God and, naturally, hope that I'm right in my belief. It's that I hope there is no God! I don't want there to be a God; I don't want the universe to be like that.*[4]

---

[2] Paul reasoned carefully with unbelievers in Acts 17:2–4, 17; 18:4, 19; 19:8 and 26.

[3] For example, in Acts 13:9–12, 40–41, 46–47; 14:15, 17:30–31, 18:5–6 and 28:23–28.

[4] Thomas Nagel is a professor of philosophy. He wrote this in his book *The Last Word* (1997).

If we want to work with the Holy Spirit and not find ourselves pushing and pulling against him, we need to recognize that the primary reasons why people disbelieve the Gospel are not to be found in the head, but in the heart and in the will.

Consequently, Paul tells us that the main person we are to preach the Gospel for is God himself. He tells us in 2:11 that when people choose to delight in wickedness and to hate the truth, God responds by *sending them a powerful delusion so that they believe the lie.* They become the biggest victims of their own rebellion, since God removes the light of his Holy Spirit from their hearts so that they cannot see that they have fallen for a lie. Since they can only be saved if God speaks *"Let there be light!"* into their heart, we need to share the Gospel in the way he has commanded. We need to push where the Holy Spirit is pushing and to pull where the Holy Spirit is pulling because only he can cure people of their spiritual blindness and enable them to see.[5]

Paul knew how to bring unbelievers to the point of conversion. He and his teammates had managed to plant a thriving church at Thessalonica through only three weeks of preaching. So we need to take him seriously when he tells us that we work against the Holy Spirit if we share the Gospel as if the major problem is that unbelievers are unhappy or confused.

But if we share the Gospel in a way that pushes and pulls with the Holy Spirit and not against him – explaining that Jesus is Lord and that he is coming back to judge the world, whether our hearers like it or not – we will be very fruitful. Whenever we push and pull with the Holy Spirit by sharing the real Gospel, we will find that people who delight in wickedness are set free from their delusion. We will find that God enables them to love the truth and to be saved.

[5] Paul teaches more on this in 2 Corinthians 4:1–6.

Stand (2:13–3:5)

So then, brothers and sisters, stand firm and hold fast to the teachings we passed on to you.

(2 Thessalonians 2:15)

The Macedonians knew a thing or two about how to advance quickly. In Daniel 7, Alexander the Great's empire is depicted, not just as a leopard, but as a leopard with two pairs of wings. In only thirteen years he created an empire that stretched 3,000 miles east from Macedonia to the Himalayas. That's why Paul is so surprising when he tells the Thessalonians how to advance as true warriors of Jesus. He tells them that the way to advance in the Christian life is to stay standing still.

It must have been a bit of a disappointment for the Thessalonians when Paul told them in 2:15 to *"stand firm and hold fast to the teachings we passed on to you."* It meant that Paul was not going to respond to the false letter by rushing back to see them in person and that, despite their nation's illustrious history of empire and advance, he believed their biggest need was simply to stand firm in the Gospel. The Greek word that Paul uses in this verse for *teachings* is *paradoseis,* which is normally translated as *traditions*. True warriors of Jesus do not advance by adding something extra to the Gospel. They advance by not seeking to modify the Gospel and by experiencing it ever more deeply.[1]

Paul tells us in 2:13 that we are to stand firm in the fact

[1] Paul says something similar when he tells us four times in Ephesians 6:11,13 and 14 that the only way for us to advance in the spiritual battle is if we learn to *stand*.

that *God has chosen us.*[2] In some Greek manuscripts Paul tells the Thessalonians that God chose to save them *ap'archēs*, or *from the beginning*. In other Greek manuscripts Paul says that God chose them to be the *aparchē*, or *first-fruits*, of his salvation. Both statements are true. If we want to advance in our Christian lives and to influence others, we need to stand firm in the fact that God chose to save us before the dawn of time[3] in order that we might spread the message of his salvation to many others.[4]

Paul tells us in 2:14 that we are to stand firm in the fact that *God has called us to have a share in his glory*. Since our salvation was based on God's initiative and not our own, we can expect its fruit to be God-sized and not man-sized. Elsewhere Paul tells us that God has transformed us by grace into his *peripoiēsis* or *treasured possession*, the word that the Greek Old Testament used for God choosing Israel to be his private treasure collection.[5] But in this verse Paul tells us something new which is just as mind-blowing as the Old Testament promise that God turns scrap metal into gold. He tells us that God has also turned his own glory into our *peripoiēsis* or *treasured possession* too! We do not advance by becoming distracted by things that are not the Gospel. We only ever advance by standing firm in what it means for us to have been granted a share in Jesus' glory.

Paul tells us in 2:16–17 that we are to stand firm in the fact that *God loves us and wants to strengthen us by giving us an eternal encouragement and hope*. He uses past tenses to remind us that God has already given us these things, but he slips in and out of prayer because we need to lay hold of them through active

2 Paul refers to the doctrine of election several times in 1 and 2 Thessalonians because he expects it to give us courage under fire.

3 Ephesians 1:4–5 and Revelation 17:8 both state this unambiguously.

4 The first-fruits which grew at the start of harvest season promised that much more fruit was on its way. Paul uses this word in Romans 16:5 and 1 Corinthians 16:15 to promise God will use us to reach many others.

5 When the New Testament uses the word *peripoiēsis* in Ephesians 1:14 and 1 Peter 2:9, it echoes Malachi 3:17.

prayer. It is tragic when Christians get distracted by things that are fascinating but which are not the Gospel, playing with fool's gold instead of the real thing. God has given us all that we need in the Gospel. We simply need to stand firm and to lay hold of it in prayer.

In the movie *Die Hard*, Alan Rickman's villain remarks that *"When Alexander saw the breadth of his domain, he wept, for there were no more worlds to conquer."*[6] The Thessalonians must have felt the same way when, despite their heritage, Paul commanded them simply to stand. However, Alan Rickman's villain is misquoting Plutarch. What he actually said was that Alexander wept and told his friends: *"It is right that I cry because the number of worlds is infinite and I have not yet fully conquered one."*[7] Paul is actually telling us that it will take us an entire lifetime to explore and to lay hold of everything that is ours through the Gospel. Standing firm in the Gospel is never passive. It means advancing rapidly. To encourage us, Paul gives us three prayer requests that show us what will happen if we stand firm in the Gospel.

Paul tells us in 3:1 that if we stand firm in the Gospel, *the Word of God will run*. Paul uses such a strange word to describe the spread of the Gospel that he must do so as a deliberate contrast to 2:15.[8] If we rest in what Jesus has done for us, spreading the Gospel is not difficult because the Gospel does the hard work for us. Whenever those around us see the contagious lifestyle, contagious hope and contagious community which the Gospel produces in those who honour its commands, they are

[6] *Die Hard* (20th Century Fox, 1988).

[7] Plutarch in his essay "On Contentedness of Mind", which forms part of his *Moralia* (33.4).

[8] The Greek word *stēkō* in 2:15 and *trechō* in 3:1 are opposites, meaning *to stand firm* and *to run*.

attracted to Jesus much more quickly than they ever are by busy evangelistic programmes.[9]

Paul tells us in 3:2–4 that if we stand firm in the Gospel, *God will deliver us from danger*. Our confidence in the face of danger, both here and in 1 Thessalonians 5:24, is firmly grounded in the fact that God is faithful.[10] Moses preached this Gospel to the panicking Israelites when he told them at the Red Sea: *"Do not be afraid. Stand firm... The Lord will fight for you; you need only to be still"* (Exodus 14:13–14). This same Gospel still turns fearful converts into fearsome warriors for Jesus.

Paul tells us in 3:5 that if we stand firm in the Gospel, *God will direct and guide us*. The problem with running quickly is that we often run in the wrong direction. We tire ourselves out and end up making far less progress than we would if we simply stood firm in the Gospel. Paul promises us that the Gospel will teach us to love like God and to persevere like Jesus. It will turn us into warriors who have all we need to keep pressing forward in the midst of persecution.

True warriors advance because they have first learned to stand firm, so let's not get distracted from the Gospel. If we stand firm in the Gospel, it will run forward very quickly.

Like a leopard with two pairs of wings.

[9] Luke uses this same phrase to describe non-Christians responding to the Gospel in Acts 13:48. Paul is linking back to 1 Thessalonians 2:13 and to his teaching in his earlier letter about how the Gospel spreads.

[10] The word for *faith* in 3:2 is *pistis* and the word for *faithful* in 3:3 is *pistos*. Paul is making a deliberate play on words here between the faithlessness of people and the faithfulness of God.

Busy Body (3:6–15)

We hear that some among you are idle and disruptive. They are not busy; they are busybodies.

(2 Thessalonians 3:11)

The Ancient Greeks despised the very idea of doing manual labour. That was what slaves were for, and the Ancient Greeks had a lot of slaves. There were roughly as many slaves as there were freemen and women in Thessalonica, so they followed the lifestyle of the philosophers in Athens who *"spent their time doing nothing but talking about and listening to the latest ideas"* (Acts 17:21). The Thessalonians lived in a culture where talk was noble and action was servile. It therefore isn't surprising that many of Paul's converts were not busy; they had so much free time that they had become busybodies.[1]

This was already a problem in the church when Paul wrote to them six months earlier. In 1 Thessalonians 5:14, he told them to warn believers who were *ataktos*, meaning *unruly* or *disorderly*.[2] This was a military term, which meant literally *absent from the ranks*, like a Greek warrior who went AWOL when he ought to be in line and fighting against the enemy. Paul saw this as such a serious issue that he reminded them in 2:9 that *"we worked night and day in order not to be a burden to anyone while we preached the gospel of God to you."* He urged them sternly in 4:11–12 to *"Make it your ambition to lead a quiet life: you should mind your own business and work with*

---

[1] This is Paul's play on words, not mine. In 3:11, he says in Greek that some people in the church were not *ergazomenoi* but *periergazomenoi*.

[2] Paul uses either the verb or the adverb of *ataktos* three times in 3:6, 3:7 and 3:11 in order to link back to his earlier instructions in 1 Thessalonians 5:14.

your hands, just as we told you, so that your daily life may win the respect of outsiders and so that you will not be dependent on anybody."

After the arrival of the false letter, the problem that had been brewing in the church at Thessalonica suddenly exploded. Some people were so confused about the second coming of Jesus that they thought there was no point in their bothering to work at all. Paul needed to warn them not to ape the folly of the Greek philosophers. The second coming had not yet happened, so this was not the time for talk instead of action. True warriors are never absent from the ranks during a battle.

In 3:6, Paul reminds the Thessalonians to take note of *his authority*. He did not begin either of these two letters by stating his credentials as an apostle, but he is not afraid to issue orders like a military officer now. *"We command you in the name of the Lord Jesus Christ"*, he tells his converts, using language that is similar to the words he used to cast out a demon in Acts 16:18. True warriors obey their leaders, so Paul and his teammates tell the Thessalonians to obey the founding fathers of their church. The word Paul uses for his *teaching* in this verse is *paradosis*, which we saw in the previous chapter can also be translated as *tradition*. We need to listen with the utmost respect to those who handed down to us the Gospel in the first place. Unruly believers may not be true converts at all.

In 3:7–9, Paul reminds the Thessalonians to take note of *his example*. He only stayed for three weeks in their city but he was determined not to freeload off his converts *"in order to offer ourselves as a model for you to imitate."* Travelling Greek philosophers did not need to work with their hands because they took money from their students, but Paul refused to copy them because he wanted to teach that Christians work hard in the ranks of the church. If a Gospel-preaching, church-planting, miracle-working, dead-raising apostle like Paul rolled up his sleeves and worked hard to put more money into the church than he took out, so must they. People who shook Paul's hands were never struck by how smooth they were from underlining verses in his Bible and from praying for the sick. They were struck by how rough they were from the harsh acids that were used by ancient tentmakers and tanners.[3]

In 3:10, Paul reminds the Thessalonians to take note of *his instructions*. While he was still with them, he had told them to resist their culture's disdain for hard work by issuing a rule that *"The one who is unwilling to work shall not eat."* This verse has often been used as an excuse for not helping the poor, but Galatians 2:10 and 1 Timothy 5:1–16 make it clear that Paul encouraged the churches he planted to support those who were unable to work.[4] He simply instructed the Thessalonians to make a clear distinction between those who were unable to work and those who were unwilling to work. They needed to feel the painful consequences of their laziness so that they would learn the meaning of Proverbs 16:26: *"The labourer's appetite works for him; his hunger drives him on."*

Paul wants to turn us into true warriors for Jesus, so these words are just as relevant for us today. The modern welfare state is designed to help those who cannot work but it can often be abused by those who prefer to work the system instead of working a job. Paul issues another solemn command in the name of Jesus in 3:12, telling us that responding to the Gospel means settling down and working hard to earn the food we eat.

These words are just as relevant to Christians who are fortunate enough not to need to earn a salary. If you are wealthy enough or at a life stage where you do not need to work, Paul

[3] Acts 18:3 tells us that Paul worked as a tentmaker in Corinth. He only stopped when a large gift from the Philippians enabled him to plant the Corinthian church full-time without the need to take any money from it (Acts 18:5; 2 Corinthians 11:9; Philippians 4:15–16).

[4] We need not be ashamed to accept help from the church if we need it, but Paul warns us in 1 Timothy 5:8 that if we take help when we could be contributing, we are even worse than an unbeliever.

warns you not to use your free time to indulge in gossip or in idle pursuits. The church should be a busy body, not full of busybodies. Even Bible study and theological discussion can become an excuse for inactivity. Like me, you may need to heed the seventeenth-century English writer Francis Bacon when he warns that *"To spend too much time in studies is sloth."*[5] Growing as a Christian means studying and praying and discussing, but Christian maturity is not measured by the calluses on our backsides. True Christian maturity always results in our getting calluses on our hands.

In 3:13, Paul tells those who have been Christians longest not to tire of doing good. They must not become idle critics or jaded cynics. They are veteran warriors who should be leading the less experienced believers forward. In 3:14–15, he ends by telling all of us to avoid idle believers, shaming them back into the ranks so that they can join us in fighting against our common enemy.

Paul is looking for true warriors for Jesus: people who will join the ranks of the Gospel army and work hard in their God-given role; people who are not busybodies but who make the church a busy body.

[5] Francis Bacon in his essay on studies in *Essays* (1625).

Converts and Warriors (3:16–18)

The grace of our Lord Jesus Christ be with you all.

(2 Thessalonians 3:18)

Paul was pleased with the Christians at Thessalonica. They had proved they were true converts by their faithful endurance in the face of persecution. He was confident that they would learn to be true warriors as they applied the teaching of his second letter. As he signs off the last of his two letters to the Thessalonians, Paul gives us four big reasons why he is confident that God will finish turning the scrap metal of their lives into gold. As we come to the end of lesson two in Paul's discipleship training school, these are also reasons why we can be confident that God will complete his work in our own lives too.

Paul is confident in 3:16 because he knows the Lord will grant them *peace*. That's an unusual way to end a letter to people who are being persecuted and who need to become warriors. Far from easing off, the persecution would get much fiercer twelve years later when the Romans started to persecute Christians for the first time. It would make their Jewish enemies seem mild in comparison, yet Paul believes the Holy Spirit will grant them peace on the inside and enable them to defy their circumstances. Paul tells us that God is *"the Lord of peace"* and that his presence is all we need to be at peace in the midst of battle and bitter persecution. We belong to the age that is yet to come, so Paul assures us that God will *"give you peace at all times and in every way."*

The Greek word that Paul uses twice in this verse for peace

is *eirēnē*. When it is used as a girl's name we translate it Irene. The church at Thessalonica would have a young girl named Irene in its youth group who experienced God's peace and was empowered to act as a true warrior for Jesus even though it cost her everything. In 303 AD, the Emperor Diocletian issued an edict that all Bibles must be destroyed and all church meetings must be closed. When Irene was found to be hiding a Bible and other Christian books in her bedroom, she was brutally persecuted. Knowing she was a virgin, the city rulers ordered that she be stripped naked and chained up in one of the brothels in Thessalonica until she renounced her faith in Jesus. When she refused to do so despite two days of this torture, her books were burnt and she was executed in April 304 AD. God made Irene live up to her name by giving her peace in the midst of this trial. She was a true convert and a true warrior.

Paul is also confident in 3:16 because he knows the Lord will grant them his *presence*. He began these two letters by making it clear that he and his teammates are merely extras in a drama in which Jesus always plays the starring role. He is therefore happy to sign off this letter and to entrust his converts to God's care because he knows that God will still be with them. Sure enough, we are told in the book of Acts that two of Paul's Thessalonian converts quickly grew strong enough to come and join his church-planting team. Aristarchus and Secundus had been pagan scrap metal, but God turned them into gold. Aristarchus remained so loyal to Paul when he was imprisoned in Rome that the Emperor Nero's soldiers saw him as a key figure in the Church and imprisoned him too.[1] Aristarchus means *"The Best Leader"*, and God made him live up to his name just like Irene. He was a true convert and a true warrior.

Paul is confident in 3:17 because he is able to give them *proof* at the end of his letter. Having dictated most of it to a scribe, he now signs off with his own hand as a mark of

[1] Acts 19:29, 20:4 and 27:2, Colossians 4:10 and Philemon 24.

authenticity which will stop his converts from falling for any more fake letters forged by their enemies. Sure enough, we discover in the pages of Church history that the church at Thessalonica remained true to the Gospel which Paul had given them. Their contagious lifestyle and contagious hope attracted the son of a local senator to join their contagious community. Demetrius was part of the ruling elite which was persecuting the Christians, but they captured his heart through the way in which they doggedly hunted him down with their love. His conversion sent such shockwaves through the city that the Emperor Diocletian ordered him to renounce his faith and offer sacrifices to the pagan gods. When he refused in 306 AD, a squad of Roman soldiers stabbed him to death with their spears. He was a true convert and a true warrior. He was also vindicated. It was partly due to his witness that the Emperor Theodosius issued an edict from Thessalonica in 380 AD which decreed that the Christian Gospel was now the official faith of the Roman Empire.

Paul is confident in 3:18 because he knows that they will never run out of God's *provision*. He began both of these letters by blessing his converts with a deeper experience of God's grace, so he ends this second letter with another blessing that they will experience God's grace even more. God's provision will never run dry towards us because there are no limits to his grace. Some readers remark that Paul's tone is less affectionate in 2 Thessalonians than in 1 Thessalonians (despite the fact that he addresses them seven times as his beloved *"brothers and sisters"*[2]), but this misses the point. He wrote this second letter to train them to be warriors. He has taught them to rely on the Lord's gracious provision and not on the one who first told them about it. As far as we know, Paul never wrote again to Thessalonica and he only went back to visit the church in

[2] 2 Thessalonians 1:3; 2:1, 13, 15; 3:1, 6, 13.

passing two or three times more before he died.[3] He prepared it to depend on God's work on the inside instead of on its founding father on the outside. Paul is confident as he signs off this letter that the Lord will turn them into true converts and true warriors.

The church at Thessalonica took to heart the words of these two letters. It became part of a Gospel chain reaction which spread from its harbour across the seas and along its busy Roman roads into the unreached hinterland. Only five years later, Paul was able to tell his friends at Rome that the Balkans north of Thessalonica had been fully reached without him.[4]

It is time for us to leave the Thessalonians behind and to embark on the final three lessons in Paul's discipleship training school. Let's not forget these first two lessons which established such a powerful church in the Macedonian capital. God used these two lessons to turn the Thessalonians into true converts and true warriors. He used these two lessons to take pagans from the scrapheap and to turn them into precious gold.

---

3 Acts 20:1–6; 1 Timothy 1:3.

4 Romans 15:19, 23. Paul never visited Illyricum, the Roman province in modern-day Croatia, but it was at the end of a busy trade route from Thessalonica.

Lesson Three – Titus:

Truly Fruitful

The Fourth Seed (1:1–5)

To Titus, my true son in our common faith.

(Titus 1:4)

The most remarkable thing about Paul's letter to Titus is the fact that he ever wrote it. Most people miss this because they place Titus on the same pedestal as Paul, but all the evidence suggests Titus was an absolute nobody. He was pagan scrap metal and his life reminds us what God can do through anyone who surrenders to him.

Let's examine the facts. When Luke summarized the first thirty years of Church history in the book of Acts, he failed to mention Titus, even in passing. He mentions a dozen or more of Paul's team members, but not Titus, which is particularly surprising since they both became Christians at the same church in Antioch and they both served for several years together in Paul's team. Luke knew Titus as well as anyone, but he clearly thought that Titus had not played a big part in the story. Paul did not write to Titus because he was exceptionally gifted, but to demonstrate how God turns scrap metal into gold.

Paul mentions Titus thirteen times in his letters, but when he does so it is clear that nobody else shares his high view of him.[1] He tells us in Galatians 2:1–3 that he took Titus to Jerusalem because the Jews doubted that Greek converts like him were converted at all. He urges the Corinthians so strongly to respect Titus that it is obvious they were tempted to despise

[1] Paul mentions Titus by name nine times in 2 Corinthians, twice in Galatians, once in 2 Timothy and once at the start of Titus. Paul calls him his *"son"* in Titus 1:4 because he was responsible for his conversion.

him. Paul is forced to remind them that *"he is my partner and co-worker among you,"* and to ask them, *"Did we not walk in the same footsteps by the same Spirit?"*[2] Paul did not write to Titus because he was a superstar in Christian ministry but because he was an ordinary and unimpressive member of his team. He entrusted great responsibility to Titus because he truly believed that God turns scrap metal into gold.

Twelve years have passed since Paul wrote his second letter to the Thessalonians. He spent four of those years conducting his third missionary journey, planting a huge church at Ephesus and strengthening the churches in Macedonia and Greece. He was arrested in Jerusalem in May 57 AD and spent the next five years in prison in Caesarea and in Rome. After his release in 62 AD, he planted churches in Spain before heading back to the Eastern Mediterranean. His first destination was the island of Crete, which he had visited briefly as a prisoner on a ship bound for Rome. He had not forgotten the pagan islanders whose faces he had seen but whose souls he had not been permitted to save. When he left the island for a second time, he told Titus to stay behind to complete the work before joining him in Greece at the end of the sailing season.[3] This letter therefore contains Paul's instructions to one of his true converts and warriors. It acts as lesson three in his discipleship training school.

The theme of this third lesson is that God wants to make us truly fruitful. Paul is able to tell his unimpressive team member in 1:5 that *"The reason I left you in Crete was that you might put in order what was left unfinished."* He has no doubt that Titus will be able to complete the job because he is confident that the Holy Spirit is at work within him. He remembers the promise

---

[2] 2 Corinthians 8:23; 12:18. Titus had acted as delivery boy for Paul's letter and the Corinthians were evidently disappointed that Titus came instead of Paul.

[3] We can piece this together from Acts 20:16, Romans 15:23–28, Titus 1:5 and 3:12, as well as from 1 Clement 5:7 (c.95 AD), the Muratorian Fragment (c.180 AD) and Eusebius in his *Church History* (2.22.2–8).

that Jesus made in the Parable of the Sower in Matthew 13. Titus is not like the first seed that was sown, since the Gospel has taken root in his heart and he is a true convert. He is not like the second seed, since he has put down deep roots into the Gospel and resisted the scorching heat of persecution like a true warrior. He is not like the third seed, since he has turned his back on everything that might suffocate his complete devotion to Jesus. Therefore, Paul reasons, he must be like the fourth seed that was sown in the parable. He is like the seed which *"fell on good soil, where it produced a crop – a hundred, sixty or thirty times what was sown."*[4] Paul is not put off by any of the weaknesses he can see in Titus. If he is a true convert and a true warrior, he can be taught to become truly fruitful. The only question is whether his fruitfulness will be thirtyfold, sixtyfold or a hundredfold.

These opening verses of Paul's letter show us why he was confident that Titus would be very fruitful. It's easy to miss this because most English translations downplay the meaning of the Greek word *doulos* and overplay the meaning of the Greek word *apostolos*. The word *doulos* did not just mean servant. It meant slave. It was one of the most despised words in the Roman Empire. The word *apostolos* means apostle when it is used in a Christian sense, but its secular meaning was simply *sent one* or *messenger boy*. Paul therefore starts the letter by reminding us that he is nothing more than the slave of God and the messenger boy of Jesus. A nobody like Titus can be just as fruitful as Paul is because he is a nobody too! Every time we write ourselves off in God's purposes and every time we refuse to trust God to work through other people, we demonstrate that, unlike Paul, we have forgotten this.

Paul is more aware of God's promises and God's purposes than he is of his team member's personal weaknesses. He is not

[4] Matthew 13:8. Jesus does not simply promise that they will reap 30, 60 or 100 more converts like themselves, but that they will reap 30, 60 or 100 times the entire quantity of seed the farmer sowed.

daunted by the fact that Crete is the largest of the Greek islands, over 3,000 square miles in size, or by the fact that he can only spare Titus until the autumn. He believes that God has an *"elect"* throughout Crete and that he has promised since before the dawn of time that he will save and transform them.[5] He fixes his eyes on *"God our Saviour"* and upon *"Christ Jesus our Saviour,"*[6] which makes him confident that now is the *"appointed season"* for their salvation.[7] If God is who God says he is, it doesn't matter if his servant is a nobody.

Paul is more aware of God's faithfulness than he is of his team member's failures. He tells Titus that the Lord's name is the *"God Who Does Not Lie"* and assures him that faith in God's words will always lead to godliness.[8] The power to change lives comes from God's Word and not from the person who preaches it, so our own lack of talent makes no difference. Paul calls Titus *"my true son in our common faith"* because he is convinced that he is like the fourth seed in the parable.[9] He is a true convert and a true warrior, so he is going to be truly fruitful.

Paul wrote this letter to Titus but he also wrote it to you and me, because we are nobodies too. Lesson three in Paul's discipleship training school teaches how God makes nobodies like us truly fruitful.

---

[5] Paul shows us in 1:1 that a proper understanding of God's election will cause us to share the Gospel more actively, not less actively. We also see this in Acts 18:9–11.

[6] Note that Paul deliberately tweaks the blessing which he uses at the start of all his letters in order to stress to Titus that Jesus is the Saviour. He assures him that his confidence for Crete is based on Jesus, not on him.

[7] Paul's description of AD history being the *right season* for salvation ties in with his teaching in Romans 5:6, Galatians 4:4, 1 Timothy 2:6 and 2 Timothy 1:9–10.

[8] When Paul calls the Lord *The God Who Does Not Lie*, he may be thinking back to Numbers 23:19 and 1 Samuel 15:29. He tells us in 1:12 that the battle for Crete is a conflict between Greek lies and God's truth.

[9] Paul uses a similar phrase in 1 Timothy 1:2. The instructions he wrote to Titus from Ephesus in 64 AD are closely echoed by a similar letter which he wrote to Timothy from Philippi in 65 AD.

A Hundred Cities (1:5–9)

The reason I left you in Crete was that you might put in order what was left unfinished and appoint elders in every town, as I directed you.

(Titus 1:5)

People often refer to the three letters that Paul wrote to Titus and Timothy as the "pastoral epistles". This name is quite helpful if it reminds us that Paul did not write these letters to churches but to individual converts. But it is very unhelpful if it makes us think these letters are nothing more than a handbook to pastoral care within the Church. They are missionary pamphlets. They tell Titus and Timothy how to establish churches that can reach an entire region with the Gospel.[1]

Establishing churches that would reach the whole of Crete was going to be very difficult. Cretans had been converted on the Day of Pentecost in Acts 2:11, but they had failed to reach the rest of their island with the Gospel. This was partly due to geography, since Crete is an island of mountain ranges and deep valleys and gorges which separate people from one another. Homer calls Crete *"the island of a hundred populous cities,"* so it could only be reached if it had a hundred fruitful churches.[2] Paul therefore begins his letter by telling Titus to appoint hundreds of church leaders. He should *"appoint elders in every town,"* just as Paul did in Turkey in Acts 14:23. Titus needed to believe that

---

[1] We see this theme most clearly in Titus 2:1–10 and 1 Timothy 2:1–4, but it runs throughout the three letters.

[2] Homer says this in his *Iliad* (2.645) and he says something similar in his *Odyssey* (19.174).

God had appointed him to be very fruitful and that God would enable him to make the Cretan believers very fruitful too.

Pioneering missionaries often refer to the "choke effect" of successful evangelism. Since converts need discipling, the first few hundred converts often bring missionary momentum to an abrupt halt. Missionaries become so busy caring for those who have been converted that they have no time to venture back into the harvest fields. They become like many church leaders, so engrossed in the needs of their congregation that they lose sight of the Great Commission. Paul tells Titus that the "choke effect" can be avoided if we remember that God turns scrap metal into gold. Paul tells him to expect his converts to be fruitful missionaries themselves. They should increase missionary momentum in Crete from the moment they are converted.

Paul wrote this letter in 64 AD from Ephesus, where he was working with Timothy to resolve some problems in the church he had planted there. The following year he wrote a very similar letter to Timothy from Philippi to teach him how to finish off his work at Ephesus. This explains why the two letters are so similar, and particularly the two lists of qualifications for church leaders in Titus 1:5–9 and 1 Timothy 3:1–7. There is one glaring difference between the two lists, however. In the established church situation at Ephesus, where many people had been Christians for ten years or more, Paul tells Timothy that church elders must not be recent converts. In the pioneering situation in Crete, Paul gives Titus no such instruction because just about every believer was a new convert! Paul tells Titus that he needs to spot which believers are true converts and true warriors so that he can quickly entrust them with leading the other Christians forward. If Titus finds people who have learned lessons one and two in Paul's discipleship training school, he can trust God to teach them this third lesson too.

William Booth believed this. People laughed at the founder of The Salvation Army when he announced his plan to re-evangelize Great Britain. They asked him where he thought he would find enough leaders, so he told them: *"We shall get them from the public houses. Men who have felt the fire will be the best men to rescue others, and we shall never fail in getting the right men."* True to his word, he successfully entrusted the management of his largest soup kitchen to a notorious bare-knuckle fighter named Peter Monk within two weeks of his conversion.[3] He turned London's thieves and prostitutes and brawlers into God's evangelists and church leaders and missionaries. Because he truly believed that God turns scrap metal into gold, he expected all of his converts to be truly fruitful. As a result, they spread the Gospel far beyond the shores of Britain. His army of ordinary believers took the Gospel to the ends of the earth.

Only once in all his letters does Paul refer to church leaders as *poimenes*, the Greek word for *shepherds* or *pastors* (Ephesians 4:11). The rest of the time he either borrows the Jewish word *presbuteroi*, which was used for the *elders* who led each synagogue, or the Roman word *episkopoi*, which was used for *overseers* in the imperial civil service. Here he uses the Jewish word in 1:5 and the Roman word in 1:7, because he is less concerned with what church leaders are called than with what they do. Their work is so important that Paul begins his letter with a call to appoint the right leaders. He believes that if Titus gets the leaders right, everything else will follow. The right church leaders will deal with false teachers (1:10–16), attract new converts (2:1–10), disciple those new converts (2:11–15) and train them to live out their Christian faith in a hostile culture (3:1–15). Crete had a hundred towns and cities but it could be reached with only a few hundred good church leaders. With the right leaders in place, Crete was as good as

---

[3] Booth also entrusted Elijah Cadman – a former chimney sweep, drunkard and prizefighter – with senior leadership within The Salvation Army very soon after his arrival in London.

converted, but without them the battle was lost before it had begun.

Christians always become like their church leaders. We are reminded of this in 2 Thessalonians 3:7 and Hebrews 13:7, but it is also pretty obvious when we look around at churches today. Although many church leaders complain that their people do not follow them, the problem is usually that their people do. When leaders indulge sin, even in secret, they create churches in which people indulge sin. When leaders fail to care for the lost or to care for the saved, they create churches that fail in those same areas. When leaders lack the faith to advance in Jesus' mission, they create weak and passive churches. That's why Paul tells Titus to appoint teams of several elders in every town. A solo leader spells danger, but a team of great leaders can spur one another on.[4]

Non-Christians always judge the Church based on its leaders. We are reminded of this in 2 Peter 2:2, but it is also pretty obvious when we talk with unbelievers. Good church leaders give unbelievers a reason to take their church's message seriously, but sinful church leaders give unbelievers an easy excuse to reject its message.[5] That's why Paul places leadership right at the start of his letter to Titus, and it's why we should prize good church leadership too. When a church is led by a team of true converts and true warriors, the whole church can learn to become truly fruitful. Missionary momentum does not stall as the church advances. It keeps on spreading across a region and to the unreached nations of the world.

[4] We need to be careful not to project our existing leadership structures onto these verses, as the older English translations do when they translate *episkopos* as *bishop* in 1:7. New Testament churches were always led by teams of elders, as we can see from Acts 11:30, 14:23 and James 5:14.

[5] This happened in 2 Samuel 12:14 and Nehemiah 5:7–9. It still happens today.

Daedalus and Icarus (1:5–9)

An elder must be blameless... so that he can encourage others by sound doctrine and refute those who oppose it.

(Titus 1:6, 9)

We become like the people we admire. Crete's most celebrated myths were about its ancient King Minos, who was such a liar that he even tried to lie to the Greek gods. When he reneged on his promise to sacrifice a bull to Poseidon, the god punished him by making his wife lust after the bull. When she gave birth to the Minotaur, half-human and half-bull, King Minos was so horrified that he paid the great inventor Daedalus to construct a labyrinth in which to hide the monster from the world. When it was finished, he swindled Daedalus out of his payment and imprisoned him so he could not reveal its secrets to anyone. In 1:12, Paul tells Titus that the Cretans have become like their most famous ruler, but first he tells him the solution. If Titus wants to attract the whole of Crete to the Gospel, he needs to appoint church leaders that the island can admire.

Paul gives Titus fifteen things to look for in potential church leaders. It is very significant that not one of them is about gifting or potential. King Minos was very gifted and had huge potential. He created the first major civilization in European history and the world's first navy. He looked set to create the world's first maritime empire too. However, because of his character flaws he was murdered in his bathtub before he was able to do so.[1] All fifteen of these leadership attributes have to do with a leader's

---

1 Thucydides tells us this in his *History* (1.4).

character and *track record*.[2] Church leaders need to be selected from among those whose lives show the most clearly that God turns scrap metal into gold.

I often meet people who are frustrated that God has not used them as much as they hoped he would. They ask why he has not entrusted them with a greater position of leadership and I usually have to reply that it is because God really loves them. We are told in 1 Peter 5:5–6 that God actively blocks people who lack the character to handle a position of leadership. Daedalus escaped from prison along with his son Icarus by making wings out of candle wax and feathers. Because he loved his son, Daedalus warned him not to fly too high, but Icarus did not listen. He flew too close to the sun and the wax on his wings melted. Because he could not handle the gift his father gave him, he fell to his death in the sea below. God is not blocking you because he does not want you to be fruitful in leadership. He wants that more than you do, but he loves you too much to entrust you with wings before you are ready to fly.

In 1:6, Paul tells Titus to look for men who have been faithful in leading their families.[3] If a husband has been unfaithful to his wedding vows, he is unlikely to be faithful if entrusted with leading the Bride of Christ.[4] If a father has been too lazy or too scared to confront and discipline his own children, he is not the man to shepherd God's flock or to protect them from the many

---

[2] Paul expects Titus to appoint elders based on a sober assessment of their current character, not based on high hopes or prophetic hunches that they will change when offered the challenge of leadership.

[3] Paul assumes in these verses that churches will be led by men rather than women. We will examine why he says this and whether it still applies today when Paul explains it in much more detail in 1 Timothy 2–3.

[4] Paul is not saying that an elder must be married or even that he must not be remarried. The Greek phrase *"husband to one wife"* was put on gravestones to state that the deceased was a one-woman man who had remained faithful to his wedding vows and to the trust that his father-in-law had placed in him. Paul uses a similar phrase in 1 Timothy 5:9 to refer to women being faithful to their husbands.

wolves who dress up in sheep's clothing.[5] Paul points out in 1:7 that the Church is the household of God. The right church leaders can therefore be found among those who are already leading their own households well.

In 1:7, Paul tells Titus to look for people who have been faithful in leading themselves. A person who has not repented of their anger, their bullying or their use of force to get what they want will never be able to handle the increased temptation which church leadership brings. A person who has not learned to say no to a drink too many or to ill-earned money will never be able to say no to the many temptations which increased church responsibility brings. Handing a leadership role to such people would be more dangerous than it was for Daedalus to hand a pair of candle-wax wings to Icarus.

In 1:8, Paul tells Titus to look for people who have been faithful in their interactions with unbelievers. Like it or not, church leaders become the face of Christianity to the world. We must therefore look for people who are *philoxenos*, a Greek word that means far more than just *hospitable* in the sense of being willing to invite church friends back for lunch after a service. A *xenos* was a *foreigner* or *outsider* (hence our own word xenophobia), so Paul is saying that no one is to be considered for eldership unless they have a track record of loving those outside the church.[6] If they fail to make room for non-Christians in their home and diary, so will any church which they lead.

If the Cretan believers were to reach the rest of their island with the Gospel, they needed leaders who had a heart to do so and the character to match. They needed leaders who were so

---

[5] Paul is not saying that an elder must have children or that he is responsible for the actions of his adult children. He is pointing out that the behaviour of a man's children while they are at home is a reflection of his leadership of his family. A man who cannot lead children will not be able to lead a church.

[6] *Xenos* is the word that Paul uses in Ephesians 2:12 and 19. Hebrews 13:1–2 also makes a deliberate contrast between *philadelphia* (love for Christian brothers and sisters) and *philoxenia* (love for non-Christian outsiders).

captivated by what is good, so self-controlled, so upright, so holy and so disciplined that they naturally made unbelievers around them want to find out more about the Jesus who had changed them. This is what Paul means by the Greek word *anenklētos* in 1:6 and 1:7. Nobody is perfectly *blameless*, but church leaders must be *above reproach* in the eyes of unbelievers for the way in which they live their lives.

In 1:9, Paul tells Titus to look for people who have been faithful with the Gospel. An elder may not be a gifted speaker but he must be honest enough not to change the Gospel in order to boost the numbers on a Sunday. He must understand the Scriptures well enough to spot false teaching and he must have the courage to confront false teachers with *"the trustworthy message as it has been taught."* The Gospel is far more powerful than the wings that Daedalus gave to Icarus. People must have proved themselves faithful with the Gospel before they are entrusted to disciple a church in it.

If you find this list of fifteen attributes quite daunting, that's a good thing. God is convicting you that any leadership position you gain through your gifting is simply a higher place from which to fall unless you have the character to handle it. These fifteen attributes are a description of what God promises to do in the life of any believer who will let him. They are an invitation to allow him to change your heart more and more through the Gospel.

God loves you far too much to treat you like Icarus. He invites you to walk more closely with Jesus so that he can enable you to fly higher and higher.

What Church Leaders Do (1:10–16)

Rebuke them sharply, so that they will be sound in the faith.

(Titus 1:13)

Paul told Titus that the way to reach Crete with the Gospel was to plant churches in every city. He told Titus that the way to make those churches strong and attractive to unbelievers was to appoint the right sort of church leaders. It isn't surprising, therefore, that he ends chapter 1 by telling us what those church leaders should actually do. They needed to do five things if they wanted to reach the rest of their island with the Gospel.

Paul tells us in 1:10 that church leaders must *define* biblical doctrine and practice for those they lead. The small Christian presence in Crete before Paul's arrival was not leaderless yet, sadly, its leaders were teaching something that sounded like Christianity but was nothing of the kind. Paul tells us that the most influential preachers on the island were *"full of meaningless talk and deception"* and refused to submit to the teaching of the apostles. Since Paul tells us that the most dangerous false teachers were part of the "circumcision group", they were probably part of the same group of Jewish false teachers that Paul confronted in his letter to the Galatians and at the Council of Jerusalem. Sheep cannot be blamed for eating nettles if they have no shepherds to feed them grass. False teaching always thrives in the absence of godly church leaders.[1]

---

[1] Paul had already been able to stop the influence of the *peritomē*, or *circumcision group*, over churches which had good elders (Galatians 2:12;

Paul therefore tells Titus that the first task of the new church leaders he appoints is to define clear biblical doctrine and practice for the Christians on Crete. They must confront *"Jewish myths"* and rid the church of *"the merely human commands of those who reject the truth."* The last of the fifteen character attributes that Paul lists for a church leader is the courage to *"hold firmly to the trustworthy message as it has been taught, so that he can encourage others by sound doctrine and refute those who oppose it"* (1:9).

Second, Paul tells us in 1:11 that church leaders must *discipline* church members where necessary. We live in an unruly and aggressively tolerant culture, much like first-century Crete, so we can tell how surprised they must have been when Paul told Titus to do more than shout above the roar of the false teachers: *"They must be silenced."* The work of church leadership is often pleasant, so it attracts people who enjoy Bible study, pastoral conversations and works of mercy, but we must never forget that first-century shepherds carried a big stick for a reason. Wolves were a constant danger to the flock, which was why Paul told the Ephesian elders in Acts 20:28–31 to

> *Keep watch over yourselves and all the flock of which the Holy Spirit has made you overseers. Be shepherds of the church of God, which he bought with his own blood. I know that after I leave, savage wolves will come in among you and will not spare the flock. Even from your own number men will arise and distort the truth in order to draw away disciples after them. So be on your guard!*

Paul says two things here: that false teachers will arise from within the church at Ephesus and that he is leaving! He believes that the right church leaders will be able to deal with troublemakers without his needing to stay. Disciplining unruly

Ephesians 2:11; Philippians 3:2; Colossians 2:16–23).

church members is such an essential aspect of eldership that Paul tells Titus not to appoint anyone who has not first learned to discipline their children.[2]

Third, Paul tells us in 1:12 that church leaders must also *display* godly character to the church and to unbelievers. Cretans were seen as immoral even by the dismal standards of the Roman Empire. The Roman historian Livy denounced their greed, and the Greek historian Polybius complained that

> *Greed and avarice are so native to the soil in Crete that they are the only people in the world among whom no stigma is attached to any sort of gain whatsoever... The Cretans by their ingrained avarice live in a perpetual state of private quarrel and public feud and civil strife... You cannot find people more steeped in treachery and deceit than the people of Crete.*[3]

Paul accepts this frank assessment of Cretan morality but in doing so he deliberately undermines and destroys it. Read carefully, because it's clever.

Paul quotes from the famous Cretan poet Epimenides, just as he did when standing before the greatest thinkers of Athens in Acts 17:28. He quotes from the poem *Cretica* in 1:12, but he does so not to reinforce popular prejudice against Cretans but to undermine it.[4] He tells us that Cretans always lie and that this must be true because a Cretan says it is the truth. Read that sentence again slowly. It's deliberately ridiculous! He knows

---

[2] It is significant Paul says these false teachers are motivated by financial gain. *"Not pursuing dishonest gain"* is the only thing mentioned in all three lists of eldership character in Titus 1:5–9, 1 Timothy 3:1–7 and 1 Peter 5:1–4.

[3] Livy in his *History of Rome* (44.45) and Polybius in his *Histories* (6.46–47).

[4] Epimenides wrote *Cretica* in the sixth century BC. These words are spoken by King Minos only two lines before the words Paul quoted in Athens in Acts 17:28. Paul does not despise Cretan culture by insisting Epimenides was not a prophet. He honours Cretan culture by affirming what was right about what he said.

that Titus is likely to complain that no one in Crete qualifies to become a church elder, so he shows him the stupidity of accepting the view that Cretans are any more sinful than other people. Epimenides had been executed by the Spartans because he refused to lie to them by prophesying blessings over their city. Crete was therefore the very place where Titus should expect to find fearless preachers of the Gospel![5]

Fourth, Paul tells us in 1:11–14 that church leaders must *direct* the mission and ministry of the church. The fundamental unit of Cretan society was not the individual but the household, so Paul tells Titus that church leaders must have a strategy to stop false teachers from leading whole households astray. We noted in 1:7 that Paul borrowed the word *episkopoi*, or *overseers*, from the Roman civil service, and this reflects the fact that God chooses those who lead their households well to train other people to lead their households better. Church leaders need to see the big picture like the men of Issachar in 1 Chronicles 12:32, who *"understood the times and knew what Israel should do."* Crete would lose its reputation as an island full of liars when its church leaders devised a strategy to move each believing household forward in the truth.[6]

Fifth, Paul tells us in 1:15–16 that church leaders must *delegate* this ministry to capable workers whom they support. The false teachers had taught the Cretan Christians that they could be purified by observing Jewish food laws and mystic rituals, and Paul tells us that this made households *"detestable, disobedient and unfit for doing anything good."* The task of church leaders is to teach people how to become truly pure through the blood of Jesus, making them fit for the work of extending God's Kingdom. Several hundred church leaders could never reach the

[5] The ancient Greek travel writer Pausanias tells us this in his *Description of Greece* (2.21.3).

[6] The tragic consequence of Cretan lying was that their minds and consciences no longer recognized the truth. This is why Paul emphasizes that God's Word is the truth that Crete needs in 1:1–2, 9, 13–14).

whole of Crete, but nothing could stop them if they delegated a share in the mission to every person in the churches they led.

When church leaders *define* biblical doctrine and practice, when they *discipline* unruly people in the church, when they *display* the godly character which they want to see replicated and when they *direct* the ministry of the church by *delegating* it to every church member, that's when whole regions are affected by the Gospel. These five things always make churches very fruitful. They are what good church leaders do.

Lights on, Windows Open (2:1–10)

> *You, however, must teach what is appropriate to sound doctrine... so that in every way they will make the teaching about God our Saviour attractive.*
>
> (Titus 2:1, 10)

When I was a teenager, I bought a Venus flytrap. It didn't take me very long to discover that the plant was very badly named. It might be able to trap flies in its fly-infested native swamplands, but not on a windowsill in England. I wasted hours looking for insects in the garden and feeding the plant with tweezers until one evening I happened to leave the lights on with my windows open. Light is so attractive to insects that, to my surprise, they quickly came to me. That's what Paul wants you to understand about the Gospel here in chapter 2. It is the bedrock of his strategy to reach the rest of Crete with the Gospel.

Most churches adopt the go-into-the-garden-and-look-for-insects method of evangelism. They organize special events and they urge church members to go out and persuade people to come in and hear the Gospel. Church members either get worn out or they tune out. Either way, they are often unfruitful. Paul tells Titus to adopt a lights-on-windows-open method of evangelism instead.

In 2:1, Paul tells Titus that, like everything else, this must start with the church leaders. They *"must teach what is appropriate to sound doctrine."* If that doesn't sound much to you like an evangelistic strategy, you haven't really understood what Paul means. "Sound doctrine" means far more than a course in systematic theology, as is evident from the verses that follow. Paul gets very practical because he sees "sound doctrine" as properly understanding how the Gospel applies to our daily lives. If church leaders spell out to people in very practical detail how the Gospel should affect their lives as men and women, as young and old, as employees and employers, they will not need to go out and drag unwilling visitors into their church services. If they let their converted lives shine brightly, their neighbours will be attracted and will want to step inside.

This is the recurring theme of these ten verses. In 2:2, Paul tells the older men that if they let the Holy Spirit change their lifestyle by the power of the Gospel, unbelievers will start to respect the words they have to say. In 2:3–5, Paul tells the older women that if they allow their faith to transform their lifestyle and train the younger women to follow their example, *"no one will malign the word of God."* In 2:6–8, Paul tells the young men that if they refuse to participate in the sins of unbelieving Cretans, *"those who oppose you may be ashamed because they have nothing bad to say about us."* Paul does not tell Titus to teach the Cretan believers to strive hard to reach the rest of their island for Jesus, like the owner of a Venus flytrap hunting for insects in the garden. He tells Titus that Christians can expect to be fruitful if they surrender to the Gospel and spend time with unbelievers. Lights on and windows open is the only way to win large numbers of people to Jesus.

This message runs throughout the New Testament. Jesus tells us in Matthew 5:14–16 that *"You are the light of the world... Let your light shine before others, that they may see your good deeds and glorify your Father in heaven."* Before he ascended to heaven, he reminded his followers in Acts 1:8 that *"You will receive power when the Holy Spirit comes on you; and you will be my witnesses."*[1] Yes, they would do his witnessing, but primarily

[1] Paul does not want the Cretans to strive harder in their own strength to become more like Jesus. He explains in 2:11–14 that such a change can only happen as a result of God's grace through the Holy Spirit.

they would ***be*** his witnesses. There is a big difference between the two. People may be sick and tired of Christian *talk*, but they never fail to stop in their tracks when they see the beauty of genuine Christian *walk*. Paul told Titus to give the Cretan believers a very simple strategy to persuade their island to surrender to the Gospel. He told them that they simply needed to surrender to it fully themselves.[2]

Martyn Lloyd-Jones writes that

> *The glory of the gospel is that when the Church is absolutely different from the world, she invariably attracts it. It is then that the world is made to listen to her message, though it may hate it at first. That is how revival comes. That must also be true of us as individuals. It should not be our ambition to be as much like everybody else as we can, though we happen to be Christian, but rather to be as different from everybody who is not a Christian as we can possibly be. Our ambition should be to be like Christ, the more like Him the better, and the more like Him we become, the more we shall be unlike everybody who is not a Christian.*[3]

Paul states this strategy most clearly at the end of these ten verses. He does so when talking to Christian slaves, the very people who were treated most badly on the island and who therefore had the chance to shine brightest in reply. Paul promises them that, if they live a godly lifestyle, *"in every way they will make the teaching about God our Saviour attractive."* The Greek word which he uses is *kosmeō*, the same word which 1 Peter 3:5 uses to describe women making themselves

[2] We also find this principle in 1 Thessalonians 4:11–12, 1 Timothy 6:1, Titus 3:8 and 1 Peter 2:12–15 and 3:1–2.

[3] Martyn Lloyd-Jones in his *Studies in the Sermon on the Mount* (1959). The Gospel always provokes a reaction: either persecution (2 Timothy 3:12) or conversion (Titus 2). We have to be ready for both.

look attractive to their husbands and which Revelation 21:2 uses to describe a bride making herself look gorgeous on her wedding day.[4] Paul is therefore telling us that the battle to reach outsiders is fought and won on the inside. How we live either makes people think the Gospel is drop-dead gorgeous, or it makes them think the Gospel is a repellent old hag.

D. L. Moody, the great nineteenth-century American evangelist, grasped the lesson of Titus 2. He taught:

> *If the whole Church of God could live as the Lord would have them live, why Christianity would be the mightiest power this world has ever seen. It is the low standard of Christian life that is causing so much trouble... A great many parents have inquired of me how to win their children. They say that they have talked with them, and sometimes they have scolded them and have lectured them, and thoroughly failed. I think there is no way so sure to win our families and our neighbours, and those about whom we are anxious, to Christ, than just to adorn the doctrine of Jesus Christ in our lives, and grow in all these graces... If we just live in our homes as the Lord would have us, an even Christian life day by day, we shall have a quiet and silent power proceeding from us that will constrain them to believe on the Lord Jesus Christ. But an uneven life, hot today and cold tomorrow, will only repel. Many are watching God's people.*[5]

God wants to make you very fruitful, but this will never happen if you only pursue a go-into-the-garden-and-hunt-for-insects method of evangelism. He encourages you to respond to the Gospel fully yourself if you want to persuade others to respond to it too. Turn the lights on and then open the windows by

[4] Paul also uses the adjective *kosmios* to teach women how to make themselves beautiful in 1 Timothy 2:9.

[5] D. L. Moody in his book *Secret Power* (1881).

wearing your faith in Jesus on your sleeve. Will your life make the Gospel look like an ugly old hag or will it make the Gospel look drop-dead gorgeous? Only you can decide.

Taste the Difference (2:1–10)

In everything set them an example by doing what is good.

(Titus 2:7)

A few years ago while holidaying in Portugal, my wife and I visited a famous port distillery.[1] The owners of the distillery produced a wide variety of ports, but they naturally wanted tourists to buy their most expensive ones. The way they went about persuading us was very clever. They did not offer us a discounted price. They simply let us taste the difference.

When I tasted the cheap port, it did not taste too bad. I could have happily drunk it after dinner. The most expensive port tasted much better, but this was when they sprang on us their surprise. After we had tasted the most expensive port, they invited us to try the cheap port one more time. The same port that had tasted pleasant a few moments earlier now tasted as horrible as vinegar. All of the tourists left the distillery with bottles of the most expensive port because they had been allowed to taste the difference.

The idols that were worshipped in Crete were evil. One of their main gods was Poseidon, whose idea of justice was forcing the wife of King Minos to have sex with a bull. Another was Dionysus, the god of wine and drunken orgies. We might therefore have expected this letter to include a long tirade against the Cretan idols, but it doesn't. Instead, Paul reacts to

[1] Paul warns us in 2:3 that wine can *enslave* us, but he adds in 1 Timothy 5:23 that it can also be a good servant.

the idols of Crete in the same way he reacted to the idols of Athens. Acts 17:16–17 tells us that *"He was greatly distressed to see that the city was full of idols. So he reasoned in the synagogue with both Jews and God-fearing Greeks, as well as in the market-place day by day with those who happened to be there."* Paul did not try to convert pagans to Jesus by badmouthing and insulting the gods they worshipped. Even the rioting mob at Ephesus was forced to concede in Acts 19:37 that Paul had *"neither robbed temples nor blasphemed our goddess."*[2] Instead of preaching negatively against their idols, Paul taught Christians to live out the Gospel. He told them to give their unbelieving friends a taste of something better.

In 2:2, Paul gives Titus some instructions for *older men*, because they were the leaders of Cretan society.[3] They complained that the young men did not respect them, but it was not easy to respect a group of tired and cynical men who were as often drunk as sober. Paul tells Titus that the way to convert the island to Christ is for older Christian men to be so sober and self-controlled that they win the respect of those around them.[4] If they refuse to grow cynical like their pagan friends and persevere in faith and love, they will be worthy of the respect which the old men of Crete long to receive. Their pagan friends will see a better way of living and will reject their idols as quickly as a tourist tasting cheap port for a second time in the distillery.

In 2:3–4, Paul gives Titus some instructions for *older women*. Like the men, they complained that young women did not respect them and did not really know how to manage their homes, but it was not easy to respect retired women who used

---

[2] We see this in 1:12, where Paul calls Epimenides a *prophet* despite the fact he claimed to serve the false god Zeus. Paul did not win over Cretans to the Gospel by insulting Zeus, but by extolling Jesus.

[3] The word which Paul uses is *presbutēs*, which means *old man* and should not be confused with the word *presbuteros*, which means *elder*. Since Cretans died younger than we do, this could refer to anyone over 40.

[4] *Nēphalios* means *sober* and *sōphrōn* means *of sound mind*. Both are linked to the consumption of alcohol.

their free time to gossip and get drunk with one another. Paul tells Titus that the best way to reach Crete with the Gospel is for older Christian women to earn the respect of younger women by living in a manner that befits God's holy People, by speaking what is good instead of gossiping[5] and by devoting themselves to good deeds instead of to fine wine. This will make the younger women want to listen to their advice, and it will also make the pagan older women sit up and listen. When they see that God has granted their Christian friends the admiration which they crave, they want to accept the Gospel too.

In 2:4–5, Paul gives Titus some instructions for *younger women*. Most Cretan women could not afford to stay at home and resented their household responsibilities at the end of a busy working day.[6] Paul points out that when a woman loves her family, submits to her husband[7] and treats her home responsibilities as an opportunity to demonstrate kindness, self-control and purity, the Gospel is powerfully proclaimed.[8] When the pagan women see how much their Christian friends are loved by their grateful husbands and children, they will taste the difference and *"no one will malign the word of God."*

In 2:6–8, Paul gives Titus some instructions for *younger men*. Since Cretan women married much younger than Cretan men, these instructions probably also apply to unmarried women today. Single adults in Crete tended to be undisciplined,

[5] The word that Paul uses for *liars* or *slanderers* in 2:3 is *diabolos*, the word that is normally used for *the Devil*, because his name means *the Deceiver*. Cretan culture would be changed if Christians modelled how attractive it is to follow the God Who Does Not Lie instead of Cretan idols (1:2, 12).

[6] Women have had jobs outside the home throughout most of history (Proverbs 31). Paul is not telling the Cretan women to be housewives but to be wives who see the value of their hard work in the home.

[7] Note that Paul does not tell women to submit to men. He tells wives literally that they need to submit *"to their own husbands."* He also makes this point clearly in Ephesians 5:22 and Colossians 3:18.

[8] 1 Timothy 5:10 says that bringing up children is a *"good work"* and not second best to pursuing a career. God also places huge value on a man's role in the home, as Paul points out in 1:6.

hard-drinking, fast-talking and flippant, so Paul tells Christian singles to model a better way of living. If they are sober,[9] hardworking, truthful and worthy of respect,[10] non-Christians of any age will *"be ashamed because they have nothing bad to say about us."* Paul tells Titus that, as a young man himself, he should model this. When the Cretan believers taste the difference in his own life, they will want to live like him too.

In 2:9–10, Paul gives Titus some instructions for *slaves*, the lowest group of people in Cretan society. He tells them not to swindle their masters like King Minos, disobeying and pilfering whenever they are not looking.[11] Paul does not condemn slavery outright as an institution because he has already laid the seeds for its demise elsewhere in his letters, and because he wants the slaves to see themselves as agents of the Gospel who have infiltrated Cretan homes.[12] If they obey their masters in spite of the evident injustices of slavery, the ruling classes will quickly taste the difference. *"In every way they will make the teaching about God our Saviour attractive."*[13]

If you want to see unbelievers converted, cities revived and nations transformed, you need to learn from Paul. Don't insult their idols or shout at them that their false gods cannot satisfy. Shout at them instead through a lifestyle that makes them taste

---

[9] Paul uses this word *sōphroneō*, meaning *to be sober* or *to be of sound mind*, or one of its sister words five times in Titus 2. Drunkenness was clearly a major issue in Crete and soberness was therefore very attractive.

[10] The Greek words *semnos* and *semnotēs* in 2:2 and 2:7 do not mean *serious* so much as *worthy of respect*. Like the old men, Titus must not demand that people respect him. He must earn their respect.

[11] The only other place in the New Testament where this word for *stealing* is used is when Ananias and Sapphira steal from the Holy Spirit in Acts 5:2–3. How we obey our earthly masters is how we obey the Lord.

[12] Paul began this letter by calling himself a slave of God. For a thorough look at how Paul undermines slavery as an institution, see the chapter "Slaves of Christ" in *Straight to the Heart of Galatians to Colossians*.

[13] Today Paul would address these verses to Christian employees, urging them to see themselves as agents who have infiltrated workplaces and schools in order to demonstrate the beauty of the Gospel.

a different way of living. Most people have not rejected Jesus because they tried him and he failed. They have rejected him because nobody has ever shown them the difference that he brings. When they taste the difference that Jesus has made in your life, they will happily throw away the cheap attractions of life without the Lord.

A Ball of Thread (2:11–14)

For the grace of God has appeared that offers salvation to all people. It teaches us to say "No" to ungodliness and worldly passions.

(Titus 2:11–12)

The message of Titus 2 is both encouraging and daunting. It is encouraging because it tells us we can win people to Jesus simply by surrendering to him ourselves. But it is daunting because it tells us that our surrendered lives need to become like a taste of Jesus. Becoming more like Jesus every day is an impossible challenge. We need help.

When the hero Theseus came to Crete to kill the Minotaur, he knew he needed help to navigate the labyrinth which had been built by Daedalus. He was forced to humble himself in order to accept a gift from Ariadne, the daughter of King Minos, who befriended him and gave him a long ball of thread.[1] She told him to tie one end to the entrance of the labyrinth and to unravel the thread until he found and killed the Minotaur at the heart of the maze. Then he would be able to retrace his steps back to the entrance by following the ball of thread. Breaking free from sin and becoming more like Jesus may seem impossible, but it isn't if we follow in his footsteps. Jesus is our ball of thread, and in these four verses Paul explains how we can follow him to freedom.

Paul tells us in 2:11–12 that we need to be humble like Jesus.

---

[1] The old English word for a ball of thread is a *clue*, which is why the word is still used to refer to any help which a person receives in order to help them solve a difficult puzzle.

We need to confess that no amount of willpower, resolutions or positive thinking can ever change us. We must place all our hope of finding freedom from sin in the same *"grace of God"* through which we found forgiveness from sin. The same Gospel message that showed us how God could justify us through Jesus (*declare* us holy) also shows us how God can sanctify us through Jesus (*make* us holy). The Greek word that Paul uses here to describe the Gospel teaching us is *paideuō*, which means literally *to train a child*. If we let Jesus teach us, we will discover that the Gospel is not just a set of facts to be believed in order to be forgiven. It is also a pathway through which the Father leads us to a life of godliness through his Son.

Paul tells us in 2:12–13 that we need to fix our gaze in the same place as Jesus. When the Devil tempted Jesus with the riches of the world, he said no. When the crowd tried to give him an earthly crown, he said no. When the prostitutes came to him with adoring eyes and hung on his every word, he said no to every temptation. That's why his Gospel also *"teaches us to say 'No' to ungodliness and worldly passions,"* because it teaches us to prioritize the same things as him. Jesus fixed his eyes on the eternal joy which the Father had set before him, and it empowered him to say no to sin and yes to the cross (Hebrews 12:2). He teaches us to fix our eyes on the great Day when we will share that eternal joy with him, and to allow it to change the desires of our hearts towards sin and towards godliness. If we follow Jesus' gaze like a ball of thread, Paul promises God will empower us *"to live self-controlled, upright and godly lives in this present age, while we wait for the blessed hope – the appearing of the glory of our great God and Saviour, Jesus Christ."*[2] Knowing what tomorrow has in store gives us strength to say no to sin today.

Paul tells us in 2:14 that we need to believe in Jesus' death

[2] Verse 13 is one of the greatest statements of Jesus' divinity in the New Testament. He is our divine helper.

and resurrection. He reminds us that Jesus died in order to *"redeem us from all wickedness."* In other words, while we were slaves to sin, Jesus paid the penalty for our sin in order that we might walk free. Employees no longer work for their employer after they die. Death terminates the job contract! In the same way, since we have died with Jesus (Colossians 3:3), we can look sin and temptation in the face and say, *"I don't work for you any more!"* More than that, Paul tells us that Jesus rose to life for us as well, in order to *"purify for himself a people that are his very own."* Since we have been raised to new life with Jesus by the power of the Holy Spirit (Romans 6:5–14), we have been empowered to live a pure life like that of Jesus. We have the Spirit of Holiness within us, making the life of Jesus triumph over the deadly power of sin as we trust in him every day.

Paul tells us in 2:14 that we need to follow Jesus closely. The more we recognize we are part of Jesus' chosen People, the more we will want to follow the lifestyle that he modelled for us during his life on earth, like a ball of thread for his People to follow. The more we are captivated by the beauty of our Saviour and of his plans for us, the more we will grow dissatisfied with the empty pleasures of the world. Paul tells us literally that anyone who follows Jesus closely will become *"a person who burns with zeal to do good works."*[3] The more we taste of Jesus, the more we will love holiness and hate sin. The more we love holiness and hate sin, the more those around us will taste Jesus through us. That's the Gospel chain reaction which Paul wants to set off on the island of Crete. Whenever Christians truly love Jesus and truly respond to the Gospel, it doesn't take long for those around them to start loving him and responding to the Gospel too.

When the Cretan Christians were tempted to lie, the false teachers had no help for them other than a reminder that

[3] This is one of Paul's big themes in his letter to Titus. True conversion always leads to true fruitfulness because the Gospel makes us want to do good works and then empowers us to do them (Philippians 2:13).

the Ninth Commandment told them not to. But reciting rules cannot sanctify us.[4] We need Jesus to be our ball of thread. We lie because we are afraid of telling the truth, but the Gospel teaches us that the truth is better than we could ever imagine. We have died to sin and been raised to a new life of holiness through the power of God's Spirit. God knows the worst truth about us yet he has decided to make us precious jewels in his private treasure collection.[5] How can we say yes to the fleeting pleasures of sin when the grace of God has already given us all we need? Because of who we are in Jesus, we can say no to sin and act like the people that we are.

Paul began this letter by telling Titus that the Gospel is not merely a message of forgiveness. If we want the scrap metal of our lives to be turned into gold, we need to grow in our *"knowledge of the truth that leads to godliness."*[6] If we want to taste like Jesus, we need to follow the Gospel as the ball of thread that he has laid down for us to help us escape the labyrinth of our sin. What willpower and resolutions and positive thinking can never accomplish, Jesus has given us as a free gift through the grace of God.

[4] Paul tells us in Colossians 2:23 that relying on rules may give us the illusion of progress, *"but they lack any value in restraining sensual indulgence."*

[5] The word Paul uses in 2:14 is *periousios*, a word that is used in the Greek Old Testament to translate the Hebrew word *segullāh*, or *treasured possession*. Paul is telling us that the Gospel makes us heirs to the promises in Exodus 19:5, Deuteronomy 7:6 and Psalm 135:4.

[6] The Greek word *epignōsis* in 1:1 means literally a *full knowledge* of the truth. The Gospel is not simply an entry-level message for unbelievers. We grow in godliness through the exact same message which saved us.

Front-line Leader (2:15)

Encourage and rebuke with all authority. Do not let anyone despise you.

(Titus 2:15)

In 1915, Douglas Haig became commander of the greatest army the British Empire had ever known. He was given complete control of the British trenches in World War One. What he did with this army over the next three years makes tragic reading. In a single day, on 1st July 1916, he sent 60,000 British soldiers to be killed or injured in no-man's-land. There are many reasons why Douglas Haig made so many bad decisions during World War One, but one of them is very simple. He and his senior commanders led the army from a chateau over twenty miles away from the front-line.

Paul ends chapter 2 by telling Titus that he needs to be a front-line general. Reaching the rest of Crete with the Gospel was not going to be easy, so he and the elders he appointed would need to lead the way. Paul tells Titus that he needs to be able to teach, encourage and rebuke the Cretans with all authority, and that he must therefore ensure that nobody can despise his lead. In order to do this, he needs to be more than an armchair general who issues orders to the Christians from the safety of a pulpit. He needs to roll up his sleeves and lead the Gospel charge himself on the front-line.

Paul tells Titus that taking an active lead will give him *clear authority to teach people*. Like the older men and women of Crete, he needed to earn people's respect instead of demanding it. He needed to show people how to follow in Jesus' footsteps and how to break out of the labyrinth of their sin. He needed to show them what it meant to taste like Jesus and how powerfully attractive it made the Gospel to unbelievers on the island. Douglas Haig was a cavalry commander who had risen to the highest rank through his shrewd use of horses on the battlefields of Africa and India. His greatest flaw in World War One was that he had no first-hand experience of fighting a very different war on the battlefields of Europe. Paul tells Titus that he must not make this same mistake himself. He must know what it is like to try to spread the Gospel to one non-Christian Cretan household after another, and he must ensure that the Cretan believers know that he knows it too. Paul tells him in 2:7: *"In everything set them an example by doing what is good."*

I am a church leader so I know how tempting it is to try and direct the church's evangelistic efforts from the comforts of an office. I winced when I read Bill Wilson describe his stubborn refusal to spend his time in the office instead of setting up Sunday schools for vulnerable children on the streets of New York: *"If I take that approach, I will become what so many other pastors, unfortunately, are – pencil sharpening, paper-pushing administrators, so alienated from the people that they really think they are ministering by sitting in an office, living in the suburbs and writing books on evangelism."*[1] I have learned that the people I lead will ignore my teaching on evangelism unless they hear me ground it in real and recent examples of how I have personally attempted to spread the Gospel.

Paul tells Titus that as he takes an active lead it will also give him *clear authority to give feedback to people.* Christians do not simply need to be sent off to share the Gospel with unbelievers. Paul tells us that they also need to receive on-the-job encouragements and challenges as they go. The historian John Keegan tells us that *"The problem of command in the circumstances of the First World War was insoluble. Generals*

[1] Bill Wilson says this in his book *Whose Child Is This?* (1992).

were like men without eyes, without ears and without voices, unable to watch the operations they had set in progress, unable to hear reports of their development and unable to speak to those whom they had originally given orders once action was joined."[2] When I read the biographies of great evangelists such as Charles Spurgeon, William Booth, D. L. Moody and Billy Graham, I am always struck by the active way in which these great platform speakers shared the Gospel one-on-one as part of their everyday lifestyle. It is as if their public success was rooted in their private first-hand experience of learning to connect with different types of unbeliever. Paul tells Titus that he will only be able to coach people in how to reach their island with the Gospel if he keeps his own experience fresh by joining them on the battlefield.

You don't have to have watched *War Horse* to know that Douglas Haig was too removed from the action to grasp that cavalry charges could no longer succeed against trenches and machine guns. Long after the war ended, he continued to argue that

> *the value of the horse and the opportunity for the horse in the future were likely to be as great as ever... He was all for using aeroplanes and tanks, but they were only accessories to the man and the horse, and he felt sure that as time went on they would find just as much use for the horse – the well-bred horse – as they had ever done in the past.*[3]

Leaders will misdirect their church's evangelism and will lose the respect of those they lead unless they can give them relevant and up-to-date directions from their personal experience.

Paul tells Titus that as he takes an active lead it will give him *clear authority to lead the charge*. As any military officer

[2] John Keegan in *The First World War* (1998).

[3] This is taken from a report in *The Times* on his speech to the Royal College of Veterinary Surgeons on 5th June 1925.

can tell you, the moment a commander loses the confidence of his troops is the moment when any hope of advance stalls. It is easy for church leaders to complain that the members of their church do not invite non-Christian friends to evangelistic events, but very often the problem is that, much as they love their leaders, they have lost confidence in their battle sense when it comes to evangelism. They have become like Douglas Haig, as Winston Churchill who was one of his junior officers, complained in 1917: *"The hopes of decisive victory... grew with every step away from the British front-line and reached absolute conviction in the Intelligence Department."*[4]

This is what Paul means when he tells Titus, *"Do not let anyone despise you."* He expects him to take a lead in modelling this evangelistic lifestyle to the Cretan Christians. He expects him to show that the Gospel really does sanctify and that a sanctified life really does attract unbelievers to the beauty of the Gospel. He expects him to act like David when he saw how afraid the Israelite army was of the Philistine giant Goliath. Instead of barking orders from the rear, David marched to meet the Philistine on the front-line and showed the rest of the army how easy it was to advance in the power of God's name. When David took the lead, 1 Samuel 17:51–52 tells us the Israelite soldiers stopped trembling and started advancing:

> *When the Philistines saw that their hero was dead, they turned and ran. Then the men of Israel and Judah surged forward with a shout and pursued the Philistines.*

[4] Winston Churchill in *The World Crisis, 1911–1918* (1931).

Nero (3:1–2)

Remind the people to be subject to rulers and authorities, to be obedient, to be ready to do whatever is good.

(Titus 3:1)

If you live in a peaceful, democratic nation, you will not find the first two verses of Titus 3 very surprising. You will think it stands to reason that Christians should make the Gospel attractive to unbelievers by submitting to the government as model citizens. But Paul was not writing to a peaceful, democratic nation. He was writing to Crete, an island that had been annexed by the Roman Empire in a brutal war which lasted from 72 to 69 BC. He was writing to an island whose ruler was the Emperor Nero, one of the worst rulers in human history.

The Roman historians Tacitus and Suetonius tell us about the Emperor Nero. They say he murdered his stepbrother, his mother and his wife, and that he generally *"showed neither discrimination nor moderation in putting to death anyone he pleased."*[1] At the very time Paul was writing this letter to Titus, Nero was beginning to execute Christians in Rome.

On the night of 18th July 64 AD, a fire broke out near the chariot-racing stadium in Rome and it quickly spread across the city. Rome burned for a week and a rumour spread that Nero had begun the fire in order to facilitate his plans to redevelop the city. Tacitus tells us that

---

1 Suetonius in his *Life of Nero* (33 and 37).

> *To quash this rumour, Nero fastened the guilt and inflicted the most exquisite tortures on a class hated for their abominations, called Christians by the populace. Christ, from whom the name had its origin, had suffered the death-penalty during the reign of Tiberius at the hands of one of our procurators, Pontius Pilate, and a most mischievous superstition, thus checked for the moment, again broke out not only in Judea, where the evil began, but even in Rome.... A large number were convicted, not so much for the crime of setting fire to the city as for the fact that people hated them. Mockery of every sort was added to their deaths. Covered with the skins of beasts, they were torn by dogs and perished, or were nailed to crosses, or were doomed to the flames and burnt, to serve as nightly illumination when daylight had expired.*[2]

Paul may not have known everything that was happening in Rome when he wrote this letter from Ephesus. However, he was not naïve. He had been Nero's prisoner in Rome and he counted as friends many members of Nero's household and the Praetorian Guard.[3] We must therefore not miss how shocking it was for Paul to tell the Cretan Christians in 64 AD that following Jesus meant submitting to the Emperor Nero and his imperial agents on the island. It is so shocking that it demands an explanation.

First, Paul is recognizing the sovereignty of God in the rise and fall of rulers. Even if Suetonius is right when he suggests that Nero gained power through poisoning his predecessor Claudius, Paul believes that he only became emperor because God ordained it should be so. The prophet Daniel tells us that God *"sets up kings and deposes them"* and that *"the Most High is sovereign over all kingdoms on earth and gives them to anyone he*

---

2 Tacitus in his *Annals* (15.44).

3 Philippians 1:13; 4:22.

wishes." As a result, Paul tells us elsewhere that *"Everyone must submit himself to the governing authorities, for... the authorities that exist have been established by God. Consequently, he who rebels against the authority is rebelling against what God has instituted."* This is why Peter tells us less than five years before he was executed by the Emperor Nero that Christians should *"Show proper respect to everyone... honour the emperor."*[4] Christians are not to be rebellious troublemakers. They should attract unbelievers to the Gospel by their perfect courtesy towards both their rulers (3:1) and their neighbours (3:2).

But this is only half the story. The prophet Daniel also warned that earthly rulers can be very wicked. He saw a vision in which the Roman Empire was depicted as a *"beast – terrifying and frightening and very powerful. It had large iron teeth; it crushed and devoured its victims and trampled underfoot whatever was left."*[5] Daniel couched this teaching in apocalyptic language so that his Jewish readers would understand and their oppressors would not, but he left them in no doubt that earthly rulers can be agents of the Devil as well as of the Lord. Paul couches his own teaching in subtle political language which teaches the Cretan converts what it really means to submit themselves to increasingly anti-Christian Roman rule.

The Emperor Nero liked to be known as the *Sōtēr*, or *Saviour*, of the world. Inscriptions found in Cyprus and Egypt hail Nero as *"the saviour and benefactor of the world."*[6] It is therefore striking that Paul emphasizes six times in this short letter that God alone is the only true *Sōtēr*, or *Saviour*, of the world.[7] He makes this particularly explicit in 2:13 when he refers

4 Daniel 2:21; 4:32: Romans 13:1–2; 1 Peter 2:17.

5 Daniel 7:7. The other three beasts in the vision represented the Babylonian, Persian and Macedonian empires.

6 See E. M. Smallwood's *Documents Illustrating the Principates of Gaius, Claudius and Nero* (1967).

7 Titus 1:3, 4; 2:10, 13; 3:4, 6. For perspective, the word *"Saviour"* is only used three times in all four gospels.

to *"the appearing of the glory of our great God and Saviour, Jesus Christ,"*[8] because the Greek word he uses is *epiphaneia*, the word that was used to refer to the official visit of an emperor to one of his provinces.[9] Paul does not put himself in danger of re-arrest by openly criticizing Nero, but he makes it clear that Jesus is the true Lord, the true Saviour and the true Messiah from whom all rule and authority is derived. The Cretan Christians are to be submissive, obedient and peaceable towards their Roman rulers, but they also need to *"be ready to do whatever is good"* in the face of evil.

I find Richard Wurmbrand very helpful in understanding what it means for followers of Jesus to submit to authorities that oppose the Gospel. As a pastor in communist Romania, he spent thirteen years in prison because he dared to teach that Jesus was the true Lord and Saviour, not the Communist Party. He argued that every government gives followers of Jesus a choice: either they can do as commanded or they can accept the punishment stipulated. Either choice is a submission to the government's authority.

> *It was strictly forbidden to preach to other prisoners. It was understood that whoever was caught doing this received a severe beating. A number of us decided to pay the price for the privilege of preaching, so we accepted their terms. It was a deal: we preached and they beat us. We were happy preaching. They were happy beating us, so everyone was happy.*[10]

---

[8] Nero also claimed to be divine, so 2:13 is a clear statement that Jesus alone is the *"great God"*.

[9] Nero only made one provincial visit and its commemorative coins were struck in Latin, but when the Emperor Hadrian made a visit to Actium the coins were struck in Greek and celebrated his *epiphaneia*.

[10] Richard Wurmbrand in *Tortured for Christ* (1967).

Three years after writing this letter to Titus, Paul was executed by the soldiers of Nero because he submitted to the consequences of declaring that Jesus is Lord. These instructions are still relevant to us, even though we do not live under imperial Rome or in communist Romania, because democracies can be as anti-Christian as dictatorships. We need to be ready to do good on all occasions as model citizens, obeying when we can and accepting the consequences gladly when we cannot. That's what it means to follow Jesus, the man who honoured Caesar and who was crucified by Caesar's soldiers.

Friend of Sinners (3:3–8)

At one time we too were foolish, disobedient, deceived and enslaved by all kinds of passions and pleasures.

(Titus 3:3)

The Roman centurion who escorted Paul as a prisoner to Rome had no intention of stopping off in Crete. He only landed on the island because the wind blew the ship off course and he did all he could to get away from the island as quickly as possible. The Romans despised Crete as an island of liars and cheats, so instead of travelling five miles east to spend the winter at the port of Lasea which served the capital city Gortyn, he wrecked his ship by trying to travel ten times further west to the port of Phoenix. Anything to avoid having to consort with the locals and to be a few miles nearer Rome.

That's a good picture of how many Christians feel towards the unbelievers who live all around them. They allow the Devil to transform their godly hatred for their former sins into an ungodly hatred for their unsaved neighbours who still practise them. The eighteenth-century Bible commentator Matthew Henry surely meant well when he wrote that *"We should not join in friendship and acquaintance with wicked men and unbelievers. Though we cannot wholly avoid seeing and hearing, and being with such, yet we should never choose them for friends. We must not defile ourselves by converse with those who defile themselves with sin."*[1] But it was a very odd way of trying to follow the one the Pharisees accused of being *"a friend of tax collectors and*

---

1 Matthew Henry wrote this when commenting on 2 Corinthians 6:11–18.

sinners."[2] The Devil pursues a policy of Gospel damage limitation by tricking devout Christians into thinking that God is pleased with their splendid isolation from the world.

That's why Paul issues a stark warning to Titus in these verses. He tried to persuade the Roman centurion to turn back and spend the winter in the Cretan capital, and he spent his time in Rome dreaming of the moment when he would go back and rub shoulders with the sinful Cretans once more. He therefore gives Titus several reasons why he must teach the Christians on the island to love unbelievers in spite of their sin. Their passion for the heavenly city must not cause them to despise the unsaved people who lived in the hundred cities of Crete.

Paul reminds Titus in 3:3 that unbelievers are no worse than we were before Jesus saved us. *"We too were foolish, disobedient, deceived and enslaved by all kinds of passions and pleasures",* he reminds us. *"We lived in malice and envy, being hated and hating one another."* If we let our godly hatred for sin morph into an ungodly dislike for sinners, we have forgotten who we used to be. We have developed the same smug sense of spiritual superiority that spoiled the Pharisees. It's repulsive to Jesus and it is repulsive to unbelievers too. Bill Hybels reminds us that *"There may be no quicker way to send an unbeliever to the hills than to play the piety card. If you want to permanently repulse a person from the things of God, try a little superiority on for size. It works every time."*[3]

Paul reminds Titus in 3:4–5 that the only reason we have been saved is that God loved us enough to extend towards us his undeserved kindness and mercy.[4] Every true believer knows

---

[2] Matthew 11:19. One of the most shocking aspects of Jesus' ministry was the friendships he made with tax collectors, prostitutes, drunkards and other sinners.

[3] Bill Hybels in *Just Walk Across the Room* (2006).

[4] The Greek word which Paul uses for love in 3:4 is *philanthrōpia*, which is the root of the English word *philanthropy*. Christians who turn their backs on unbelievers show that they lack God's *love for people*.

deep down that *"He saved us, not because of righteous things we had done, but because of his mercy"*, so we must extend this same mercy towards others.

Philip Yancey reminds us that churches can all too often be like the unforgiving servant in Matthew 18:21–35. He tells the story of a worker on the streets of Chicago:

> *A prostitute came to see me in wretched straits, homeless, sick, unable to buy food for her two-year-old daughter. Through sobs and tears, she told me she had been renting out her daughter – two years old! – to men interested in kinky sex. She made more renting out her daughter for an hour than she could earn on her own in a night. She had to do it, she said, to support her own drug habit. I could hardly bear hearing her sordid story... At last I asked if she had ever thought of going to a church for help. I will never forget the look of pure, naïve shock that crossed her face. "Church!" she cried. "Why would I ever go there? I was already feeling terrible about myself. They'd just make me feel worse."*[5]

Paul wants us to imagine what the streets of our cities would be like if people believed that churches were a place where they would find the love and mercy of Christ instead of self-righteous Christians.

Paul reminds Titus in 3:5–7 that the Gospel is powerful enough to transform anyone. If we find it easier to imagine respectable unbelievers turning to Jesus than rogues and liars, it simply shows we have forgotten the power of the Gospel. Jesus' death and resurrection offers *"the washing of rebirth"* to the dirtiest of sinners. His ascension to heaven means that he now pours out the Holy Spirit on anyone who believes. Nobody is too sinful to break out of the labyrinth of their sin if God helps

[5] This story is taken from Philip Yancey's book *What's So Amazing About Grace?* (1997).

them. Paul tells us to have confidence in the power of *"renewal by the Holy Spirit, whom he poured out on us generously through Jesus Christ our Saviour,"* and to believe that Jesus makes even the foulest sinners *"heirs having the hope of eternal life."* We do not honour Jesus by turning our backs on unbelievers and longing for our heavenly home. We honour him by getting close to sinners out of a belief that Jesus died for them as much as he died for us.

Finally, Paul reminds Titus in 3:8 that our calling in this life is to live such godly lives that sinners are attracted to God by our lifestyle and are saved. It is so important that we understand this that Paul uses the phrase *pistos ho logos*, the same Greek phrase he also uses four times in his letters to Timothy as a way of underlining a matter of vital importance.[6] *"This is a trustworthy saying"*, he emphasizes. Those who have trusted in God need to devote themselves to doing what is good and to sharing the message of the Gospel with everyone. The Gospel is not just excellent and profitable for Christians. It is profitable for *everyone*.[7]

The Roman centurion could not wait to get away from the sinful Cretans. Paul could not wait to get back to them. Which are you more like? Which is your church more like? Charles Wesley taught believers at the start of the Methodist revival to sing, *"His blood can make the foulest clean."*[8] When we start to sing it and to believe it in our churches, we will also see a revival of our own.

[6] See 1 Timothy 1:15, 3:1, 4:9 and 2 Timothy 2:11.

[7] Paul does not say that our good works are simply profitable to *hēmeis*, meaning to *us*, but to *hoi anthrōpoi*, meaning to all *people*. This deliberately ties in with his call for us to imitate God's *philanthrōpia* in 3:4.

[8] This is one of the lines in his hymn "O, for a Thousand Tongues to Sing" (1740).

Truly Fruitful (3:9–15)

Our people must learn to devote themselves to doing what is good, in order to provide for urgent needs and not live unproductive lives.

(Titus 3:14)

Paul has reached the end of his letter to Titus. He is about to give the letter to Zenas and Apollos so that they can take it to Crete on their way to Egypt or Rome. These final seven verses are therefore very important. They show us the biggest priorities that filled Paul's mind for his Cretan converts as he drew his letter to a close. The priorities are varied but they all share one overriding theme. It is the theme of lesson three in Paul's discipleship training school. He wants them all to become truly fruitful.

In 3:9–11, Paul reminds Titus that the big priority is to deal with the false teaching that has infected the church in Crete. All this talk about Old Testament genealogies and strict adherence to the Law comes from false teachers who are unfruitful both in terms of their own lifestyle (1:16) and in terms of the converts they make.[1] Their teaching is *"unprofitable and useless"* because the people it attracts are like the first three types of seed in the Parable of the Sower and not like the fourth type of seed – converts who reap thirty, sixty or a hundred times what was sown.[2]

---

[1] The *"Jewish myths"* Paul warned against in 1:14 were based on the Old Testament genealogies. The false teachers took obscure characters from a genealogy and invented mythological stories about them.

[2] Paul makes a deliberate contrast between the false teachers and the good works he describes in 3:8. Whereas good works were *ōphelimos*, or *profitable*, their false teachings are *anōpheles*, or *unprofitable*.

People who push strange ideas on others can be so harmful to the church that Paul uses three of these final seven verses to remind Titus to deal with them firmly. If they refuse to listen to his warnings, he should put them out of the church in the way he instructed in 2 Thessalonians 3:6–15.[3] Paul gives parallel instructions in 1 Timothy 5:8 when he says that any unfruitful Christian who asks "what can I get out of the church?" rather than "what can I contribute to the church?" has *"denied the faith and is worse than an unbeliever."* These are sobering words but they remind us of Jesus' promise: *"I chose you and appointed you so that you might go and bear fruit – fruit that will last."*[4] There is no such thing as a healthy but unfruitful Christian. Church leaders need to challenge and disciple unfruitful church members to find out if they are true disciples at all.

In 3:12, Paul reminds Titus that he expects him to be very fruitful too. Most of us would consider planting healthy churches in each of the hundred cities of Crete the task of a lifetime, but not Paul. He expects Titus to be able to appoint church elders who can lead the evangelistic push to the remaining cities without him, because he needs him to leave the island within weeks of receiving this letter. He is sending Artemas and Tychicus, two members of his wider team, to relieve him so that he can join Paul at Nicopolis on the west coast of Greece. From there, he will travel up the Adriatic to Dalmatia (modern-day Albania and Croatia) as soon as the seas are safe for sailing at the start of 65 AD.[5] Crete is not to define the scope of his vision. Titus must never forget that his parish is the world.

---

[3] Paul is talking specifically about disruptive false teachers, but these instructions also reflect more general teaching in Matthew 18:15–17 and 1 Corinthians 5. Church leaders who are weak in dealing with unfruitful Christians are unloving towards them, towards the church, towards the unbelievers who see them, and towards God himself.

[4] John 15:16. Whenever Jesus makes a promise, he always delivers on it unless we resist him.

[5] The port of Nicopolis connected Greece to the regions to which Titus went in 2 Timothy 4:10.

In 3:13, Paul reminds Titus that the Cretans should quickly learn to bear fruit beyond the borders of their own island too. Apollos was an apostle who ministered in Ephesus and Corinth but who was never part of Paul's team. He had an apostolic team of his own which included the accomplished orator Zenas, a fact that the troublemakers in the church at Corinth tried to use to stir up rivalry between the two apostolic teams.[6] Far from responding to their troublemaking, Paul tells Titus to see this short visit from a new apostolic team as a perfect opportunity for the Cretans to give financially to world mission – not just to reach Crete and the rest of Paul's apostolic sphere of influence, but to reach the different parts of the world which were being reached by another team of workers. Paul is not jealous to keep all of their giving to himself because he expects the Cretan believers to be fruitful in their generosity towards everyone.

In 3:14, Paul reminds Titus that his basic message to the Cretan believers is that the Gospel must make them truly fruitful. He emphasizes one last time that real converts must *"not live unproductive lives."* He uses the Greek word *akarpos*, which means *unfruitful*, because the message of this third lesson in his discipleship training school is that true converts must become truly fruitful. Believers who do not devote themselves to doing all they can to strengthen the church and to further its mission in the world are like barnacles on the hull of a warship. They slow it down. Worse, they make the Gospel unattractive to the world because they do not taste like Jesus at all. It is very significant that Paul never refers to how many converts he and Titus have made in Crete, because he does not believe that the key to converting an island lies in numbers. He would rather have a group of small churches that attract unbelievers to the Gospel than a group of larger but far weaker churches, riddled with hypocrisy and compromise.

In 3:15, Paul signs off his letter by reminding Titus that

[6] See Acts 18:24–19:1 and 1 Corinthians 1:12, 3:4–6 and 3:21–23.

Christian fruitfulness means being generous. He talks to him about Christian *friendship*, Christian *love*, Christian *faith* and Christian *grace* – four things which mark every true believer and which are never exhausted in the giving. Christian fruitfulness is not like an apple tree, which runs out of apples once it is harvested. It is like the feeding of the five thousand – the more we give away, the more we find we have left over. Paul tells us to live on a daily diet of friendship and love and trust and grace.[7] John Wesley told his converts to *"Do all the good you can, by all the means you can, in all the ways you can, in all the places you can, at all the times you can, to all the people you can, as long as ever you can."* God will make us truly fruitful if we do this, looking everywhere for opportunities to give ourselves away.

So as we end Paul's letter to Titus, we need to ask ourselves if we are truly fruitful. We live in communities that have not yet been transformed by the message of God's salvation. We live in communities that are crying out, not just to have a church on every corner, but to have a fruitful Christian presence which tastes like Jesus. Paul promises us that if we devote ourselves to doing what is good, we will not live unproductive lives. We dare not satisfy ourselves with fruitless Christianity. We must learn this third lesson in Paul's discipleship training school. We must pray and act and give and trust that the Lord will make us truly fruitful.

[7] Paul uses the Greek word for *you (singular)* to greet Titus and to tell him to greet the Cretan Christians for him. He uses the Greek word for *you (plural)* to wish grace on the Cretan Christians directly.

Lesson Four – 1 Timothy:

Truly Mature

Same Difference (1:1–2)

Paul, an apostle of Christ Jesus... to Timothy, my true son in the faith.

(1 Timothy 1:1–2)

Paul wrote his first letter to Timothy shortly after he wrote to Titus. The two letters are very similar, but don't let that make you miss the fact that they are also different in some very important ways.

The two letters are similar because Paul wrote them to individual converts, addressing both Timothy and Titus as *"my true son in the faith."*[1] They are similar because Paul tells both of them that he has left them behind to complete his work in the cities of the Eastern Mediterranean by appointing elders who will give an effective lead to the churches he has planted. They are similar because Paul tells both Timothy and Titus to deal with dangerous false teachers and to defend *"the truth"* and *"the faith"* – not just *"truth"* or *"faith"* – reflecting the fact that these are second-generation Christian leaders who need to defend the revelation that was given to them by the apostles.[2] They are similar because Paul tells them that they will find this truth, not just in the Old Testament, but also in his own apostolic teaching. Although he does not begin all of his New Testament letters by stating that he is an apostle, he does so at the start of all three letters to Titus and Timothy. They knew he was an apostle better than anyone, so this can only be because he wants to emphasize

---

1 Compare 1 Timothy 1:2 with Titus 1:4.

2 Compare Titus 1:1, 13, 14 and 3:15 with 1 Timothy 1:2, 14, 2:4, 3:9, 15, 4:1, 3, 6, 5:8, 6:5, 10, 12 and 21.

that the words he writes to them are Holy Scripture. Five times in these three letters, he assures them that he is writing *"a trustworthy saying that deserves full acceptance."*[3]

These "pastoral epistles" therefore have a great deal in common, but they are also different, and it is in the differences that we discover the major theme of 1 Timothy. For a start, Timothy was a much more impressive leader than Titus. Whereas Luke saw no reason to mention Titus in the book of Acts, he mentions Timothy six times – more than any other member of Paul's team except for the apostles Barnabas and Silas. Paul mentions him eighteen times in his letters, co-authoring six of his thirteen letters with him, and he reflects in Philippians 2:20 that *"I have no one else like him."* If Titus was a nobody, Timothy was very much a somebody. He had been ministering alongside Paul non-stop for fifteen years when he received this letter and he was the closest thing Paul had to a spiritual heir and successor.[4]

Another big difference is that, whereas Paul left Titus in Crete to appoint elders for many churches which would reach a hundred cities, Paul left Timothy in Ephesus to appoint elders for a single church in a single city. Ephesus was the fourth or fifth largest city in the world, and the church Paul planted there twelve years before he wrote to Timothy had become a megachurch with tens of thousands of members.[5] It could hardly have been more different from the churches of Crete. Paul wrote to Titus to help him to make several newly planted churches truly fruitful, but he wrote to Timothy to help him to make one

---

[3] See Titus 3:8, 1 Timothy 1:15, 3:1, 4:9 and 2 Timothy 2:11.

[4] Having said this, Colossians 1:1 tells us that Timothy was not an apostle. We must not place him on a pedestal as somebody unlike us. Paul wrote 1 Timothy as a lesson for us as well as for Timothy.

[5] We can tell the size of the church at Ephesus from the fact that the scrolls it burnt in Acts 19:19 were worth 100,000 days' wages for an unskilled labourer. It is quite feasible that a church could number tens of thousands of people in a city of 250,000 freemen and women and 400,000 slaves, although they would have needed to meet at multiple times and in multiple locations.

well-established megachurch truly mature. This letter gives us the clearest summary in the New Testament of how established churches and church leaders should behave. It is the fourth lesson in Paul's discipleship training school and it teaches us how we too can become truly mature.

Another big difference is the challenge that it posed for Timothy when Paul told him to appoint godly elders in Ephesus. The problem for Titus was that the Cretan believers were so newly converted that it required great faith to entrust leadership to any of them. The problem for Timothy was that there were already elders in place at Ephesus; it was just that they were not necessarily the right ones! Paul had established a strong team of elders by 57 AD, but he warned them in Acts 20 that their team was about to go through a period of high turnover. He warned them *"that they would never see his face again,"* which means that the team he discovered on his return to Ephesus in 65 AD must have been unrecognizable. Timothy needed to unappoint as well as appoint elders at Ephesus. This was going to stretch him and require all of the Christian maturity he had.

A final big difference is that Paul wrote to Timothy several months after he wrote to Titus. If we piece together Paul's itinerary from the various clues he gives us in his letters, it appears he wrote to Titus late in the summer of 64 AD and shortly after his arrival in Ephesus from Crete. He then sailed from Ephesus to Philippi at the end of 64 AD and took the Egnatian Way through Thessalonica and Berea in order to rendezvous with Titus at Nicopolis.[6] He wrote his first letter to Timothy somewhere along the way, perhaps as late as 65 AD, by which time it had become clear that Nero's persecution of Christians was not a temporary measure. Paul had begun to sense that time was running out for him. He wrote 1 Timothy in order to prepare his converts to continue as truly mature believers without him.

---

6 We can deduce this from 1 Timothy 1:3 and Titus 3:12.

Paul's first letter to Timothy continues to teach us how God turns scrap metal into gold. It helps us to grow into Christian maturity personally and it shows us how to bring churches to maturity so that they can reach the rest of the world. It teaches us how to produce mature disciples of Jesus and how to lead them in a Gospel charge into unreached communities. God still *"wants all people to be saved and to come to a knowledge of the truth,"* and he still promises that if we are *"rich in good deeds,"* it will ensure that *"God's name and our teaching may not be slandered."*[7] Whatever the differences between Ephesus and Crete, our God remains the same. He wants to turn us into true converts and true warriors who are truly fruitful and truly mature.

Paul reminds us in these two opening verses that God is still the Saviour, Jesus is still the Lord, the Gospel is still our hope, and it still promises us grace, mercy and peace.[8] God is still the same in every place and at every time. He still invites us to let him turn the scrap metal of our lives into precious gold.

7 1 Timothy 2:4; 6:1, 18.

8 While Paul normally begins his letters by blessing his readers with grace and peace from God, one of the distinctive features of the start of his two letters to Timothy is that he also blesses him with *mercy*.

The Enemy Inside (1:3–10)

As I urged you when I went into Macedonia, stay there in Ephesus so that you may command certain people not to teach false doctrines any longer.

(1 Timothy 1:3)

The Chinese emperors of the Ming Dynasty were seriously paranoid. They lived in fear that the tribes to the north of their borders would renew the days when Genghis Khan and his Mongol horde swept suddenly through China. As a result, they started building the largest fortress in world history. They built the Great Wall of China – 9 metres wide, 5,500 miles long, and boasting 25,000 watchtowers – but they were unprepared for the enemy inside. In May 1644, a general named Wu Sangui cut a deal with the Manchus and opened up a gate in the wall to let them through. Within weeks of his act of treachery, the Ming Dynasty had fallen. Paul begins his letter to Timothy by warning him not to be so foolish. The biggest danger to the church has never been its enemies on the outside. It has always been the threat posed by false friends on the inside.

Paul tells Timothy in 1:3 that leaders need to be wary of what is happening within the walls of their churches. Timothy's calling to *"stay there in Ephesus so that you may command certain people not to teach false doctrines"* might not sound as glamorous as Paul's calling to move on to help the churches of Macedonia, but it was every bit as essential. Paul had warned the Ephesian elders in Acts 20 that *"After I leave, savage wolves will come in among you and will not spare the flock. Even from your own number men will arise and distort the truth in order to draw away disciples after them. So be on your guard!"* Paul warns Timothy that the biggest danger for the church at Ephesus is not the threat that Nero's persecution might come to its walls. It is the false teaching of its enemies on the inside.

In 1:3, Paul tells Timothy that leaders have to be strong enough to spot false teaching and to put a stop to it very quickly. He doesn't just tell him to command the Ephesian Christians not to listen to them. He tells him to stand up to the false teachers and to silence them.[1] We know from the final verses of Titus that this means warning them once, warning them twice and then, if necessary, putting them out of the church entirely, but the implication throughout 1 Timothy is that these false teachers are not merely oddballs on the edge of church life. They are senior leaders who have gathered a real following. Paul tells us in 1:7 that they see themselves as gifted Bible teachers, and he reminds Timothy in 1:20 that two of the individuals he has already excluded were prominent leaders within the church.[2] There is a reason why Paul tells Timothy in 3:4 not to appoint elders who are unable to stand up to their own children. Church leadership is not for the weak. It means being willing to stand up to friends and to loved ones who unwittingly place the church in danger.

A. W. Tozer warns us that

> *Many tender-minded Christians fear to sin against love by daring to inquire into anything that comes wearing the cloak of Christianity and breathing the name of Jesus. They dare not examine the credentials of the latest prophet to hit their town lest they be guilty of rejecting*

---

[1] Paul tells us in no uncertain terms in 1:3 that these people are *heterodidaskaleō*, or *teaching something different* from the Christian Gospel. They are to be silenced as troublemakers, not lauded as free thinkers.

[2] If this is the same Alexander who is mentioned in Acts 19:33, he was one of Paul's closest allies in Ephesus. 2 Timothy 2:17 tells us more about what Hymenaeus was teaching the Ephesian Christians.

something which may be of God. They timidly remember how the Pharisees refused to accept Christ when He came, and they do not want to be caught in the same snare, so they either reserve judgment or shut their eyes and accept everything without question. This is supposed to indicate a high degree of spirituality. But in sober fact it indicates no such thing. It may indeed be evidence of the absence of the Holy Spirit. Gullibility is not synonymous with spirituality... We may sin as certainly by approving the spurious as by rejecting the genuine.[3]

In 1:4–7, Paul tells Timothy that false teaching is often the result of people majoring on minors and losing sight of the Gospel.[4] The false teachers at Ephesus appeared to be Christian. They created stories about the exploits of characters they found in the Old Testament genealogies. Since the Ancient Greeks loved myths and storytelling, the teachers looked like the church's most gifted communicators.[5] It would take courage for Timothy to confront their *"controversial speculations"* about obscure passages and their *"meaningless talk"* about side issues – just as it still requires courage for us to confront falsehood today. But Paul tells Timothy that mature Christians must stand up against such teachers, regardless of their position or their gifting. We must have the courage to say *"they do not know what they are talking about or what they so confidently affirm."*

In 1:8, Paul tells Timothy that the antidote to dangerous distraction from the Gospel is for church leaders to keep the focus of their preaching on what really matters. The false teachers

---

3 A. W. Tozer in a sermon on 1 John 4:1 entitled "Testing the Spirits" (first published in 1978).

4 The Greek word *astocheō* in 1:6 was used to describe archers *missing the mark*. For all their self-confidence, the false teachers had lost sight of the Gospel and were way off target. Paul uses the same word again in 6:21.

5 Paul tells us in 4:1–5 that people can teach from the Bible and yet entice people to *"abandon the faith and follow deceiving spirits and things taught by demons."*

were abusing texts from the Old Testament, so Timothy needed to remember that *"the law is good if one uses it properly."*[6] Paul modelled this in Galatians 3 by responding to false teachers who misquoted the Law of Moses by quoting from the Law correctly six times in only sixteen verses. He tells Timothy to do the same, safeguarding the Christians at Ephesus by teaching them what the Scriptures really mean.[7] He must show them that the whole Bible points people to faith in Jesus alone (1:4), and that faith in Jesus is always seen by our love and good deeds (1:5), not by our idle talk (1:6). Teaching the truth and keeping people's focus on the Gospel is the best way to expose error and empty speculation for what they are.

In 1:9–11, Paul tells Timothy that what we are taught always affects how we behave. People fed on genealogies and myths soon start taking their morality from their man-made heroes, just as people fed on Hollywood movies and TV dramas soon start taking their morality from the stories on which they have fed their minds. Stories have great power to change our views on sexual immorality, gay relationships, deceit and violence,[8] but proper Bible teaching carries an even greater power to expose the people in those stories as *"lawbreakers and rebels, the ungodly and sinful, the unholy and irreligious."*[9] Paul reminds Timothy that God entrusted *"the sound doctrine"*

[6] Paul uses a play on words in Greek in 1:8–9. He tells us that the *nomos* is good if it is used *nomimōs* for the *anomoi*, meaning literally that the *Law* is good if it is used *lawfully* to expose *lawbreakers*.

[7] Paul repeats in 4:13 that reading and teaching Scripture is the best defence against false teachers.

[8] The Greek word *arsenokoitēs* means literally *going to bed with men*. Both Tacitus (*Annals*, 15.37) and Suetonius (*The Life of Nero*, 28–29) tell us that Nero tried to normalize gay sex and same-sex marriage. There is nothing new about most false teaching today.

[9] The list in 1:9–10 appears to be a description of people breaking each of the Ten Commandments in order.

of the Gospel to the apostles and that he needs to teach it to the Ephesians so they can stand their ground.[10]

The biggest danger to the Church has never been persecution on the outside. It has always been false teaching and sinful practice on the inside. So don't be like the Ming Dynasty and ignore the dangers of the enemy inside the walls. Paul and Timothy saved the church at Ephesus through their courage. Now Paul charges us to do the same: *"Stay... so that you may command certain people not to teach false doctrines."*

[10] The slaves at Ephesus outnumbered the free citizens, so Paul could not simply demand their instant freedom. Instead, he says the slave trade is an act of theft. Without the slave trade, slavery would slowly die.

The Friends Outside (1:12–20)

Here is a trustworthy saying that deserves full acceptance: Christ Jesus came into the world to save sinners – of whom I am the worst.

(1 Timothy 1:15)

Nobody shocked people's religious sensibilities quite as much as Jesus. He knew full well that devout Jews hated the Samaritans for their semi-pagan worship, yet he asked a Samaritan woman if she would let him share a drink with her. When he learned she was a five-time divorcee and was living with her latest boyfriend, he didn't walk away. Instead, he told her that God wants to save sinners and to turn them into better worshippers than the devout Jews on the Temple Mount in Jerusalem.

On another occasion, he shocked the people of Jericho by choosing not to stay at the house of any of their respectable religious leaders. Instead, he invited himself to stay at the home of Zacchaeus, the crooked tax collector who was hated by everyone for using his friendship with the Romans to steal his neighbours' money. *"All the people saw this and began to mutter, 'He has gone to be the guest of a sinner.'"*[1] That's what often happens when God extends his grace towards the sinful and undeserving. Religious people can be quick to overlook the sins of insiders and to spot the shortcomings of outsiders. Even as Paul warns us to beware of enemies inside the church, he

---

[1] See John 4:4–42 and Luke 19:1–10. See also 1 Corinthians 5:1–13.

urges us to be constantly on the lookout for potential friends of God who are as yet still on the outside of the church.

If it was going to be difficult for Timothy to confront the false teachers in the church at Ephesus, it was going to be even harder for him to persuade the church to extend love towards outsiders. Paul and Timothy had been forced to flee Ephesus in 55 AD because a pagan mob rioted and attempted to lynch them. Although Nero's persecution of Christians had not yet reached their city, the Ephesian believers were concerned that what was happening to their Roman brothers and sisters might soon happen to them as well. When Tacitus talks about the persecution, he uses language to describe the Christians that nowadays is reserved only for paedophiles. He tells us that ordinary Romans were pleased to see the slaughter of *"the notoriously depraved Christians"* because the whole *"human race detested them"* and hoped it would put an end to their *"deadly superstition."*[2] If any generation of believers might have been justified to batten down the hatches and withdraw from contact with their non-Christian neighbours, it was this one. That's why Paul spends the second half of this opening chapter giving Timothy some reasons why we need to love unbelievers as much as Jesus does.

In 1:12–14, Paul tells us to love non-Christians because of our own background. He reflects on his conversion testimony in order to encourage us to reflect on our own. If he was *"a blasphemer and a persecutor and a violent man"* and yet *"was shown mercy because I acted in ignorance and unbelief,"* we cannot refuse the same grace to other people. When sinners are sinful, they are simply acting out what they believe. We need to sacrifice our comfort, our reputation and even our lives in order to tell them about Jesus and to call them to a different way of living. Our hearts grow cold towards unbelievers whenever we forget

[2] Tacitus does not try to conceal his hatred of Christianity. He says these things in his *Annals* (15.44).

the miracle of our own conversion. Paul's love for his persecutors comes from the fact that he has never lost his sense of wonder that the Lord *"considered me trustworthy, appointing me to his service"* or that *"the grace of our Lord was poured out on me abundantly, along with the faith and love that are in Christ Jesus."*

In 1:15, Paul refuses to let us rush on from this insight. He uses a phrase which he uses five times in the pastoral epistles in order to highlight vital creedal statements.[3] He warns us that *"Here is a trustworthy saying that deserves full acceptance: Christ Jesus came into the world to save sinners – of whom I am the worst."* The fact that Paul was one of the unlikeliest people to be converted in his generation made him precisely the kind of person God wanted to save! We must never write anyone off from a share in the Gospel, because it is good news for sinners and Samaritans and adulterers and brawlers and tax collectors. It is the news that God has come down to save us because he loves us in spite of our rebellion and sin.

In 1:16–17, Paul develops this thinking further by telling us that God particularly wants to save out-and-out sinners in order to showcase his glory. Paul may or may not have been objectively *"the worst of sinners"*, but he feels he was and he is convinced that ***"for that very reason*** *I was shown mercy."* Far from discounting him from salvation, his terrible sins made him an ideal candidate to become a trophy of God's immense patience towards people who deserve nothing but death. Paul is so excited about this that he cannot contain his worship. He laughs at Nero's pretentious lust to be revered as a mighty king and god, celebrating that Jesus alone is the *"King eternal, immortal, invisible, the only God."*[4] Looking back on God's mercy towards you should make you want to raise the roof in worship. It should also break your heart for the sinners outside the church who as yet have no idea that they can become friends of God.

---

3 Titus 3:8; 1 Timothy 1:15; 3:1; 4:9; 2 Timothy 2:11.

4 The most reliable Greek manuscripts say *"the only God,"* but some manuscripts say *"the only wise God."*

In 1:18–20, Paul warns Timothy that living out this Gospel is never easy. It is always easier to remain in the comfort and safety of the church community than it is to see each day as a chance to make fresh evangelistic sorties into the unbelieving world.[5] Paul suggests later that Hymenaeus avoided the laughter of the serious thinkers of Ephesus by persuading himself that the Christian hope of resurrection was simply a metaphor. He suggests that Alexander turned away from the faith because he could make more money by softening his stance against idols.[6] Paul reminds Timothy that he was forced to put these two friends out of the church because they denied the Gospel for the sake of comfort.[7] He tells Timothy that he will only *"fight the battle well"* if he clings to the prophetic encouragements which God has given him to help him.[8]

Every Christian faces the temptation to be too soft towards Christians in the church and too harsh towards non-Christians outside the church. Having dealt firmly with the enemy on the inside, Paul now deals firmly with us and warns us not to forget that Jesus still has many friends for us to gather on the outside. Despite hostility and persecution, Paul encourages us to expect the Lord to save a great many sinners. The more sinful and the less likely they are to be saved, the more glory Jesus will receive when he turns his fiercest enemies into friends of God.

---

[5] Paul warns us in 1:5, 1:19 and 4:2 that we need to resist this temptation with *faith* and *a good conscience*.

[6] Compare Acts 17:32 with 2 Timothy 2:17–18. Compare Acts 19:23–27 with 1 Timothy 6:10 and 2 Timothy 4:14.

[7] Paul uses this same phrase *handing someone over to Satan* in 1 Corinthians 5:5 to describe putting somebody out of the church. Paul jolted people into repentance by making it clear to them that they were siding with the Devil, although neither man had repented by the time Paul wrote 2 Timothy. He does not tell us whether they were ever truly converted; he simply warns us to hold onto a good conscience ourselves.

[8] Paul uses a military metaphor in 1:18 to warn Timothy up front that evangelism always means wounds and setbacks and discouragements. Scripture and prophecies remind us that, in spite of these, we will win.

When Two Kingdoms Collide (2:1–7)

I urge, then, first of all, that petitions, prayers, intercession and thanksgiving be made for all people – for kings and all those in authority.

(1 Timothy 2:1–2)

On Monday 1st July 2013, a man was arrested for preaching the Gospel in the street a block away from the church I lead in London. I didn't know him and I was not linked to him, but very soon I became involved in the fall-out from the incident. After all, to my knowledge, it was the first time that a Christian had been arrested for preaching the Gospel in London for over a century.

One thing that became clear very early on was that Christians do not respond to incidents of public hostility towards their faith in the same way. Some local Christians responded very angrily and cast themselves in the role of victim. Others sought to distance themselves from the street preacher, arguing that he was unwise to have chosen to preach from such a contentious Bible passage. Others sided with the police, arguing that it was worth accepting a bit less freedom of Christian expression if it meant silencing the spiteful preaching of radical Muslim clerics who come from overseas. This was nothing compared to the major persecution that was taking place in Rome when Paul wrote to Timothy, but it is enough to illustrate one thing: the Christians at Ephesus must have had different views on how to respond to the news that was reaching them from Rome. They must have been very eager to read about Paul's reaction.

Perhaps the most surprising thing about 1 Timothy is that Paul does not refer explicitly to the start of Nero's persecution at all. He wrote freely to the Thessalonians about persecution from their Jewish neighbours, but he is much more wary of writing about persecution from the Roman emperor in a letter that might be intercepted by one of his officials. A few unwise sentences might cause problems for the church at Ephesus, and they might give an ambitious official a pretext on which to re-arrest him and send him back in chains to Rome. That's why Paul adopts the same subtle approach in this letter to Timothy that he used in his previous letter to Titus. He does not refer explicitly to the emperor or his persecution, but he gives Timothy some clear direction on how he should help the believers at Ephesus to respond to their present crisis.

First, Paul says in 2:1–2 that Christians should remain positive about the government even when they are being persecuted by it. He urges the church to pray *"for all people – for kings and all those in authority."* They should not simply pray for help against them. They should also give thanks for them and pray for their blessing and well-being. The early Christians model this for us in Acts 4:24–30 by the way in which they pray for help against their government using the words of Psalm 2. They use the psalm to guide their prayers but stop before its final verses, which say that the Lord will smash his enemies to pieces like pottery. Instead of asking God to destroy their rulers, they ask him to empower them to perform miracles that smash through unbelief so that their rulers and their entire city can be saved. However hostile your government may be towards the Gospel, Paul urges you to pray positively for them, both in your public gatherings and in your private prayers.

Second, Paul reminds us in 2:2 that we need good government so that *"we may live peaceful and quiet lives in all godliness and holiness."* The Emperor Nero was one of the worst rulers in history, but Paul points out that even his government was not entirely bad.[1] Paul's successful missionary journeys during the reigns of Claudius and Nero owed much to the Roman administration, which produced well-ordered cities where he could preach the Gospel, an excellent travel network between them, and protection from highwaymen and pirates along the way. He would have been murdered by the mob had he not used his Roman citizenship to call on Caesar's soldiers to save him, and we are told in Acts 19 that he was protected from death in Ephesus by the city clerk and by *"some of the officials of the province, friends of Paul."* Paul therefore warns us not to be naïve. Bad governments can sometimes serve the spread of the Gospel, just as the crumbling of an evil regime can sometimes spell very bad news for the safety of Christians. Even the worst rulers are better than no rulers at all.

Third, Paul reminds us in 2:3–7 that our prayerful support for the government – however flawed that government may be – *"is good, and pleases God"* because he is *"our Saviour, who wants all people to be saved and to come to a knowledge of the truth."* When my Zimbabwean friends prayed publicly for President Robert Mugabe and honoured him as their ruler during the darkest moments of his regime, it pleased God. It gave them the freedom to keep preaching the Gospel in Zimbabwe and it gave them a hearing whenever they spoke out against the worst atrocities of his rule.[2] Paul tells Timothy that Jesus came to earth *"at the proper time"* because the Roman Empire, for all its faults, offered a brilliant context for world evangelism. The early Christian thinker Origen pointed out that

[1] In Ephesians 6:11–12, Paul teaches the Ephesians not to blame the Devil's work in the world on his earthly agents. We may disagree strongly with politicians, but we must not demonize them.

[2] In a democracy we are all rulers in a limited sense, so we can speak out for and against the policies of the elected government. Paul was not writing to Timothy in a democracy, but under a totalitarian dictator.

God prepared the nations for his teaching, that they might be under one Roman emperor so that the unfriendly attitude of the nations to one another, caused by the existence of a large number of kingdoms, might not make it more difficult for Jesus' apostles to do what He commanded them when He said, "Go and teach all nations."[3]

Fourth and finally, Paul gives us subtle reminders throughout 2:1–7 that we need not panic, because Jesus is the true King of kings. He told us in 1:1 that Jesus is the Christ, the Messianic king whose coming was prophesied in Daniel 7 and whose *"kingdom is one that will never be destroyed."*[4] He told us in 1:17 that Jesus alone is the eternal King. Now he tells us in 2:3–5 that Jesus alone is the *Saviour* and *Mediator* between humankind and God.[5] He uses the political language of the Roman Empire to tell us that God has made him a *herald* of Jesus' reign to people from every nation. Paul did not need to confront the empty boasts of Caesar. He simply needed to proclaim that Jesus was the real King.

Christians will always react differently to persecution, but make sure that your reaction fits within these four guidelines from Paul. If we continue to appreciate whatever is good about our rulers, if we continue to give thanks for them and to ask God to bless them, and if we proclaim the positive message that Jesus is the true King of kings, we will find that the Gospel spreads even in the midst of fierce persecution.

---

[3] Origen wrote this in c.248 AD in *Contra Celsum* (2.30). It echoes Paul's statement that Jesus came "at just the right time" in 2:6, 2 Timothy 1:9–10, Titus 1:3, Romans 5:6 and Galatians 4:4.

[4] Paul emphasizes that Jesus is the *Son of Man* prophesied in Daniel 7:13 when he tells us that, even now in heaven, he is still *"the man Christ Jesus."* Paul states the superiority of the Lord's reign even more clearly in 1 Timothy 6:15 when he refers to him as *"God, the blessed and only Ruler, the King of kings and Lord of lords."*

[5] We saw in Titus 3 that one of Nero's favourite titles was that of *Sōtēr* or *Saviour*. He also called himself the *Pontifex Maximus*, which meant the *Greatest Bridge-Builder* between humans and the gods.

The One and Only (2:3–7)

For there is one God and one mediator between God and mankind, the man Christ Jesus.

(1 Timothy 2:5)

One of my friends works for the biggest art auction house in London. Part of her role is to distinguish between original works of art and forgeries. What I find fascinating is that she had to study for three years before she could be trusted to spot counterfeit works of art, yet she spent none of that time looking at forgeries. Her employer was convinced that if she studied the originals in enough detail, she would easily be able to spot forgeries when they came. That's why Paul does not mind that he cannot point out the shortcomings of the Emperor Nero to Timothy. He doesn't feel he needs to talk about false gods or trumped-up rulers. All he needs to do is help his readers to fall in love with the One and Only.

The opening verses of chapter 2 contain a remarkable amount of detail about who Jesus is. They are the perfect antidote to the modern and completely unhistorical idea that *"Jesus was viewed by His followers as a mortal prophet… a great and powerful man, but a* ***man*** *nonetheless… Jesus' establishment as 'the Son of God' was officially proposed and voted on by the Council of Nicaea… A relatively close vote at that."*[1] Paul is writing at the start of 65 AD, only thirty-five years after the death and resurrection of Jesus, and he is in no doubt whatsoever about who Jesus is. He believes that true Christian maturity means

[1] Dan Brown makes this wildly unhistorical claim in his novel *The Da Vinci Code* (2003).

getting to know Jesus better and better. By the time he finishes, he will make us want to put down this book and worship.

First, Paul tells us that Jesus is *the only true Saviour*. We have already seen that the name *Sōtēr* was one of the Emperor Nero's favourite titles, but an inscription to the Emperor Augustus that was found in the ruins of the Greek city of Priene gives us a deeper insight into Roman imperial propaganda. It claims that *"Providence has filled Augustus with virtue that he might benefit mankind, sending him as Saviour both for us and for our children... The birthday of the god Augustus marked the beginning of the Gospel regarding him for the world."* Paul does not need to tell us that the Roman emperors are impostors. He simply uses the emperors' own language to describe Jesus as the One and Only. He tells us ten times in the pastoral epistles that the Lord is the *Sōtēr*, the one and only *Saviour* – that's five times more often than in the rest of his letters put together. He also uses the word *euangelion*, or *Gospel*, dozens of times throughout his letters to tell us that the good news is not that an emperor has been born but that Jesus is on the Throne.

Second, Paul tells us that Jesus is *the only true God*. He is more than just our Saviour; he is *"our great God and Saviour"*. On six of the ten occasions that Paul uses the Greek word *Sōtēr* in his pastoral epistles, he refers to God the Father being the Saviour rather than Jesus the Son.[2] This is not an incidental point. It is absolutely crucial. Paul will not allow us to treat God the Father as a stern Judge and Jesus as the loving Saviour who rescues us from his angry dad. The three persons of the Trinity play different roles in our salvation, but all three persons are the same Triune God and Saviour. Paul refers to both God the

---

[2] Paul calls God the Father *Sōtēr* in 1 Timothy 1:1, 2:3, 4:10, Titus 1:3, 2:10 and 3:4. He calls Jesus the Son *Sōtēr* in 2 Timothy 1:10, Titus 1:4, 2:13 and 3:6.

Father and to Jesus as Saviour in order to help us understand that Jesus is the one and only God.[3]

Third, Paul tells us that Jesus is *the only true Mediator*. The word for a pagan priest in the Roman Empire was *pontifex*, which meant literally a *bridge-builder*. One of the most important titles of the Roman emperors was *Pontifex Maximus*, which meant *The Greatest Bridge-Builder*. Nero claimed to be both human and divine, the living mediator between the gods and humankind. Paul mocks his claim by telling us that there is only *"one mediator between God and mankind, the man Christ Jesus."* He alone is the Pontifex Maximus.[4] What is more, Paul reminds us that Jesus did not stop being human when he ascended to heaven. Nero might boast that a god is on the throne in Rome, but in Jesus there is a human being on the Throne of heaven! Jesus alone is fully God and fully man, so he is the one and only bridge-builder between the holy God and his sinful creatures.

Fourth, Paul tells us that Jesus is *the only true ransom for sin*. The Greek word Paul uses is *antilutron*, a word that was used to describe the *redemption price* that was paid to free a slave or a mortgaged property. Whereas Nero taxed his subjects and demanded that they serve him, Jesus poured out his blood for his subjects when he suffered on the cross to pay the price of God's just punishment towards our sin.[5] Nero claimed to be emperor of the world, but over half of the known world was outside his empire. Jesus' blood is so precious that it has paid *"a ransom for all people,"* whether they are part of the Roman Empire or in the barbarian lands beyond. People may reject Jesus' act of redemption and choose to bear God's punishment

[3] Paul's statement that God wishes all people to be saved ties in with Ezekiel 18:23, 33:11 and 2 Peter 3:9. He sees no contradiction between this and God allowing people to reject the Gospel if they want to.

[4] Although many Popes have also called themselves the "Pontifex Maximus", I am convinced this is a bad idea. It sounds more like the boasting of Nero than the Gospel of the one and only King Jesus.

[5] Romans 3:26 tells us that the ransom price was paid to God's justice, not to Satan. The Gospel doesn't reward Satan; it destroys him!

themselves.[6] However, 2,000 years after Nero was forced to commit suicide by his disillusioned subjects, Jesus is still able to save anyone who asks God for forgiveness through his blood.

That's why fifth, Paul tells us that Jesus is *the only true Gospel for the world*. The Roman state would send a *kērux*, or *herald*, to every corner of the empire whenever a new emperor took to the throne or a great victory was won on the battlefield. Paul uses the same word here to tell us that God has appointed him to be his *herald* and messenger boy to the nations. Paul does not need to say anything that could be construed as seditious by a Roman official who intercepted his letter to Timothy. He does not need to say that Nero is a forgery at all. He simply needs to hold up Jesus as the One and Only for every other rival claim to be exposed as a shabby imitation.

This is important in our multifaith society today. Paul shows us that we do not need to badmouth prophets like Muhammad. We do not need to rail against secular idols such as sex and self and money. We simply need to explain to people why Jesus is the One and Only. He is the only Saviour. He is the only God. He is the only Mediator, the only Ransom and the only Gospel for the world.

This should make you want to worship and it should make you want to persuade other people to worship him too. Don't slander the gods which they worship. Tell them instead why Jesus is the One and Only.

---

6 Paul adds in 4:10 that Jesus is the Saviour of everyone potentially but not everyone receives him as Saviour.

Real Men and Women (2:8–15)

I do not permit a woman to teach or to assume authority over a man; she must be quiet.

(1 Timothy 2:12)

Paul was very careful not to offend any Roman official who read his letter. He isn't so careful not to offend us. Having taught us to be wary of false teachers inside the Church and loving towards unbelievers outside the Church, he now turns to address specific issues within the church at Ephesus. He starts with one of the most controversial topics in our culture. He teaches Timothy how to turn the Ephesian believers into real men and real women.

Elsewhere in his letters, Paul tells husbands to take a lead in their marriages and wives to submit to their husbands' lead. Men and women are equal before God, but God has made them different because he wants them to worship him in different ways.[1] Here, Paul teaches Timothy how these gender differences ought to be reflected in the Church. As members of one of the largest and most established churches in the Roman Empire, Paul expects the Ephesian believers to model to the world a new way for men and women to work together. Paul takes us back to the early chapters of Genesis in order to show us that it isn't really a new way of working at all.

In 2:8, Paul teaches *Christian men to be real men*. God

[1] See Ephesians 5:22–24, Colossians 3:18, Galatians 3:28, 1 Corinthians 11:1–16 and 14:34–38. Importantly, Paul only ever tells wives to submit to their own husbands, not women to submit to men in general.

instructed Adam and Eve to *"Fill the earth and subdue it"* together in Genesis 1:28, but he specifically *"took the man and put him in the Garden of Eden to work it and take care of it"* in Genesis 2:15. He expected Adam to take the lead, which is why he came looking for Adam rather than Eve when she sinned (Genesis 3:9).[2] She sinned because Adam was passive and failed to protect her from the Devil, even though he was with her when she was tempted (Genesis 3:6). Paul tells us that the Gospel does not neuter men. It restores them to who they were always meant to be. It stops them using their hands to harm others and causes them to raise their hands in prayer for their government and for the world.[3] Sinful men are passive, working hard at their day jobs and their hobbies while ignoring their calling to care for their wives and children by taking a lead in the home and in the Church. Christian men are real men. They do not abdicate their responsibility. They take a lead as Adam did before the Fall.

In 2:9–10, Paul teaches *Christian women to be real women.* Eve sinned because she judged the snake's temptation too superficially. *"The woman saw that the fruit of the tree was good for food and pleasing to the eye"*, so she ate it. Paul therefore urges the Christian women at Ephesus not to make the same mistake by running after expensive clothes and jewellery and hairstyles in order to be beautiful in the eyes of the world. He tells them to adorn themselves with good deeds in order to be beautiful in the eyes of God. When women allow men and fashion magazines to define whether or not they are beautiful, they become miserable. But when they find their beauty in reflecting the character of God, they find true happiness and they make their husbands truly happy too.

---

2 Romans 5:12–19 also treats Adam rather than Eve as the main guilty party in her sin.

3 We are meant to see the link between 2:8 and 2:1. Paul's reference to *"holy hands"* echoes the message of Proverbs 28:9, James 5:16 and 1 Peter 3:7. How we live our lives affects our authority in prayer.

In 2:11–12, Paul teaches *men to be men and women to be women within the church.* This is where he really starts to offend our twenty-first-century sensibilities. God created men and women as equals (Galatians 3:28) but he did not create them identical because they have different roles to play. God created Eve to be Adam's *"helper"* in Genesis 2:18, not because she was inferior to him (the same Hebrew word describes God as our Helper in Exodus 18:4), but because he needed her to complement what was lacking in his gifting as he led. She wouldn't do this by pretending to be just like him, but by enjoying the fact that God had made her different.

We can fall into two extremes when we read Paul's instruction that *"a woman should learn in quietness and full submission."* Some people forbid women from contributing to public church meetings (even though 1 Corinthians 11:3–16 and 14:26 make it clear that Paul cannot be instructing any such thing), while other people try to explain away the instruction altogether (even though Paul reinforces it by adding that *"I do not permit a woman to teach or to assume authority over a man."*) Arguments that Paul uses the Greek word *authenteō* to mean *usurp authority* or *abuse authority* rather than *exercise authority* deliberately ignore the fact that the word is never used that way in any ancient Greek literature.[4] Both of these two extremes are foolish. They miss what Paul is saying about how the Gospel frees us to be who God always created us to be.

In 2:13–14, Paul teaches us that *Christian men always take a lead in the church.* God made Adam first and commissioned him to be the spiritual leader of his family. Sinful men copy Adam's passivity which allowed Eve to be deceived.[5] Where this sin isn't dealt with at conversion, Christian men remain passive and

[4] The Greek word *didaskō* simply means *to teach* and *authenteō* simply means *to exercise authority*. These are two key aspects of church eldership, which is why Paul assumes elders should be men in 3:1–7.

[5] 2:14 is not saying women are more sinful than men! It is pointing out that Adam knew that Eve was in trouble but was too passive to stop her.

the eldership tasks of teaching and governing the Church fall onto the shoulders of women. Where this sin is dealt with, men rise up to take an active lead, both in their own homes and in the Church.

In 2:14–15, Paul teaches us that *Christian women always play a vital role in the church*. Genesis tells us that Adam could not lead effectively without his helper, and that God made Eve the solution to human sin by affirming the unique role that women have to play in God's purposes for the world. Men produce the seed for human reproduction, yet God prophesied about the woman to the snake in Genesis 3:15 that *"I will put enmity between you and the woman, and between* ***your seed and hers****; he will crush your head and you will strike his heel."* From the very outset, God prophesied that Jesus the Saviour would be born to a virgin woman. Male eldership does not make women second-class Christians. It releases them to play the vital role that God has given them to play.

Let me put my cards on the table. I find this one of the hardest passages in the Bible to submit to. I grew up in a nation that was ruled by a queen and a female prime minister, so I instinctively want to stress the equality of Galatians 3:28 over the diversity of 1 Timothy 2. However, where Scripture offends us most is usually the place where it has most to teach us. Our culture is very confused about gender and surveys show that women's happiness has plummeted in comparison to that of men over the past forty years.[6] We need these verses more than most of us would like to admit. As a man, I need to be challenged about the dangers of passivity. As a church elder, I need to be challenged about the dangers of treating women like men and therefore devaluing the unique role that God has fitted them to play.

Paul promises us that if we let God turn us into mature

---

[6] See *The Paradox of Declining Female Happiness* by the US National Bureau of Economic Research (2009).

men and women – the people he always intended us to be – the world will sit up and take notice of the Gospel. When men are real men, taking the lead instead of living passive lives, and when women are real women, working hard with men to reach a common goal, the Church becomes the beautiful Bride of Jesus. She gives glory to the true and better Adam who was born as the seed of Eve.

Elders and Deacons (3:1–13)

If anyone does not know how to manage his own family, how can he take care of God's church?

(1 Timothy 3:5)

When Paul wrote to Timothy he did not divide his letter into chapters and verses. These were added many centuries later and they make an unhelpful division between 2:8–15 and 3:1–13. It is important that we read them as a single body of teaching because they deal with the same issue in the church at Ephesus. Are you confused and offended by Paul's teaching about real men and women in chapter 2? Then it will help you to see his teaching worked out in practice in chapter 3. Are you surprised that Paul seems to assume that all elders will be male in chapter 3? Then you need to understand why from his reasoning in chapter 2. Paul takes his general teaching on real men and women and he applies it to leadership roles within the church.

Paul begins by telling us that church leadership is vitally important. This was obvious at Ephesus where weak church elders had allowed false teachers to infect the whole church body. In case we think it is less important today, Paul uses his distinctive phrase to emphasize that *"Here is a trustworthy saying: whoever aspires to be an overseer desires a noble task."*[1] God expects every Christian man to want to be an *episkopos* – an *overseer* or *elder* or *church leader* – so they must never abdicate

[1] Paul is not saying everyone who aspires to church leadership has noble motives, just that it is a noble task.

this privilege to their wives as something unwanted.[2] Paul says that being a church elder is literally *"a good work."* It is therefore one of the best ways for men to respond to the charge which he gave us in Titus 3:14.

Paul assumes that we will understand from 2:8–15 why church elders must be male. He gives no further justification for this. He simply uses male pronouns throughout 3:2–7 and tells us that an elder must be *"faithful to his wife,"* rather than that an elder must be *"faithful to his or her spouse."* We saw in the chapter "What Church Leaders Do" that church elders *define* the church's beliefs and practice, that they *discipline* those who wander from it and that they *direct* the church forward in Jesus' mission. Having told us in 2:12 that he only appoints men to *teach* and to *exercise authority,* Paul expects Timothy to grasp why he needs to look for new elders among the men who lead the best Christian households in the city.[3]

Having settled this, Paul assumes that we will understand from 2:8–15 why the wider church leadership must be both male and female. Having told us that churches must be overseen by male elders, Paul spends as many verses talking about the deacons who must help them. The word *deacon* means *servant* or *minister,* so these are people who manage key church ministries for the elders. In Acts 6:1–7 a group of deacons are appointed to manage a ministry which helps poor widows in the church at Jerusalem.[4] Paul does not devalue this role in comparison with that of eldership. He tells us in 3:8–10 that deacons must be people of great character, such as Stephen

---

[2] They cannot all be elders in the same church, but Genesis 1:28 commands us to *"Fill the earth and subdue it."* Paul expects men who aren't elders to be willing to take a lead in planting new churches elsewhere.

[3] First-century women stayed in their father's household until they married. Widows sometimes led their own households (5:14), but Paul still assumes that only male household leaders will be chosen as elders.

[4] The word *diakonos*, or *deacon*, is not actually used in Acts 6:1–7 but the sister words *diakonia* and *diakoneō* are. The three types of church leader mentioned in the New Testament are *apostles*, *elders* and *deacons*.

and Philip in Jerusalem, and he emphasizes in 3:11 that many of them will be women of great character, such as Phoebe who served as a deacon in the church at Cenchrea (Romans 16:1–2).[5] Male elders must take a lead in defining and directing the church's mission, but they are fools if they fail to mobilize the complementary gifting of men and women when they delegate their authority to others.

Paul's instructions in 3:1–13 are the outworking of his teaching in 2:8–15. He reasserts that church elders should be the best men in a church, active and available men whom God can empower to define doctrine and practice for the church as a whole. Once this is in place, Paul reasserts that men and women both have a vital role to play by complementing one another's gifting in order to accomplish the church's mission. Paul placed such a high value on the role of deacons that when he wrote to the Philippians he addressed his letter to both the elders and the deacons. He valued their contribution so highly that he says Phoebe *"has been the benefactor of many people, including me."* He prizes the contribution of women so highly that over a quarter of the people he greets as co-workers in Romans 16 are *"women who work hard in the Lord."* Our objections to Paul's teaching about male eldership are not a sign that we are enlightened and he is not. They are a sign that we devalue the vital role that deacons and faithful church members – both men and women – have to play. Eldership isn't everything.

I have not found it easy to apply these verses to the church I lead in London. Some people decide not to join the church when they discover that the team of elders is exclusively male. But whenever people are patient enough to discover the whole breadth of Paul's teaching in 2:8–3:13, they come to admire the fact that we submit to the commands of Scripture, even when they clash strongly with the sinful thinking of our city.

[5] Paul simply refers to *"the women"* in 3:11, but this cannot mean the wives of deacons since he says nothing about the wives of elders. He is telling Timothy to raise up many female deacons like Phoebe.

Men whose idea of leadership is to unlock a new level on a computer game are being transformed by Paul's promise that the Gospel will turn them into real men of God. Women are thriving as deacons and ministry leaders and speakers and worship leaders and small group leaders through the support and encouragement of a strong team of male elders. The Church is the Bride of Jesus and she always flourishes when he gets to decide who leads it and how they should release every single member towards fruitfulness. When everybody plays the role that God has assigned to him or her, the Gospel forcefully advances.

It's just as Deborah, one of the greatest female leaders of the Old Testament, promised when she submitted her gifting to Barak and helped him to save God's People in a mighty battle: *"When the princes in Israel take the lead, when the people willingly offer themselves – praise the Lord!"*[6]

[6] Judges 5:2. It is significant that God judged Barak for his male passivity in Judges 4:8–9.

The Devil's Trap (3:6–7)

He must also have a good reputation with outsiders, so that he will not fall into disgrace and into the devil's trap.

(1 Timothy 3:7)

The Devil does not mind when many Christians are given positions of leadership within the Church. In fact, he rather likes it. He knows that the wrong leaders will enable him to inflict greater damage on the Church in the long run. That's why Paul mentions the Devil twice in 3:6 and 3:7 as he talks about appointing elders and deacons, because a leader who falls brings down many others. Paul therefore warns us that the Devil is very cunning and that he tries to trap us by targeting our character, conceit and consistency.

The first trap of the Devil targets our *character*. Like the list in Titus 1:5–9, almost all of these qualifications for elders and deacons have to do with a person's character.[1] Fourteen of the fifteen qualifications for elders and all eleven of the qualifications for male and female deacons focus on their character, and only one of them focuses on their skill or know-how. As General Norman Schwarzkopf said after he led his troops to victory in the First Gulf War: *"Leadership is a potent combination of strategy and character. But if you must be without one, be without the strategy."*

In June 1812, Napoleon Bonaparte invaded Russia. The

---

[1] A new character attribute, which was not on the list in Titus 1:5–9, is that a deacon must not be *dialogos*, which means literally *double-tongued* or *saying two things* (3:8). Sincerity and honesty are vital in leadership.

Russian commander was outnumbered three-to-one, so he laid a trap for Napoleon by allowing him to advance very rapidly. Napoleon looked as though he was winning when he marched into Moscow after only eleven weeks of fighting, but he realized too late that his successes had all been an illusion. The Russian troops had burnt 80 per cent of the houses in Moscow and had taken all of the food out of the city. Napoleon was forced to retreat over hundreds of miles that had been torched by the Russian army so that his men were unable to forage for any food. Some historians estimate that only 40,000 of the 700,000 soldiers that Napoleon led into Russia were still with the army by the time it staggered back to France.

The Devil loves to do what the Russian commander did to Napoleon. He loves to see Christians who lack character entrusted with leadership, because such false advances always benefit him in the end. He leaves the leaders unmolested in their position, often for years, knowing that their character flaws will soon be replicated throughout the church they lead. Then, when they have reached a stage where public failure will inflict more damage on the church than leaving them in place, he calls time on their character. When a church leader falls through lack of character, it is as tragic as Napoleon's retreat from Moscow.

Napoleon told his lieutenants, *"Never interrupt your enemy when he is making a mistake."*[2] Paul urges Timothy to interrupt his friends at Ephesus before it is too late. By appointing weak and passive men as elders, they have spelt disaster for the church and Paul warns Timothy not to repeat this mistake when he replaces them with better men. It is tempting to compromise on a leader's lifestyle, their love for unbelievers or their ability to handle money.[3] It is easy to rely on wishful thinking or on

---

[2] He said this in 1805, quoted by General Jomini in his *Political and Military Life of Napoleon* (1827).

[3] The ability to handle money faithfully is the only item mentioned in all four lists in 1 Timothy 3:1–7, 8–13, Titus 1:5–9 and 1 Peter 5:1–4. 1 Timothy 6 tells us that this was a big issue for the false teachers.

a prophetic hunch that they might change. That's why Paul tells Timothy to reflect soberly on a person's character. Promotion without character is simply being given a higher platform from which to fall.

The second trap of the Devil targets our *conceitedness*. Paul didn't warn Titus not to appoint recent converts as elders in Crete because almost all of the believers were recent converts. But this list is different. In the more established church at Ephesus, Paul tells Timothy to find some more mature believers. Since the Devil was an angel who fell from heaven because he allowed his position to go to his head,[4] a recent convert who is fast-tracked too quickly will face the same temptation. There is no substitute for walking with Jesus through periods of doubt and failure and defeat to remind us that we know nothing without Jesus and that all our hopes of fruitfulness lie entirely with him.

In 3:2, Paul tells us the only skill we are to look for in a potential elder. Every other item on the lists he gives to Titus and Timothy focus on character rather than skill, but here he says that an elder must be *"able to teach."* Paul clarifies in 5:17 that elders do not all need to be accomplished preachers, but they do all need to have a deep grasp of the Scriptures so that they can spot error before it damages the church. A recent convert is less likely to be able to spot this error, but having been a Christian longer is no guarantee that a person is mature. Each church needs to reflect on whether its situation is more like that of Crete or that of Ephesus. If people are coming through to eldership despite having been following Jesus for less time than you, it is probably more constructive to examine your own maturity than to criticize theirs.

The third trap of the Devil targets the *consistency* of our Christian walk. Paul echoes the list in Titus 1:5–9 by telling Timothy that *"the overseer is to be above reproach."* An elder

[4] Isaiah 14:12–17; Ezekiel 28:11–19; Luke 10:18; Revelation 9:1; 12:7–12.

must be *philoxenos*, or *loving towards unbelievers,*[5] and *"He must also have a good reputation with outsiders, so that he will not fall into disgrace and into the devil's trap."* It is easier to act like a Christian in the church than it is in the outside world, but both are crucially important. Only those who live consistently at church and at work and at play will escape the Devil's trap of hypocrisy and shameful exposure as a liar. If in doubt, Paul's advice to Timothy is that a leader should undergo a period of testing before they are formally appointed.[6]

If you find Paul's warning about these three traps of the Devil very alarming, be encouraged in 3:1 that *"whoever aspires to be an overseer desires a noble task."* It is worth it. But if you find his warning over-intense, be warned. The Devil is far smarter and far more ruthless than a Russian general. James 3:1 warns us that *"Not many of you should presume to be teachers, my brothers, because you know that we who teach will be judged more strictly."* If we are truly mature, we will lead truly mature churches. If we are immature but are promoted into leadership, our speedy advance may be the prelude to disaster.

Let's be challenged but not intimidated. In 3:13, Paul encourages us that, if we avoid these three traps of the Devil, we will be refined through the privilege of serving as leaders among God's People: *"Those who have served well gain an excellent standing and great assurance in their faith in Christ Jesus."*

---

[5] Although the Greek word *xenos* was sometimes used to refer to Christian strangers (1 Peter 4:9; 3 John 5), it was more commonly used to describe outsiders to the Christian faith.

[6] Paul is not saying that people need to be appointed as *elders-in-waiting* or as *deacons-in-waiting*. He is saying that they should be tested before they are even proposed as elders and deacons at all.

The Jewel and the Ring (3:14–4:7)

Beyond all question, the mystery from which true godliness springs is great.

(1 Timothy 3:16)

Paul had left Ephesus to visit Philippi, a city famous for its goldmines, but his attention was firmly focused on the jewel of the Gospel. He delights in its beauty in 3:16 when he tells us that *"Beyond all question, the mystery from which true godliness springs is great."*[1] Paul is so captivated by the beauty of the Gospel that he sings an early Christian song or recites an early Christian creed to celebrate it in the second half of 3:16.[2] He treats the Gospel like an exquisite jewel, and he is desperate for Timothy to guard it from the Devil and his conmen.

Paul's appeal is made all the more poignant by his statement in 3:14–15 that he is writing to Timothy in case he is delayed in coming back to Ephesus. We can tell that Paul was arrested at Troas, a major port on the way back from Philippi to Ephesus, since 2 Timothy 4:12 tells us he left in such a hurry that he left his books and travelling cloak behind. Paul would therefore not make it back to Ephesus at all. He would be taken in chains to Rome and executed. This makes it very moving

---

[1] The Greek word *mustērion* means a *mystery* or a *secret thing revealed by God*. Paul uses it 20 times in his letters, including here in 3:9 and 3:16.

[2] The second half of 3:16 is evidently poetry from the way in which its six pithy statements each contains a passive verb which summarizes an aspect of Jesus' ministry.

when we read his charge for Timothy to guard the jewel of the Gospel and to protect the ring in which it is set.

In 4:1–2, Paul urges Timothy not to let the Gospel be replaced with a *paste jewel*. The false teachers at Ephesus were trying to switch the truth of the Gospel for a man-made imitation. Timothy must not be so afraid of appearing closed-minded or intolerant that he falls for their jewel heist by allowing their teaching to continue. He must remember the Holy Spirit's warnings throughout Scripture and through prophecies that in the last days *"some will abandon the faith and follow deceiving spirits and things taught by demons."*[3] It makes a good movie when a gang of clever conmen leave substitute gems in place of real ones so that the jeweller does not even know he has been robbed, but it spells disaster when the Devil's gang of demons con unwitting Christians out of the jewel of the Gospel.

Paul uses very strong language here because he wants to grab our attention. False teachers are usually gifted communicators who appear plausible. Conmen always are. Paul explains that false teachers seem sincere because they are the first victims of their own deception. Because they have ignored Paul's warnings in 1:5 and 1:19 to keep a *"pure heart and a good conscience,"* their *"consciences have been seared as with a hot iron."* Demons have numbed their hearts so that they can no more sense the inner promptings of the Holy Spirit than a burns victim can feel sensations with his badly damaged hand. They do not look like the *"hypocritical liars"* that they are because they genuinely think that they are led by the Holy Spirit. They have no idea they have been deceived into preaching a paste jewel instead of the Gospel.

In 4:3–5, Paul urges Timothy not to let the Gospel be replaced with a *dirty jewel*. If the Devil's gang of demons cannot steal the Gospel altogether, they will try to cover it with enough

3 Some people say that the pastoral epistles are less focused on the work of the Holy Spirit than Paul's other letters. I cannot understand this. Paul says the Spirit who vindicated Jesus (3:16) still speaks for him (4:1).

grime to stop it shining in all its glory. Some of the false teachers at Ephesus affirmed the Gospel but then added certain rules. It seemed harmless and even virtuous when they persuaded church leaders and devout believers to take a vow of celibacy and to abstain from any food that was not kosher or had been sacrificed to pagan idols when it was slaughtered. But the Gospel is perfect, which means that anything we add to it makes it less perfect and more polluted. Paul reminds Timothy that the Gospel is not just *"truth"*; it is *"**the** truth"* which God has given us. We dare not add any modifications of our own to the Gospel. We enjoy marriage and food as good gifts from God which are to be received with thankfulness and praise.[4]

In 4:6–7, Paul urges Timothy not to let the Gospel be replaced with a *flawed jewel*. The Devil's conmen want Christians to be ignorant of the Scriptures so that they will not notice that something is missing from the Gospel. They want to fill people's heads with *"godless myths and old wives' tales"* instead of deep truths about Jesus. Paul urges Timothy to devote himself to reading Scripture as diligently as an athlete preparing for a big race, so that he can show the Ephesians what they are missing. Only if he is *"nourished on the truths of the faith"* will he be able to *"point these things out to the brothers and sisters."* If the Devil cannot switch the Gospel for a paste jewel or add to it so that it becomes a dirty jewel, he will try to detract from it so that it becomes a flawed jewel. We must not be deceived by any of these three strategies. We must resist the Devil's heist and guard the true Gospel which alone can save.

Understanding that Paul treats the Gospel as a precious jewel in 4:1–7 helps us to understand what he is saying in 3:15. The beauty of a jewel is only truly seen when it is set correctly on a ring. Paul tells us in 3:15 that the Church is the ring on which God wants to display his Gospel to the world. Having

[4] These verses and Acts 27:35 and 1 Corinthians 10:30 are why many Christians say grace before a meal. One of the tests for whether something is beneficial for us as Christians is to ask, *"Can I thank God for this?"*

fought off the paste jewel, the dirty jewel and the flawed jewel of the Devil, we need to display the beauty of the true jewel for all to see. Paul reminds us that the Church is the showcase for the Gospel, the perfect setting in which it can attract unbelievers to the beauty of Jesus. Paul tells Timothy that the Church is *"God's household"* and *"the pillar and foundation of the truth."* It is the thing that holds up the Gospel for all the world to see.[5]

Paul was so excited when he wrote about the Gospel as a jewel and about the Church as a ring that he started singing. He was so impassioned that he wrote these verses to warn Timothy and us, so do not be deceived. The Devil has a team of demonic conmen who want to steal away the message of God's salvation. They have already hoodwinked many in the Church, but you are still able to stop their heist from working. If you train yourself through Bible study to appreciate the Gospel jewel in all its glory, you will be able to teach those around you in the church to wear the jewel in all its glory. If you protect the jewel and the ring, as Paul urged Timothy, you will see the Devil's conmen thwarted in your generation.

[5] The word *hedraiōma* can mean either a *buttress* (an external pillar) or a *foundation*. Either way it holds up the Gospel for all to see. Galatians 2:9 tells us that key leaders in the Church can act as *stuloi*, or *pillars* too.

Ring-Bearers (4:7–16)

Be diligent in these matters; give yourself wholly to them, so that everyone may see your progress.

(1 Timothy 4:15)

In the first *Lord of the Rings* movie, the hobbit Frodo complains to the wizard Gandalf about the solemn responsibility of having been entrusted with a Ring of Power.

Frodo: *I wish the Ring had never come to me. I wish none of this had happened.*

Gandalf: *So do all who live to see such times. But that is not for them to decide. All we have to decide is what to do with the time that is given to us.*[1]

Timothy must have felt the same way when Paul wrote to him about the jewel of the Gospel and the ring of the Church while dropping hints in 3:15 and 4:13 that he might not be able to rejoin him in Ephesus quite as quickly as planned. Timothy was young and in danger of feeling crushed by the weight on his shoulders. That's why Paul gives him several simple ways in which he can take a lead as a ring-bearer of the Gospel.

Paul tells Timothy in 4:7–10 that he should start by *training himself in the Gospel*. The young men of Ephesus were obsessed with athletics, so Paul uses several sporting terms in these four verses. He uses the Greek verb and noun from which we get our word gymnasium when he tells him to *"train yourself to be godly"* as diligently as his friends trained

---

1 *The Lord of the Rings: The Fellowship of the Ring* (New Line Cinema, 2001).

themselves to play sport. Paul emphasizes how important this is by saying once again that *"This is a trustworthy saying that deserves full acceptance."* It is God's will and not just Paul's good idea. Growing in godliness means *exhausting ourselves through hard work* like a long distance runner and *struggling like a competitor in the games.*[2] If we want to defeat passivity and protect the Gospel, it's very simple. We need to get active in studying the Gospel straightaway.[3]

Church leaders need to get radical about their responsibility as ring-bearers for the Gospel.[4] The word *gymnazō* means literally to *exercise naked* because first-century athletes always stripped off to run. Paul is therefore telling Timothy that he needs to throw off everything that might hinder him from running well.[5] Growing in godliness is not a passive thing which happens to people who have good intentions. It is an active thing which happens to people who devote themselves to Bible study, worship and prayer. When I first started getting up in the dark every morning to study the Bible, I used to be encouraged by the regular sight of one of my friends jogging past my study window. Every athlete knows that public success only comes through private diligence and early mornings. Every Christian leader knows the same thing too.

Paul tells Timothy in 4:11–12 that this will enable him to *model the Gospel*. It does not matter that he is young – the best athletes often are. If he trains himself in godliness through time alone with God in studying the Scriptures and in prayer,

---

[2] Paul uses these same sporting terms *agōnizomai* and *kopiaō* to describe athletes running hard in 1 Corinthians 9:25 and Philippians 2:16.

[3] 2 Peter 2:14 states this same principle negatively, using the same Greek word *gymnazō* for false teachers exercising their hearts in greed and lust. Whatever we train our hearts in today affects the Church tomorrow.

[4] 4:10 ties in with 2:6 to remind us that Jesus is the Saviour of all but not everyone receives him. God has written a blank cheque with Jesus' blood, so we need to do all we can to encourage people to cash it.

[5] Hebrews 12:1. Growing in godliness is also presented as a very active thing in 2 Peter 3:14 and Jude 20–21.

he will be able to *"set an example for the believers in speech, in conduct, in love, in faith and in purity."* Christians need more than sermons to make them truly mature. They also need to see an example of true maturity in practice. It was going to be difficult for Timothy, a young man in his thirties, to unappoint some of the old but immature elders at Ephesus, but he could do it if he personally demonstrated a Christian maturity which went way beyond his years.[6]

Paul tells Timothy in 4:13–14 that this will make people take him seriously when he *teaches the Gospel*. He tells him to make Bible reading,[7] preaching and teaching core components of the church's public meetings.[8] Most of the slaves and some of the free citizens in Ephesus were illiterate, so reading the Bible out loud to one another was essential in the first century, but this instruction is still relevant for us today. For all their claims to be Bible-based, the services in many Protestant churches contain less Scripture reading than their Catholic counterparts, where liturgical readings and historic creeds still ensure that Paul's instruction is obeyed.[9] What is more, there is tremendous pressure for church leaders to make their sermons shorter, catchier and less committed to a systematic exegesis of the Bible. Paul reminds Timothy that he received a charismatic gift when the eldership team prayed and prophesied over him,[10] and that he must use it, because charismatic gifts grow

---

[6] Timothy started travelling with Paul in 50 AD, so he must have been about 35 by the time he received this letter. The Ephesian elders must have been old to despise a 35-year-old for his youth!

[7] Paul simply refers to *"the reading."* Since public reading of the Scriptures formed part of synagogue services, most translators assume that this is what Paul means. See 1 Thessalonians 5:27 and Colossians 4:16.

[8] The Greek word which Paul uses for preaching in 4:13 is *paraklēsis*, which means literally *encouragement*. Put together with 4:11, this reminds us that balanced preaching should command, instruct and encourage.

[9] They also tend to contain more public prayers of intercession, following Paul's instructions in 2:1–2.

[10] This Greek word *presbuterion* in 4:14 is also used for the body of Jewish elders in Luke 22:66 and Acts 22:5.

as we train ourselves to use them and they diminish through neglect.[11] Paul does not tell us what the gift is, but the context suggests that it is a gift for authoritative Bible teaching.

Paul tells Timothy in 4:15–16 that if he perseveres, he will also *train others in the Gospel.* Even in a church of tens of thousands of people, this is the only way to change a congregation. The more church leaders pray and study the Bible, the more the church learns to pray and study the Bible. The more church leaders love unbelievers and those who are poor, the more the church will eventually love them too. The word Paul uses at the start of 4:15 is a word that the Greeks used to describe great thinkers like Socrates pondering diligently over a problem and the New Testament uses to describe leaders devising plans of action with painstaking care.[12] Paul encourages Timothy that if he gives his whole attention to training himself in godliness, he will spur the whole church to do so. If you *"watch your life and doctrine closely,"* it will naturally benefit *"both yourself and your hearers."*

When the hobbit Frodo complains again, this time to the elf Galadriel, that *"I cannot do this alone,"* she reminds him that *"You are a Ring-bearer, Frodo. To bear a Ring of Power is to be alone."* When he confesses that *"I know what I must do, it's just that I'm afraid to do it",* she reminds him of the principle which Paul gives us in these verses: *"Even the smallest person can change the course of the future."* It may be challenging to train a church to wear the jewel of the Gospel in a way that makes the unbelieving world sit up and listen, but it is not impossible. Leaders simply have to be exemplary ring-bearers themselves.

---

[11] God never revokes a charismatic gift (Romans 11:29), but our gifting will either grow or stagnate depending on how much we train ourselves to use the gifts we have received (2 Timothy 1:6).

[12] This Greek word *meletaō* is used in Acts 4:25 and in some manuscripts of Mark 13:11. Growing in godliness is a work of God's grace but it requires all of our best mental effort too.

People Are Different (5:1–2)

Do not rebuke an older man harshly… Treat younger men as brothers, older women as mothers, and younger women as sisters.

(1 Timothy 5:1–2)

People are different. That may not sound very profound, but it is absolutely crucial for anyone who wants to bring a group of Christians to true maturity through the Gospel. As he charges Timothy to set an example, Paul gives him two verses of practical instruction which remind us that wise leaders lead different people in different ways.

The hardest group of people that Timothy needed to help was *the team of elders*. The Greek word *presbuteros* means both *elder* and *old man*, so it isn't clear whether Paul's instructions in 5:1 concern old men in general or elders in particular.[1] But since we know from chapter 3 that he left Timothy in Ephesus to deal with significant issues within the eldership team, his ambiguity is probably deliberate. Timothy had a major challenge on his hands.

Paul will give Timothy some specific instructions on how to help the elders in 5:17–22, but for now he simply reminds him that he must not deal with them harshly. Although Paul has not stipulated in his list of qualifications that elders need to be old men, it appears from 4:12 that most of the Ephesian elders were. He therefore warns Timothy not to be arrogant as

---

[1] This does not mean that church elders need to be old men, or Paul would have said so in 3:1–7. The Hebrew word for servant means literally a *boy*, yet a 60-year-old servant is called a "boy" in 2 Samuel 19:17.

he models for those elders how a true ring-bearer of the Gospel should behave. He must remember he is little more than a hobbit in their eyes.

The second group of people that Timothy needed to help was *older men in general*. As any young pastor or small group leader can tell you, it is very difficult to disciple a person who is old enough to be your father or grandfather. It requires real humility, both on the part of the older person and on the part of the young leader. We must not chide older people like children. We must respect them as fathers even when they are in the wrong. We must not give them any justifiable reason to take offence over our manner.

The third group of people that Timothy needed to help was *the young men* of the church. On one level this was easier, since he could talk to them as brothers, but on another level it was harder because a leader's example is always tested most severely by his peers. They are the people who see us when we are relaxing and who give our private indiscretions as much weight as our public instructions. When we see them sinning and fail to challenge them as loving brothers, they take our indulgence as a statement that their sins are not in fact as deadly as we tell them in our preaching. The seventeenth-century church leader Richard Baxter warned that

> *All that a minister does, is a kind of preaching; and if you live a covetous or a careless life, you preach these sins to your people by your practice. If you drink, or game, or trifle away your time in vain discourse, they take it as if you said to them, "Neighbours, this is the life you should all live; on this course you may venture without any danger." If you are ungodly, and teach not your families the fear of God, nor contradict the sins of the company you are in, nor turn the stream of their vain talking, nor deal with them plainly about their salvation, they*

will take it as if you preached to them that such things are needless, and that they may boldly do so as well as you. No, you do worse than all this, for you teach them to think evil of others that are better than yourselves... Is that man then likely to do much good, or fit to be a minister of Christ, that will speak for him an hour on the Sabbath, and, by his life, will preach against him all the week besides, yes, and give his public words the lie?[2]

The fourth group of people that Timothy needed to help was *the older women*. Paul will give him some detailed instructions about widows in 5:3–16, but first he gives him general instruction, which is similar to what he said about older men. One of the most difficult tasks that fell to me in my first weeks as a church elder was confronting an older lady in the church who had started sleeping with her lodger. She was old enough to be my mother (in fact, she was probably old enough to be my grandmother!), but I had to meet her with another woman in the church to ask her questions and to challenge her about her sexual sin. It wasn't easy, but even young men can bring older women to true maturity if they treat them with the respect they would show to their own mother. I respect my mother, so I was careful not to ask questions in a manner that shamed her or made it hard for her to confess her sin. But I also love my mother, so I did not hold back my challenge for fear of offending her sensibilities.

The fifth group of people that Timothy needed to help was *the younger women*. Again, this was easier on one level than dealing with older Christians and yet it was also much harder. Nothing in Acts or in Paul's letters suggests Timothy was married, so his interactions with younger women cannot have been easy. Some of them must have put him on a pedestal

---

[2] Richard Baxter writes this in his excellent book for church leaders, *The Reformed Pastor* (1655).

as Paul's closest friend and ally, and a few of them must even have dreamed of becoming his wife and joining him on his travels. Timothy needed to guard his heart towards the single girls at Ephesus. He needed to act with complete purity towards them, treating them like sisters until he was sure which one of them, if any, he would eventually marry. God knows what you think about the pretty girls in your church and it matters to him deeply. He hates it when leaders fantasize or flirt with the girls he has entrusted to their pastoral care.

Elders, older men, younger men, older women, younger women – people are all different. But Paul assures us that one thing remains the same with everyone: the way in which we conduct ourselves towards them is just as important as the words which we teach them. The great Scottish church leader Robert Murray M'Cheyne wrote a warning to church leaders while he was still in his twenties:

> *Study universal holiness of life! Your whole usefulness depends on this. Your sermon on Sabbath lasts but an hour or two, – your life preaches all the week. Remember, ministers are standard-bearers. Satan aims his fiery darts at them. If he can only make you a covetous minister, or a lover of pleasure, or a lover of praise, or a lover of good eating, then he has ruined your ministry forever... Dear brother, cast yourself at the feet of Christ, implore His Spirit to make you a holy man. "Take heed to thyself and to thy doctrine."*[3]

[3] *Memoir and Remains of the Rev. Robert Murray M'Cheyne* (1845).

Real Widows (5:3–16)

Give proper recognition to those widows who are really in need.

(1 Timothy 5:3)

Things had been so simple in the early days of the Church. When the first believers gathered together in Jerusalem, it was easy to be a church family. Christians with money looked out for Christians who were in need and they gave generously so that the elders could help the poor. It was easy to care for one another in those early days and everyone could see that *"there was no needy person among them."*[1]

Then something happened that made church life a lot more complicated. God started saving thousands of people. When most Christians pray for revival, they imagine it will make their church the same, only bigger, but these new believers broke the structures of the little church they joined. Some of the people who have prayed hardest for revival throughout Church history haven't liked it when it came. Sure enough, many of the Christians in Jerusalem were soon complaining that their needs were being overlooked, so seven deacons had to be appointed. The problems were even more complex in the megachurch at Ephesus. A church with tens of thousands of members required more administration than most first-century villages! Paul needed to help Timothy appoint scores of deacons and a series of systems. The first half of chapter 5 is all about good church

---

[1] Acts 2:44–45; 4:32–37. We never read of people in another local church sharing their possessions in such an informal way. When a church grows, its structures, systems and procedures have to grow with it.

administration, with particular reference to helping those church members who are in need.

First, Paul tells Timothy that *church leaders must be caring.* The apostles had not meant to ignore the needs of widows in the church at Jerusalem, but they had fallen into the trap which Job 29:16 warns us to avoid. Job tells us literally that *"I was a father to the poor and I sought out any case of need I did not know about."* The apostles ought to have had systems in place that enabled them to find out quickly who was in need, and Paul tells Timothy that he needs even better systems in place at Ephesus. Inadequate church administration isn't godly or spiritual. It is just plain inadequate.

Many of the biggest needs in the first-century church were financial. The Roman Empire was not a welfare state, so its poorest subjects either begged or became slaves or died. Paul tells us elsewhere in his letters that church leaders ought to help poor believers, just as the Old Testament commanded the rulers of Israel to help the poor of Israel.[2] In Ephesus, as in many urban situations where extended families live far away from one another, the biggest group who were in need were widows who had no relatives to care for them and for their children. Paul makes it clear that leaders have a responsibility to marshal the church's resources to help such people. He expects them to pull together a formal list of those who are in need so that they can help them. Caring isn't enough. Care must be turned into well-organized activity.

Paul's words are very challenging because every church has its poor and needy people. Jesus told us in Matthew 26:11 that *"The poor you will always have with you,"* so if we do not have them with us, there is something badly wrong. Poverty is far broader than a lack of money. Paul says in 5:3 that some people lack honour and he warns in 5:14 that some people's

---

[2] Deuteronomy 15:4 provides the background to Galatians 2:10 and 6:2.

life circumstances expose them to excessive temptation.[3] These verses about poor widows should challenge us about how we care for single people, divorcees, new parents, recent immigrants, the unemployed and those who are poor in many different ways.

Next, Paul tells Timothy that *church leaders must be wise.* Help could be given to people informally in the early days in Jerusalem because everybody knew one another, but in the large church at Ephesus this was impossible. Paul needed to warn the Thessalonians against freeloaders even though their church was much smaller.[4] Paul therefore tells Timothy to create a list of *"those who are really widows"* (5:3, 5, 16) and to do so formally (5:9).[5] If a person has no family to rely on (5:4) and if they live for prayer rather than pleasure (5:5–6), they should not be embarrassed about receiving aid from richer people in the congregation. But if they are able to swallow their pride by appealing to family members (5:7–8) or by doing what they can to change their circumstances (5:9), the formality of the list should make them think twice about abusing the church's financial provision. If anyone places an unnecessary drain on the church, they hinder its mission and are therefore worse than an unbeliever (5:8).[6] Paul expects individual church members to take this so seriously that they will volunteer to help their friends without their needing to go on the formal list at all (5:16).

Finally, Paul tells Timothy that *church leaders must take a long-term view.* It always sounds like Christian compassion to

---

[3] The Greek word *aphormē* in 5:14 is a military term that was used for the base from which an enemy launched its raids. Well-intentioned but unwise help towards those in need can actually destroy them.

[4] Paul is very firm with freeloaders in the church in 1 Thessalonians 4:9–12, 5:14 and 2 Thessalonians 3:6–15.

[5] The Greek verb *katalegō* in 5:9 means *to enrol on a list*, and it is the root of the English word *catalogue*. This list would help the church deacons to ensure that nobody deserving was ever overlooked (Acts 6:1).

[6] Mature believers don't ask "what can I get out of the church?", but "what can I contribute to the church?"

give money to someone in need, but Paul warns that we can give in a way that promotes an unhealthy dependency. If a church gives money to its poorest members with no conditions attached, it puts them in grave danger of having too much time on their hands and not enough to do (5:13). Paul therefore tells Timothy that able-bodied people should only go on the list of people the church cares for if they take a pledge to do some work in return (5:11–12).[7] We see an example of this in Acts 9:36–41, where Dorcas is part of a group of widows who receive funding from the church at Joppa in return for working to make clothes for the poor. The aim of helping those in need should always be to get them off the list again as soon as possible (5:14–15). Feeling like we are helping is not always the same thing as helping.

Paul does not tell Timothy to extend this support system to unbelievers. There were a dozen unbelievers in Ephesus for every believer, so Paul recognizes that the need would be simply overwhelming. Instead, he instructs Timothy to turn the church into a prophetic community which prefigures the justice and grace that God's People will enjoy in the age to come. This will attract the world to take Jesus seriously because the church displays the beauty of the Gospel.[8]

Paul tells us in Galatians 6:10 to *"do good to all people, especially to those who belong to the family of believers."* Having put these systems in place to ensure that they cared for one another, the Ephesian church would be freed up to meet the spiritual and social needs of the wider city. Good administration of their church would enable them to see the same fruit that the appointment of deacons brought in Jerusalem in Acts 6:7: *"So the word of God spread. The number of disciples in Jerusalem increased rapidly."*

---

[7] Even the very frail can give themselves to prayer (5:5), evangelism (5:10) and discipling others (Titus 2:3–4).

[8] The formal list and the fact that recipients were charged with doing good works safeguarded against false conversions in the hope of handouts. Nobody would receive help without the converted lifestyle of 5:9–10.

What Leaders Deserve (5:17–23)

The elders who direct the affairs of the church well are worthy of double honour, especially those whose work is preaching and teaching.

(1 Timothy 5:17)

The area of London where I live boasts the largest density of Koreans outside Korea. I've therefore made a lot of Korean friends at church and among the parents at my children's school. We live in the same city and lead similar lives but I've noticed something: my Korean friends don't view the world in the same way that I do.

On some of the differences, I'm pretty sure I'm right. My Korean friends seem to have an excessive fear of challenging people in authority. Some of them come from North Korea, so that's not surprising, but it does not do justice to the warnings throughout Scripture that we should not follow leaders blindly. On the other hand, there are some differences where I'm pretty sure my Korean friends are right and I am wrong. They have a respect for people in authority that is much more in line with Paul's teaching in Titus 3 and 1 Timothy 2 than my own culture. Mine is the culture which produced the songs "Anarchy in the UK" and "Revolution", so there is no danger of it slavishly kowtowing to leadership. Its biggest danger is that it does not give its leaders what they truly deserve.

Paul tells Timothy in 5:17 that *church leaders deserve honour*. The context of these seven verses is the fact that Timothy needs to stand down some of the weak elders at Ephesus who have failed to resist the false teachers. Paul warned Timothy in 5:1 that he needs to honour these men as fathers, and now he returns to this in greater detail.[1] He points out that some of the elders at Ephesus are actually leading well and that *"the elders who direct the affairs of the church well are worthy of double honour."* Some of them have resisted the false teachers, so Timothy must honour *"especially those whose work is preaching and teaching."* Even though Timothy needs to retire some of the Ephesian elders, Paul tells him that he needs to do it in a manner that honours them and reinforces eldership authority for the long term.

Paul tells Timothy in 5:18 that *church leaders deserve their pay*. That's another area where my neighbours from other cultures have a lot to teach me. When I see an African pastor driving a flashy car and enjoying a better standard of living than those he leads, I get indignant. I find it easy to quote 1 Thessalonians 2:9–10 back at him. But, however wrong it may be, it highlights the opposite extreme in British culture, where churches have a history of paying their leaders badly in order to keep them humble and reliant upon God. Paul tells Timothy outright that this is a sin. He takes a verse from the Law of Moses[2] and a statement by Jesus in Luke's newly published gospel to show that churches ought to honour their leaders by paying them well enough for them to enjoy a similar standard of living to the people that they lead.[3]

Paul tells Timothy in 5:19 that *church leaders deserve their people's trust*. It is easy to slander leaders because it places them

[1] 5:17–23 is separated from 5:1 by instructions on how to help widows. However, it belongs to a longer section of teaching on how to relate to different groups within the church (5:1–6:19).

[2] Paul also quotes from Deuteronomy 25:4 in 1 Corinthians 9:4–15, telling us that this verse was not included in the Law for the sake of oxen but for the sake of church leaders!

[3] Galatians 6:6. Luke only finished his gospel in around 60 AD yet Paul refers to Luke 10:7 as *graphē*, or God-inspired *Scripture*, just like Deuteronomy 25:4. Paul's letters are treated similarly in 2 Peter 3:15–16.

in a no-win situation. If they fight to clear their name, they seem proud and authoritarian, but if they do nothing, people begin to assume the slander must be true. Paul therefore takes Timothy back to another verse in the Law of Moses, Deuteronomy 19:15, where God commanded that accusations either be made formally, backed up by two or three witnesses, or not be made at all. As soon as Timothy began to stand down some of the elders, it would unleash a critics' free-for-all against the remaining elders. Timothy was to make it clear that, unless an accusation was lodged formally and with proof, it was nothing more than sinful gossip against leaders.

At the same time, Paul tells Timothy in 5:20–21 that *church leaders deserve public discipline*. If people minister publicly, they need to be disciplined publicly if an accusation is proven to be true. Paul is not talking in the realms of theory here. Timothy was about to stand down elders because they had failed to resist false teachers and had fallen into sin. Paul tells Timothy that the leadership changes at Ephesus must not take place behind closed doors. He must be transparent with the congregation about why some of their leaders were no longer part of the eldership team. This would not only prevent speculation, but it would also issue a strong warning to the church. When an elder is stood down for tampering with the jewel of the Gospel or for character failure, it preaches more loudly than any sermon. Paul issues Timothy with a very solemn charge – in the sight of the God the Father, God the Son and all the angels[4] – not to let his fear or his friendships stop him from acting as transparently as he should.[5]

Paul tells Timothy in 5:22 that *church leaders deserve very*

[4] It should strike you as very unusual that Paul refers to the *elect* angels. He is reminding Timothy that, if God dared to discipline Lucifer and his angels when they sinned, he must also discipline his friends.

[5] Paul warns Timothy not to succumb to *prokrima*, or *prejudice*, which makes us say *"I can't believe he would do that!"*, and to *proklisis*, or *partiality*, which makes us say *"But he's my relative!"* or *"We go back such a long way!"*

careful choosing. When he tells Timothy not to be hasty in the laying on of hands, he is not talking about praying for the sick or for the poor. The context means that he is talking about laying hands on new elders to replace those he has stood down. Since churches become like the people who lead them, these potential elders need to be tested every bit as well as Paul told Timothy to test potential deacons in 3:10. Timothy must not copy the sin of impatience that led to the wrong elders being appointed the first time around. Appointing an elder is easy, but unappointing an elder is very hard. Paul therefore urges Timothy to check the purity of his motives and his sense of having heard God before proceeding. The Ephesian church would become like its leaders, so he owed it to them to take his time.

Finally, Paul tells Timothy in 5:23 that *church leaders deserve to be protected.* Paul models this by telling Timothy to stop abusing his own body. He is making himself ill by not eating and drinking well.[6] Church leaders often make themselves ill by not taking holidays or days off or a time each day when they can exercise. They often neglect their families for the sake of a ringing phone or an urgent email. They can feel under so much pressure to be the life and soul of every aspect of church life that they starve themselves of time to give *"attention to prayer and the ministry of the word"* (Acts 6:4). Since the health of leaders is of vital importance to the health of the church as whole, we need to give them time to refresh their bodies, their minds and their spirits.

Paul tells Timothy that leaders deserve our honour and our care. We haven't always been very good at this in Western culture. That's why I am so grateful to my Korean and African friends for challenging me to give leaders what they deserve.

---

[6] Paul tells leaders not to overindulge in wine in 3:3 and Titus 1:7, but he is not advocating a harsh ascetic regime in which wine and fine foods are forbidden in an unhealthy way.

Payday (5:24–6:2)

The sins of some are obvious, reaching the place of judgment ahead of them; the sins of others trail behind them.

(1 Timothy 5:24)

My first job was working as a machine operator in a factory. The machine I operated produced a part for tractor engines and I earned a penny for every part I made. But I didn't call the foreman over to my machine and ask him for a penny every time I made one. I knew that he would tell me: *"Son, it isn't payday until Friday."*

I know that sounds obvious, but it's surprising how easy it is to forget. It is easy to look at the way that many wicked people prosper and to take offence at God for not judging their evil deeds. It is easy to look at our own hard work for the Gospel and to grow despondent that, so far at least, we don't seem to have reaped too much reward. Timothy must have felt this temptation acutely as he rolled up his sleeves to deal with the problems in the church at Ephesus, because Paul does not catch his breath between talking about standing down elders and fixing our eyes on the payday which is coming. He tells Timothy not to judge events too early. It isn't payday until Friday.

Some of the elders who needed to go looked as if they were living under God's blessing. They had tolerated false teaching in the church, but there was no sign that God was displeased with them for doing so. Paul has to remind Timothy in 5:24 that God does not judge every wicked deed in this lifetime: *"The sins of some are obvious, reaching the place of judgment ahead of them."* In other words, some people's sins are judged before they ever stand before Jesus on Judgment Day. On the other hand, *"the sins of others trail behind them."* In other words, they prosper in this life and only reap judgment at the very end. Good fortune has never been a good gauge of whether or not a person's life is pleasing to God, as the story of the Rich Man and Lazarus reminds us in Luke 16:19–31. The rich man looked like the luckiest man alive, but he was hurtling towards judgment. Lazarus looked unlucky, but he pleased God. Paul encourages Timothy not to judge the outcome of people's lives too early. Payday doesn't come until Friday.

Some of the elders who were to remain in place did not appear to be living under God's favour. We do not know what was happening in their lives but we can guess. Perhaps one had a child who was sick.[1] Perhaps another had a business that was going under or was finding his walk with God a daily struggle. Paul has to remind Timothy in 5:25 that God does not reward every godly action in this lifetime. Some good deeds are obvious, receiving an instant reward, but other good deeds will not be rewarded until the Final Day. This should encourage you if you are serving God faithfully but everything in your life seems to be going against you. Paul assures you that payday is coming and that none of your faithful deeds will go unrewarded in the end.

This forms a bridge into Paul's teaching in 6:1–2 about slaves and their masters. Paul spends the whole of chapters 5 and 6 teaching Timothy how to deal with different groups of people in the church. He started with the old and the young in 5:1–2, he moved on to widows in 5:3–16, he came back to elders in 5:17–25, he deals with slaves and their masters in 6:1–2 and he finishes with the wealthy in 6:3–19. If anybody in the church

[1] We were reminded in 5:23 that, although Paul performed extraordinary miracles in Ephesus in Acts 19, healing was not automatic for every Christian even in Paul's day.

needed to know that payday is Friday, it was these final groups of people.

We often forget how big an issue slavery was in the Early Church. So many slaves were converted that one of the earliest opponents of Christianity complained that *"they plainly show they only want to and only can win over the foolish, the low-born, the stupid, slaves, women and little children."*[2] The slave population of Ephesus was greater than the free population, so it is likely that half of the church members were slaves. If anybody had a right to complain that their faithful work was going unrewarded, it was Christian slaves. Some of them had remained faithful to the Gospel while their freeborn masters ran after the false teachers, and yet they were still enslaved. It simply wasn't fair. Paul sided with their plight by condemning the slave trade (1:10) and by calling himself a slave of God (Titus 1:1), but they needed something more.[3] Paul therefore tells Timothy that he needs to encourage the slaves in the church at Ephesus that their payday is coming too. God has not forgotten their faithful work, even if their masters have.

Paul says that slaves who are owned by pagan masters are in line for a great reward. God has enabled them to infiltrate pagan households across the city in order to hold out the beauty of the Gospel for everyone to see. If they honour their oppressive masters because they trust that they have a heavenly Master who will reward them justly in the end, then it will mean that *"God's name and our teaching may not be slandered."*[4] Paul says that slaves who are owned by Christian masters are also in line for a great reward, because they can make their Christian

[2] *Contra Celsum* (3.44). Although Origen wrote in c.248 AD, he is quoting from Celsus in c.170 AD.

[3] For a thorough examination of how Paul fatally undermines slavery as an institution throughout his letters, see the chapter "Slaves of Christ" in *Straight to the Heart of Galatians to Colossians*.

[4] Paul's promise is very similar to the one he makes to slaves in Crete in Titus 2:10. He encourages slaves to see their workplace as a platform for evangelism. The same is true for unhappy Christian employees today.

brothers prosper, which will in turn be a blessing to the church as a whole. Although Paul addresses slaves rather than their masters, his words contain a pointed message for their masters too. Paul reminds them that their payday is coming, and the thought that they will one day stand before their own heavenly Master should make them devoted to the welfare of their slaves.[5]

Timothy was nervous. Some of the elders he needed to stand down and some of the false teachers he needed to silence appeared to be living under the blessing of God. Some of the people he needed to commend and affirm looked as though God had forgotten them. He needed to listen to Paul's reminder that payday is coming and that we must not think that temporary prosperity or momentary setbacks are proof of God's approval or displeasure. He needed to remember that the Day of Judgment will be full of surprises.

So don't rely on midweek assessments of what God is doing in your life and in the lives of others. Payday is Friday. No sin will ever go unpunished and no faithful act of obedience will ever go unrewarded.

[5] Paul taught Christian masters that if they did not care for the slaves in their household, they were *"worse than an unbeliever"* (5:8). Philemon 16 even suggests that he urged some to set their slaves free.

False Profits (6:2–21)

For the love of money is a root of all kinds of evil. Some people, eager for money, have wandered from the faith and pierced themselves with many griefs.

(1 Timothy 6:10)

Paul's first letter to Timothy does not end like most of his other letters. There are no personal greetings to friends in Ephesus because Paul was there recently and hopes to be back again soon. There are none of the social interactions that mark the end of most of Paul's letters, because Paul is single-mindedly focused on the job in hand. If the letter appears to end abruptly, don't be surprised. Timothy had work to do and he didn't have any time to lose.

In 6:2–5, Paul issues Timothy with a final warning about the false teachers. He strengthens his arm by charging him not to be apologetic in his dealings with them or with any of the elders they have led astray. He tells him that he should *"teach and encourage"* people into line with the instructions in this letter,[1] but he also warns him that he needs to prepare for a fight. Those who oppose him *"are conceited and understand nothing."*[2] Their main problem is not that they have failed to grasp the truth with their heads, but that they have failed to submit to the truth in their hearts. Their minds have been corrupted

---

[1] Even though some English Bibles translate the Greek word *parakaleō* at the end of 6:2 as *to insist*, its meaning is actually a little bit softer. It means *to encourage* or *to urge*.

[2] The word which Paul uses for *conceited* in 6:4 is exactly the same word that he used to warn against new converts becoming elders in 3:6. The only other place in the Bible where this word is used is in 2 Timothy 3:4.

because their hearts were corrupted first. They have failed to grasp the truth because they deliberately chose to embrace silly, semantic debates over things that do not really matter. Worst of all, they have forgotten that payday is Friday and they *"think that godliness is a means to financial gain."* They are motivated by greed, like the wicked prophet Balaam in the Old Testament.[3] They are false prophets who can be seen as such by the way in which they run after false profits.[4]

In 6:6–10, Paul issues Timothy with a final warning about his own attitude towards money. He reminds him that he was born naked and that anything he acquires in this life is his on loan. There is no baggage allowance for our journey past death, so all we need is enough money to pay for our vital necessities between cradle and grave. The madness of the Ephesians chasing after false profits was that right under their noses there were true profits to be had. Paul deliberately uses the same Greek word to warn against ungodly *gain* in 6:5 and to promise great *gain* in 6:6, because there is eternal profit in store for those who serve God faithfully in this world. Those who run after false profits are in for a shock, however. They will end up with nothing.

Since one of the hallmarks of false teachers is their attitude towards money, Paul warns Timothy to beware of this trap.[5] Billy Graham was right to say that *"If a person gets his attitude toward money straight, it will help straighten out almost any other area of his life."*[6] The ability to handle money is the only

---

[3] Numbers 22:7; 2 Peter 2:15; Jude 11. Titus 1:11 says the false teachers in Crete were also after false profits.

[4] The most reliable Greek manuscripts of 6:5 end with *"think that godliness is a means to financial gain,"* but in some Greek manuscripts Paul continues by telling Timothy to *"Withdraw from such people."*

[5] The Greek word Paul uses for *trap* in 6:9 is the same one he used for the Devil's trap in 3:7. The word he uses for *eagerly desiring* money in 6:9 is the same one he used for eagerly desiring eldership in 3:1.

[6] Harold Myra and Marshall Shelley in *The Leadership Secrets of Billy Graham* (2005).

aspect of character that is mentioned in all four lists of leadership attributes in the New Testament.[7] It caused Paul and Timothy's friend Alexander to shipwreck his faith, and it is a constant danger to any other Christian too.[8] *"The love of money is a root of all kinds of evil."* False profits actually lead to *ruin* and *destruction* – often in this life and always in the age to come.[9]

In 6:11–16, Paul tells Timothy to fix his eyes on the true profits which will await him if he is faithful. If he trains himself like an athlete as Paul instructed him in 4:7–10, he will reap the reward of eternal life in all its fullness.[10] If he remains faithful to his confession of devotion to the Lord (this is probably a reference to his baptism or to a later commissioning service[11]), he is a true imitator of Jesus who confessed to Pontius Pilate at his trial that he is the Lord. If he continues in this good confession, he has truly turned his back on the Emperor Nero's crumbling kingdom and allied himself with the Kingdom of *"God, the blessed and only Ruler, the King of kings and Lord of lords, who alone is immortal and who lives in unapproachable light."* If he serves the right Master, he can rest fully assured that his Master will reward him when he finally appears.[12]

---

[7] 1 Timothy 3:1–7; 8–13; Titus 1:5–9; 1 Peter 5:1–4.

[8] Acts 19:23–27 explains 2 Timothy 4:14. Alexander was a leader within the church at Ephesus (Acts 19:33) who threw it all away for the sake of money (1 Timothy 1:19–20). The word Paul uses for *plunged* in 6:9 means literally *to sink underwater*, so it deliberately links back to *shipwrecking* in 1:19.

[9] Paul's first word *olethros* refers to earthly ruin in 1 Corinthians 5:5 and 1 Thessalonians 5:3, and to eternal ruin in 2 Thessalonians 1:9. His second word *apōleia* usually refers to eternal destruction.

[10] When Paul tells Timothy to *"fight the good fight of the faith"* in 6:12, he deliberately uses the same word that he used in 4:10 – *agōnizomai*, or *to struggle like a competitor in the games*. See also 2 Timothy 4:7.

[11] Paul's double reference to *"the good confession"* in 6:12 and 6:13, plus a scribal addition of Acts 8:37, suggests that early baptisms were not generally private affairs but involved a public confession of faith.

[12] Not only is 6:15 an amazing statement of Jesus' superiority to the Emperor Nero, but Paul also uses the Greek word *epiphaneia* when he refers in 6:14 to Jesus' *appearing*. We noted in the chapter "Nero" that this was the word used for an official visit by the Roman emperor. He also uses this word in Titus 2:13.

In 6:17–19, Paul tells Timothy to command the Christians at Ephesus to run after such true profits too. Paul is not implying that all rich Christians must have compromised their faith. On the contrary, he tells us that the Lord's name is *The One Who Richly Provides Everything for Our Enjoyment.* The God who loves widows and slaves also loves the very wealthy and he gives them a crucial part to play in his purposes. Paul is positive about the rich believers in Ephesus, but he tells Timothy to warn them firmly because they face temptations that their poorer brothers and sisters do not. Rich Christians can easily grow arrogant and confident in their bank balances rather than in their God. They can be tempted to hoard their wealth and to accumulate treasures in this life instead of investing it in good deeds which will grant them treasure in the life to come. They can become so contented with their lot in this life that they fail to *"take hold of the life that is truly life."*[13] Timothy needs to teach them to view their money as a gift from God with which to bless others. The only way for them to keep their money is for them to learn how to give it away.

In 6:20–21, Paul ends his letter abruptly. He has said all he needs to say, so it is time for Timothy to stop reading and to start praying and acting. Paul gives him one last charge to guard the Gospel from false teachers and then he prays that God's grace will be upon Timothy and the rest of the church at Ephesus.[14]

We have reached the end of lesson four in Paul's discipleship training school. We have learned what it means to be truly mature believers. This abrupt ending reminds us that reading this letter is only the beginning. We need to put it down and surrender to its challenge every day if we want to live truly mature Christian lives.

---

[13] Paul uses a similar phrase to describe *"real life"* in 6:19 as he used to refer to *"real widows"* in 5:3 and 5.

[14] The Greek word for *you* at the end of 6:21 is plural. The Ephesians would need as much grace as Timothy.

Lesson Five – 2 Timothy:

Truly Ready

Leaders Die (1:1–7)

I am reminded of your sincere faith, which first lived in your grandmother Lois and in your mother Eunice and, I am persuaded, now lives in you also.

(2 Timothy 1:5)

Paul never made it back to Ephesus as planned. He was arrested at the port of Troas, about 100 miles short of finishing his journey. By the time he wrote 2 Timothy, the last of his thirteen New Testament letters, he was back in jail in Rome. He knew that he was about to die.

Paul's death would have spelt disaster for the Church had he not poured his life into working with God to turn his converts into mature Christian leaders. Because he believed that God turns scrap metal into gold, his ministry had never been about creating large churches in his own generation. It had always been about working with God to create churches full of leaders for the next generation. Faced with death, this was now the moment of truth when it would be revealed whether Paul truly believed God turns scrap metal into gold. He passed the test, because this death-row letter expresses his faith that his converts are truly ready to step into his shoes.

Paul tells us in 1:1 that what really matters is *God's big picture*. Paul does not begin every letter by stating that he is an apostle, but he does so here in order to teach Timothy that even he has only been *"an apostle of Christ Jesus by the will of God."* He has shone brightly in his own generation, but it has all been about the will of God rather than the skill of Paul. He preached in Acts 13:36 that *"when David had served God's purpose in his own generation, he fell asleep; he was buried with his ancestors and his body decayed,"* and now he draws comfort from the fact that the same thing is about to be said of him. He has played a vital part in God's purposes for his own generation but now it is time for him to cash in *"the promise of life that is in Christ Jesus."*[1] He is confident that God has made Timothy and many others ready to carry on without him.

Paul tells us in 1:2–4 that what really matters in this life is *the people we disciple*. He calls Timothy *"my dear son"* and tells him that *"I long to see you, so that I may be filled with joy."*[2] We can sense their deep affection for each other from Timothy's tears for Paul and from Paul's constant prayers for Timothy.[3] We enter this world naked and leave it naked, but that does not mean we leave no trace of our ever having been here. Paul has spent his life working with God to turn scrap metal into gold, so in his final days he finds comfort in the leaders he is leaving behind. Paul's discipleship training school teaches us how to be transformed by the power of God, but that is only half the story. It also shows us how to work with God to transform the lives of many others. God wants us to see ourselves as one link in the great chain of Church history. He wants us to be able to say with Paul in the face of death: *"I thank God, whom I serve, as my ancestors did."*

Paul tells us in 1:5 that what really matters in this life is *the faith we impart to others*. Timothy was the son of a Greek man from Lystra who married a Jewish girl and was so hostile to her

[1] Though Nero can kill him, Paul is confident that Nero cannot take away his life.

[2] In the first two pastoral epistles, Paul greeted Titus and Timothy as *gnēsion teknon*, or as his *true son*. In this final letter, he greets Timothy even more affectionately as *agapēton teknon*, or as his *beloved son*. He tweaks his normal greeting to wish Timothy *mercy* along with grace and peace, just as he did in 1 Timothy 1:2.

[3] Paul continued praying for Timothy, even in a cold and lonely dungeon. If we pray as fervently as Paul, we shall not fail to see our converts grow as quickly as Timothy.

faith that he refused to allow their baby to be circumcised. The Lystrans tried to stone Paul to death, so Timothy's father was probably as hostile towards the Christian faith as his neighbours and friends. But Timothy's Jewish mother Eunice and his Jewish grandmother Lois were not intimidated by his father. They gave the baby a Greek name that means *Honouring God* and from a very young age they read him stories from the Jewish Scriptures in order to teach him to follow the God of Israel. When Paul arrived at Lystra in 48 AD, Timothy was speedily converted. The faith that had been imparted to him became his own. He defied his father's wishes, was circumcised and joined Paul for the next fifteen years as a travelling companion.[4]

Some Christian leaders struggle to hand things over to the next generation. Deep down, they believe that those they lead are not yet ready. They lack Paul's confidence with Timothy that the faith of previous generations *"now lives in you also."*[5] People who gather a following but who never empower new leaders show that they do not truly believe God turns scrap metal into gold.

Paul tells us in 1:6 that what really matters in life is *the gifts we impart to others.* He reminds Timothy that he received a charismatic gift from the Holy Spirit when Paul laid hands on him in prayer. If this is the same gift that Paul mentions in 1 Timothy 4:14, the Ephesian elders were involved in this prayer too. Paul does not tell us what the gift was, but he tells us that spiritual gifts are like muscles: they grow with exercise and they shrivel with neglect. Paul says that the main thing that stops Timothy from exercising his gifting is fear, so he urges him to *kindle up*

---

[4] 2 Timothy 3:15; Acts 14:8–20; 16:1–3. Note how Paul emphasizes in 1:3 and 1:5 that the Christian faith is the true continuation of the Old Testament Jewish faith, and not Messiah-less modern Judaism.

[5] Paul sees faith as something alive. Timothy does not simply have the faith of his ancestors. It *lives* in him.

the spark into a flame.[6] Paul's own preaching ministry is over. He will reach no new nations with the Gospel. But he is ready to die because he knows he has passed that gifting on to many others.

Paul tells us in 1:7 that what really matters in life is *the character we impart to others.* Paul is not saying that Timothy is a shrinking violet who struggles with fear and timidity. He would not have left a coward in Ephesus to confront false teachers and to stand down respected elders. He is actually expressing his confidence that the Holy Spirit lives in Timothy and that he is changing him from the inside out so that he can step into Paul's shoes. Christians grow old and die but the Holy Spirit doesn't, so Paul is confident that Timothy will grow more and more in courage and power and love and self-discipline as time goes on. Leaders who struggle to hand over to the next generation have either lost sight of the role that God's Spirit played in their own achievements or of how much that same Spirit is now at work in other people too.

Not Paul. He has spent his entire Christian life working with God to turn his converts into mature Christian leaders. He is grateful that he can thank God with a clear conscience that he has been faithful in turning scrap metal into gold. He has not simply trained Timothy to do certain things *with* him or *for* him. He has made him truly ready to do everything *without* him.

---

[6] The Greek word *anazōpureō* means either to *re-inflame* or *to bring fire to life*. God holds us accountable for how we use the gifts he gives us (1 Timothy 4:14). We do not have a spirit of fear but a Spirit of fire.

Under Guard (1:8–18)

Guard the good deposit that was entrusted to you – guard it with the help of the Holy Spirit who lives in us.

(2 Timothy 1:14)

Paul knew what it was like to be under guard. He had spent two years in prison in Caesarea and two more years under house arrest in Rome. His Roman jailers watched his every move so closely that he wrote in Philippians 1:13 that *"it has become clear throughout the whole palace guard and to everyone else that I am in chains for Christ."* Now Paul found himself under guard once again, probably this time in the Mamertine Prison in the north-west corner of the Roman forum. It was a gloomy dungeon which housed prisoners briefly before they were executed, and its guards had been brutalized by the things they had seen. Nevertheless, as Paul writes his final letter he draws comfort from the fact that he has three guards who do not work for the Emperor Nero.

Paul tells us in 1:8–12 that the first guard is God himself. Even though the Roman soldiers swooped on him so suddenly in Troas that he had no time to go to his lodgings to fetch his travelling cloak and books, they were not able to rob him of the things which really matter.[1] Paul tells us in 1:12 that *"I know whom I have believed, and am convinced that he is able to guard what I have entrusted to him until that day."* Paul uses the Greek word *parathēkē*, which was used for anything entrusted

---

[1] See 4:13. Nobody went on a long journey without their cloak unless the journey was unplanned.

to Roman guards, and Acts 12:19 tells us that if they lost such a charge, they were put to death. Paul trusts that God is more reliable than a Roman soldier. He never loses whatever we entrust to him.

Paul knows that God is guarding him because God took the initiative to save him, not because of anything Paul had done, but simply because of God's plan and grace towards him *"before the beginning of time."* God chose to give him the priceless calling of heralding the Gospel to the different ethnic groups of the Roman Empire,[2] a Gospel which proclaims that Jesus is the only true Saviour and that he made the only imperial visit which matters when he came down to earth from heaven.[3] He destroyed death and revealed God's promise that those who follow him will live forever, so even the executioners at the Mamertine Prison have no power to take Paul's life away. Nero's own adviser Seneca told him that *"The man who is not afraid to die will always be your master."* Nero's prisoner has become Nero's master because his life is guarded by God.

Paul tells us in 1:13–14 that the second guard is Timothy. He uses the same two Greek words that he used in 1:12 when he tells Timothy to *"Guard the good deposit that was entrusted to you."*[4] He has spent the past fifteen years training Timothy to preach the Gospel, so he urges him to guard what he has heard as *"the pattern of sound teaching."* Paul is more conscious than ever as he faces death that the task of Christian leaders is not just to preach the Gospel to their own generation, but to preserve it so that it can be preached to the generations after them. The Gospel must be *heralded* for people to be saved, it

2 Paul tells us literally in 1:9 that he received *a holy calling*. He was called to lead a holy life but this is not what he is saying. He is saying that the call itself was holy and beyond compare.

3 We have already seen that Nero tried to claim for himself the three Greek words Paul uses in 1:10–11: *Sōtēr* or *Saviour*, *epiphaneia* or *royal arrival*, and *kērux* or *herald*.

4 Paul also refers to the Gospel as the *parathēkē*, or *entrusted thing*, in 1 Timothy 6:20.

must be *taught* for people to be discipled and it must be used by *apostles* to lay good foundations for healthy churches. Timothy needs to guard this Gospel with his life.

Paul is confident that Timothy will succeed because he tells us in 1:14 that the third guard is the Holy Spirit. Some theologians argue that Paul places less emphasis in the pastoral epistles on our need to be filled with the Holy Spirit than in his earlier letters, but I think they must be reading a different Bible. Paul only expects Titus to be able to reach Crete with the Gospel because of his *"renewal by the Holy Spirit, whom God poured out on us generously through Jesus Christ our Saviour"* (Titus 3:5–6). He tells Timothy that the work of the Holy Spirit is a vital aspect of the Gospel (1 Timothy 3:16), that he has only been fruitful in ministry because Jesus is *"the one who has given me strength"* (1 Timothy 1:12), and that Timothy needs to rely on the Spirit's prophecies (1 Timothy 1:18; 4:1) and on the charismatic gift he received through the laying on of hands (1 Timothy 4:14; 2 Timothy 1:6–7). Paul continues this theme throughout the pastoral epistles when he tells us that the Gospel is under guard by the Holy Spirit.

We have an enemy who wants to snatch the Gospel from us. He bribed his way past Alexander the metalworker. He manipulated Hymanaeus through the laughter of his intelligent friends.[5] He intimidated Phygelus and Hermogenes, two leading members of the church at Ephesus who were in Rome, into keeping quiet about their faith in the Gospel for fear of being persecuted along with Paul.[6] The only person from the church at Ephesus who was in Rome and was prepared to be known to the prison guards as a friend of Paul was a man named Onesiphorus, whose name means *Bringing Usefulness*. He can

[5] Acts 17:32 sheds light on 2 Timothy 2:17–18. Acts 19:23–27 and 1 Timothy 6:10 shed light on 2 Timothy 4:14.

[6] Ephesus was the capital of the Roman province of Asia, so Paul is not saying everybody in the church there has abandoned him. We can tell from 1:16–18 that he is talking about the Asian Christians who are in Rome.

only have been in Rome for a brief visit because 4:19 tells us that he left his family behind in Ephesus, but he made the most of the short opportunity to be counted as a guardian of the Gospel. The Holy Spirit empowered him to live up to his name.

You may not live in a country where you are likely to be thrown into a dungeon for your faith like Paul, but you do live in a country where you face the daily temptation to tweak and modify the Gospel to make life easier and to silence people's laughter. Paul names Phygelus and Hermogenes with horror because they were the last people he would have expected to sell out the Gospel, so none of us should think that we are immune to this danger.[7] Paul pleads with us in 1:8, *"Do not be ashamed of the testimony about our Lord or of me his prisoner. Rather, join with me in suffering for the gospel, by the power of God."* He pleads with us to guard the Gospel and he gives us a marvellous promise. He tells us to *"guard it with the help of the Holy Spirit who lives in us."*

This is encouraging whenever we are laughed at or despised or threatened because we believe the Gospel. The Holy Spirit promises to help us guard the Gospel just as safely as God the Father is guarding our reward until the Final Day.[8] On that Day, when Alexander and Hymenaeus and Phygelus and Hermogenes shed tears of regret and sorrow, we can reap a sure reward. We can reap the reward that God is guarding for those who guard the Gospel with the help of the Holy Spirit.

---

7 *Hermogenes* means *Son of the Messenger God*, so he did not live up to his name. *Phygelus* means *Little Fugitive*, so he did live up to his.

8 Paul refers to *"that Day"* in both 1:12 and 1:18. Facing Nero's judgment, he drew comfort from the fact that a very different judge would make decisions on the final Judgment Day.

Rise of the Guardians (2:1–7)

The things you have heard me say in the presence of many witnesses entrust to reliable people who will also be qualified to teach others.

(2 Timothy 2:2)

Matt Busby was on track to become the most successful manager in Manchester United's history. He had coached his team to win the League in 1956 and 1957, and it was on track to win it again in 1958. Then on 6th February 1958, the team's plane crashed in Munich on the way back from playing in the European Cup. Busby suffered multiple injuries. Eight of his team died and two were so badly injured that they never played again. Manchester United had so few surviving players that they plummeted in the League and there were rumours that the club would have to fold.

But Matt Busby recovered and oversaw one of the most astonishing turnarounds in sporting history. He raised up so many world-class players that Manchester United didn't just survive the Munich Air Disaster. In the next ten years they won the League twice, as well as the FA Cup and even the European Cup.

Paul wrote his second letter to Timothy during the Christian equivalent of the Munich Air Disaster. James, the leader of the church in Jerusalem, had died. Peter had died. Countless numbers of their friends in Rome had died as well. Paul was about to join them in the roll of Christian martyrs, and he appeals to Timothy to learn from his lifestyle of raising up new leaders and to replicate it. He urges him to believe that God turns scrap metal into gold.

It wasn't going to be easy, so Paul reminds Timothy about the three guards he has just talked about in chapter one. Even after Paul died, God would still be Timothy's guardian because of *"the grace that is in Christ Jesus,"* and the Holy Spirit would still be there to help him guard the Gospel. Although many English translations tell us that Paul commands Timothy to *"be strong,"* what he actually says is *"be empowered."*[1] That's very important, because Paul isn't saying that God's grace replenishes our strength. He is telling us that it gives us divine strength through the Holy Spirit. It didn't matter how many Christians the Devil managed to kill off in Nero's persecution. God would empower his Church to rise above it because he is the God of resurrection.

With these two guards in place, Paul reminds Timothy that he needs to act as the third guard and to raise up a whole army of new guardians too. The Greek word he uses to urge him to *entrust* the Gospel to these new leaders is the root of the word he used to describe *"the good deposit that was entrusted"* to Timothy in 1:14.[2] Paul had trained up Timothy to be a guardian, and now Timothy must train up a third generation of guardians and teach them how to raise up a fourth generation of guardians too.[3]

Paul is up front with Timothy that this is going to require *clear focus*. One of the main reasons mature Christians do not raise up more leaders like themselves is that they become bogged down in other priorities. They get caught up in what Paul describes in 2:4 as "civilian affairs" – anything that is appealing but isn't our main calling. Even full-time church leaders who leave their jobs to devote themselves to raising up an army of new leaders get distracted by an avalanche of emails, wall-to-

[1] The Greek work is *endunamoō*. The root word *dunamis*, or *power*, is often used to describe the Holy Spirit.

[2] The verb *paratithēmi* is the root of the noun *parathēkē*.

[3] Paul tells Timothy to raise up *pistoi* people, which can mean either *faithful* or *faith-filled*, and which therefore probably means both. The size of the leaders we create affects the size of the leaders they are able to create in turn.

wall meetings and a host of unnecessary appointments. Paul tells Timothy to avoid such civilian affairs like a soldier eager to please his commanding officer.[4] New leaders only get created when existing leaders get focused, as John Stott observed:

> *We long to see the members of our congregation grow up into independent, adult, spiritual maturity in Christ, looking to Him for the supply of all their needs, since it is "in Christ" that God "has blessed us... with every spiritual blessing" (Ephesians 1:3)... There are in every church some weak and feeble souls who love to fuss round the minister and are constantly seeking interviews with him to consult him about their spiritual problems. This should be resisted, and that strenuously. Gently but firmly we should make it clear that God's purpose is that His children should look to Him as their Father, and not to men.*[5]

Paul is also up front with Timothy that this is going to require *humility*. Another major reason mature Christians do not raise up more leaders like themselves is that they like feeling important. They may not admit it even to themselves, but they fear new leaders will squeeze them out of the ministry they love. In a static organization, that would be understandable but inexcusable. In a body that has been tasked with taking the Gospel to the ends of the earth, it is simply criminal. When church leaders are afraid of releasing leaders more gifted than themselves, they make the Church like the opening of a Russian doll: each new generation of leaders is smaller than the one which went before. Paul reminds Timothy in 2:5 that athletes do not win a race unless they compete by the rules, and that

---

[4] The word *stratologeō* means literally *to enlist a person into the army*, because Roman commanding officers often recruited their own men. We want to please Jesus who recruited us into his army.

[5] John Stott in *The Preacher's Portrait* (1961).

Christians will not be rewarded for a lifetime of ministry if, deep down, it was more about maintaining their leadership position than it was about reaching the world.

Paul is up front with Timothy that this is going to require *hard work*. Training new leaders takes time and can often be disappointing. If one of Jesus' twelve disciples didn't make it, we should not be surprised if some of our potential leaders do not make it either. Thankfully, we can comfort ourselves in 2:3 that this gives us a share in Paul's sufferings, albeit a small one. The more we work hard, Paul assures us in 2:6, the more we will reap a bumper crop of leaders.[6]

This task is so important that Paul ends this section in 2:7 by issuing Timothy with a solemn charge which reminds him that this is the Lord's command.[7] It isn't just a call to raise up more leaders. The command in 2:2 is to raise up leaders and empower them to raise up even more leaders. Nor is it just a call to raise up more elders. The command in 2:2 uses a Greek word that applies to women as well as men.[8] It is a call to raise up an army of men and women who will guard the Gospel and who will raise up an even bigger army of men and women who will do the same. It will require the focus of a soldier, the sacrifice of an athlete and the hard work of a farmer, but it is worth it.

In the movie *Rise of the Guardians*, the evil villain Pitch hisses, *"That dream is over! It is time for fear to rule the world!"*[9] Paul writes to Timothy in the Church's darkest hour and tells him that it isn't true. The rise of the guardians has just begun.

---

6 Proverbs 20:4 reminds us that all church leaders want to raise up new leaders. The problem is that sluggards think they can harvest them without doing the hard work of farming for them.

7 The charge reminds us that the Holy Spirit teaches us when we meditate on Scripture, not in order to save us the trouble of meditating on Scripture! If Timothy reflects on Paul's words *then* God will give him insight.

8 He uses the Greek word *anthrōpoi*, or *people*, rather than the Greek word *andres*, or *men*.

9 *Rise of the Guardians* (Paramount Pictures, 2012).

One Word (2:8–13)

Remember Jesus Christ, raised from the dead, descended from David. This is my gospel.

(2 Timothy 2:8)

If somebody had stopped Paul while he was writing to Timothy and asked him to define the Gospel that must be guarded, he would have answered with one word. In 2:8, he tells us that his Gospel in a single word is *Jesus*.

The Gospel we are to guard is *news about who Jesus is*. Paul tells us in 2:8 that the Gospel is *"Jesus the Messiah... the Son of David."* The Greek word *Christ* is not a surname. It translates the Hebrew word *Messiah*. It reminds us that Jesus is the central figure of the Old Testament and the hope of Israel because he is the heir of King David. He is the Saviour promised throughout the Old Testament who would be fully God and fully human, and who would therefore be the only one who can reconcile people to God.

Paul wants us to grasp that the Gospel is not a spiritual formula: sin plus the cross plus repentance equals salvation. It is good news about a person, so if we want people to follow Jesus, we need to introduce them to him properly. Paul began his letter to the Romans by summarizing the Gospel as God's message *"regarding his Son, who as to his human nature was a descendant of David, and who through the Spirit of holiness was declared with power to be the Son of God by his resurrection from the dead"* (Romans 1:3–4). Jesus isn't just the bridge to life; he is the destination. He is not just the one who balances a spiritual equation; he is the answer to it as well. He is not just the one who died so that we can be forgiven; he is the one who lives and reigns as Lord and who empowers us to follow.

The Gospel we are to guard is *news about what Jesus has done*. In these few short verses, Paul talks about his death, his resurrection, his reign and his return to judge the world. The book of Acts models for us how to share the Gospel when Peter stands up in Acts 2 and, after dealing with the crowd's immediate questions, gives them a fifteen-verse summary of what Jesus has done. He describes Jesus' life, his miracles, his crucifixion, his resurrection, his ascension, his vindication as Messiah and Lord, and his return for those who have repented and been baptized. As a result of this biography 3,000 people decide to follow him. The apostles model the same message in Acts 3, 4, 5 and 10. In fact, Acts tells us over and over again that their message was always *"the good news about Jesus."*[1] Paul quoted from Luke's gospel in 1 Timothy 5:18, and he expects us to read it and to tell the story of Jesus' life to others.

The Devil's Gospel jewel heist is going rather well. There are lots of interesting evangelistic messages out there, but there isn't a lot of talk about Jesus. We tend to present the Gospel as a series of theological statements to which people need to nod the head, instead of as a series of facts about a person before whom people need to bow the knee. Even when they gain an audience, our messages do not fully convert our listeners. When they pray a prayer at the end of a message that tells them Jesus is the solution to their needs, they open their eyes wondering whether he will prove to be as helpful to them as they were promised. But when people pray a prayer at the end of a message that declares Jesus is the Lord of the universe who died and rose again to save them and to give them an opportunity to follow him, they open their eyes wondering what they must do to follow. They understand that Jesus is the answer to all their

[1] Examples are in Acts 4:2, 33, 5:42, 8:5, 35, 9:20, 22, 11:20, 17:3, 18, 18:5, 28, 24:24, 28:23 and 31.

needs but, more fundamentally, they understand that life is no longer about themselves. It's all about the Son of God and living for his glory.

The Gospel we are to guard is *the news that Jesus commands us to decide*. Paul was not in chains in Rome because he preached a spiritual formula but because he heralded a new King. He was not in the Mamertine Prison for preaching abstract theological statements but for commanding Nero's subjects to surrender to Jesus. Paul gives us the last of his "trustworthy sayings" in 2:11–13 in order to stress that these are the words of God and not of any man.[2] People need to choose to live or die, to rule with God or throw in the towel, to accept Jesus or be rejected by God, to have faith in God or be proved wrong.[3] These are stark choices because that's what the Gospel is. Paul did not ask the Athenians in Acts 17:30–31 whether they felt they needed Jesus in their life. He informed them that *"Now God commands all people everywhere to repent. For he has set a day when he will judge the world with justice by the man he has appointed. He has given proof of this to everyone by raising him from the dead."*

When we resist the Devil's Gospel jewel heist and preach who Jesus is, what Jesus has done and what Jesus commands us to do, it changes everything. Unbelievers want to listen to us when they grasp that we aren't just offering them opinions about how we can help them – we are telling them incontrovertible facts about the greatest man who ever lived and we are passing on his command. Believers stop complaining that they find Gospel sermons boring, because those sermons make them fall more and more in love with Jesus. They grow in their discipleship by reflecting afresh on who Jesus is and on what he has done. Their excitement that God has saved them *from* a life of sin grows into

---

[2] This is the fifth and final "trustworthy saying" after Titus 3:8 and 1 Timothy 1:15, 3:1 and 4:9.

[3] These things were particularly relevant to Paul. Nero was about to kill him for threatening his rule, but he drew comfort from the fact that he had already died with Christ and begun to reign with him.

even greater excitement about the new life with Jesus that God has saved them *for*.[4]

Ultimately, a Gospel that is all about Jesus creates believers who are truly ready to carry on Paul's mission. A false gospel fails to deal with the root of our sin by flattering our self-centred souls that God sacrificed his Son to improve our lives because he couldn't bear to see good folks like us die. The real Gospel tells us that our self-centred souls lie at the root of the problem and that God calls us to die to self and to start living for the glory of his Son. Since Paul's trustworthy saying in 2:11–13 is structured like a poem, many people believe that this is one of the worship songs which the first-century believers sang.[5] The real Gospel gets people singing about dying and enduring and suffering for Christ's cause. When was the last time you sang a song like that? It may have been the last time that you reflected on the real Gospel.

The Gospel is so simple that it can be summarized with one word: *Jesus*. Don't let the Devil trick you into thinking that it's anything else.

[4] They also get excited instead of offended by the doctrine of election. Like Paul in 2:10, it motivates them to share the Gospel much more actively, convinced the great King Jesus must have a greater Kingdom.

[5] We find other possible first-century worship songs in 1 Timothy 3:16 and Philippians 2:6–11.

Gangrene (2:14–21)

Their teaching will spread like gangrene.

(2 Timothy 2:17)

Sir Ranulph Fiennes surely has to qualify as the maddest of mad Englishmen. He tried to walk to the North Pole in 1990 but was forced to turn back when part of his frostbitten foot fell off in his boot. He gave up on a second attempt on the North Pole in 2000 after his hand became seriously frostbitten. After a heart attack, he bounced back by climbing the north face of the Eiger in 2007. Then at an age when the majority of his friends were retiring, he became the oldest man to climb Mount Everest – all missing part of his foot and part of his hand. It's hard to know whether to admire him or to offer him psychotherapy.

But Sir Ranulph Fiennes is no fool when it comes to the dangers of gangrene. He knows that when necrosis starts in one part of the body, it is only a matter of time before it spreads throughout the entire body. It will corrupt the neighbouring flesh before corrupting the bones too, so death is inevitable unless the gangrene is dealt with quickly and radically. Sir Ranulph Fiennes is famous for chopping off part of his own fingers and thumb using a fretsaw when his hand was frostbitten on the way to the North Pole. He may be mad, but he isn't mad enough to ignore gangrene in his body.

Sadly, however, Paul warns Timothy that many Christians are. Church leaders who spot false teaching and false practice in their congregations often think it virtuous to tolerate diverging views. Those who are radical with error in the church often face accusations that they are unloving and intolerant, which is the cardinal sin in our pluralist culture. Paul tells Timothy not to hesitate: No matter what it costs him, he must deal with the false teaching in the church at Ephesus as he would deal with gangrene.

Paul mentioned Hymenaeus in his first letter to Timothy because he put him out of the church at Ephesus while he was there. He did the same to Alexander the metalworker who is mentioned in 4:14.[1] Neither of them had repented by the time Paul wrote this second letter, and now Paul tells us in 2:17 that another man named Philetus is teaching error too. For the first time Paul tells us the substance of Hymenaeus' false teaching, and it sounds very similar to the heresy that he addressed in 1 Corinthians 15. Educated Greeks and Romans greeted the idea of a bodily resurrection with scorn and derision, and this was too much for Hymenaeus who was eager to earn the respect and admiration of the Ephesian chattering classes.[2] He traded in the Jewish hope of resurrection, which runs throughout the Old Testament, for a Greek hope instead. He claimed that Christians have already received the fullness of their resurrection, because it is just a clever philosophical metaphor for how new it feels to be a follower of Jesus. There was no need for Greeks and Romans to be offended. Following Jesus was just like following Plato, only a bit better.

Paul deals with this false teaching even more sternly in his second letter to Timothy than he did in his first. He tells him that this is not a case of open-minded Christian thinkers expanding the boundaries of debate. They *"have departed from the truth"* and *"they destroy the faith of some."*[3] Even though Timothy has stood down some of the elders and appointed godly leaders in

---

[1] We saw in 1 Timothy 1:20 that *"handed over to Satan"* means *"expelled them from the church."*

[2] See Acts 17:32, 26:8 and 23–24.

[3] The word Paul uses for *departing* from the truth is *astocheō*, a word from archery that means *missing the mark*. The only other places where this word is used in the New Testament are in 1 Timothy 1:6 and 6:21.

their place, the battle is still far from over. Unless he deals with the lingering damage that remains in the church, *"their teaching will spread like gangrene."*

Paul told us in Titus 3:10 how to deal with false teachers. We should warn them once, before giving them a brief period to repent. We should warn them a second time, making it clear that the entire body of elders thinks that they are in error. If they still refuse to listen, we should put them out of the church so that they may *"be taught not to blaspheme."*[4] If this seems harsh to you, it does not mean you are more compassionate than Paul. It means you are more naïve, because he had more first-hand experience of dealing with false teachers than most of us will have in a lifetime. It also means you think you know better than Jesus in Matthew 18:15–17. Gangrene spreads fast.

Paul now adds some further instructions about how to deal with false teachers. He says that the best way to ensure that false teaching does not spread in a church is to fill the church with right teaching! The opposite of *gangrenous* is *healthy*, and Paul uses that word nine times in the pastoral epistles, charging Timothy and Titus to plant good seed in their hearers' hearts and minds so that there will be no room for evil weeds to grow.[5]

Paul tells Timothy in 2:14 that this means reminding people of what they already know. We need to keep repeating old truths in fresh ways because people all too easily forget.[6] Paul also tells Timothy in 2:14 and 2:16 that he needs to warn people about the dangers of debating. Reasoned discussion is vital but theological quarrels and godless chatter ruin those who engage

---

[4] See 1 Timothy 1:20, Matthew 18:17 and 1 Corinthians 5. See also Ecclesiastes 8:11.

[5] He uses the word *hugiēs*, which means *healthy* or *sound* in 2 Timothy 1:13. He uses the word *hugiainō*, or *to make healthy* or *sound* in Titus 1:9, 13 and 2:1–2, in 1 Timothy 1:10 and 6:3, and in 2 Timothy 1:13 and 4:3.

[6] The apostles are absolutely unapologetic about repeating truth in Philippians 3:1 and 2 Peter 1:12–15.

in them as well as those who listen to them.[7] Paul tells Timothy in 2:15 that he needs to be seen to handle Scripture correctly so that the proof texts used by the false teachers may be exposed for the contortionism that they are.[8] Preachers who use Bible passages as mere springboards for their own blessed thoughts invite false teachers to hijack their untrained congregations. In a world of the internet and Christian TV, church leaders cannot close the ears of those they lead to all false teaching. They need to train them to spot it by teaching them how to handle the Bible correctly.

Paul tells Timothy in 2:19 that he needs to remember that the Gospel belongs to God and not to us. The Lord gets to decide who is and isn't part of his People, and he says that those who refuse to repent when their church leaders tell them that their teaching or their actions are wicked cannot truly have surrendered to the Gospel.[9] Paul tells Timothy in 2:20–21 that he needs to remember that a small but faithful church has a greater impact on the world than a big but compromised church. The worst thing that could happen to the church at Ephesus was not decline in numbers but decline in faithfulness towards the Gospel. Paul urges Timothy to be prepared to risk losing people if necessary to build a church that is *"holy, useful to the Master and prepared to do any good work."*

So don't be madder than Sir Ranulph Fiennes. Deal with deadly gangrene quickly in your own life and in your church before it spreads.

---

[7] The Greek word *katastrophē* in 2:14 is the root of our English word catastrophe. It is used in many manuscripts of 2 Peter 2:6 to describe the catastrophe that fell on Sodom and Gomorrah.

[8] The Greek verb *orthotomeō* in 2:15 means literally *to cut straight*. Paul tells Timothy to work hard on carving Bible texts correctly. Preparing sermons requires perspiration as well as inspiration.

[9] The first of Paul's two quotations in 2:19 comes from Numbers 16:5, and the second may be a loose reference to Numbers 16:26. Paul likens the trouble at Ephesus to Korah's rebellion. See also Jude 11.

Rear Attack (2:22–26)

Opponents must be gently instructed… that they will come to their senses and escape from the trap of the devil, who has taken them captive to do his will.

(2 Timothy 2:25–26)

Judged on results, General George S. Patton was the most successful military commander of all time. In the final nine months of World War Two, he led the American Third Army further and faster than any other army in history. They liberated 12,000 European cities, towns or villages, and they did so with surprisingly few casualties. They took 1.5 million German lives in return for 160,000 of their own. After the war General Patton revealed the secret behind his astonishing victories. He had learned to distract the enemy and then to hit him with a surprise attack upon his rear.

"The enemy's rear is the happy hunting ground for armour. Use every means to get it there", he explained. *"Battles are won by fire and movement. The purpose of movement is to get the fire in a more advantageous place to play on the enemy. This is from the rear."*[1] Having warned Timothy to guard against full-frontal attack on the Church from false teachers, Paul now teaches him how to guard against the Devil's surprise attack on his rear.

Paul warns Timothy in 2:22 that those who deal with false teaching and false practice in the Church face a very subtle danger. The Devil loves to sneak up behind them while they are

---

[1] All of the Patton quotes in this chapter are taken either from General George S. Patton's "Letter of Instruction" to his troops on 3rd April 1944 or from his memoir *War As I Knew It* (1947).

dealing with the sins of others and to plant sins in their own hearts even as they do so. Paul warns Timothy that, as he deals with indulgent elders, he must beware of his own *"evil desires of youth."* He tells him to run away from such sins, just as he told him to do so in 1 Timothy 6:11, but this time he spells out why. Unless Timothy is careful in the way he deals with false teachers, he will become self-righteous instead of righteous, frustrated instead of faith-filled, resentful instead of loving, and angry instead of peaceful. If you have ever had to point out somebody else's sin, you will know why Paul has to say this. As we deal with the Devil's attack on the church, it is very easy to get distracted from his rear attack on our own hearts.[2]

That's why Paul tells Timothy to launch a rear attack of his own. Having told him to run away from temptation, he reminds him that he has potent weapons in his armoury. If he keeps his heart pure, he can call on the name of the Lord and launch the Gospel he has protected onto the unsaved world.[3] Patton instructed his troops before D-Day that *"When soldiers are caught in a barrage, either from mortars, rockets or artillery, the surest way to get out of it is to go forward fast, because it is almost the invariable practice of the enemy to increase rather than decrease his range."* Paul tells Timothy that the best way to defend the Gospel in the church is to send the church out to preach the Gospel to the world.

Paul warns Timothy in 2:23 that those who deal with false teaching are always in danger of getting distracted. He could easily get sidetracked into *"foolish and stupid arguments,"*[4] thinking he is defending the Gospel when he is simply giving

2 This may be why Paul warns us in 1 Corinthians 5:4 to do so when *"the power of our Lord Jesus is present."*

3 Paul hints in 2:22 that how much we submit to Jesus' authority affects how strongly we can wield his authority in our prayers. See 1 Timothy 2:8, James 5:16, 1 Peter 3:7 and Proverbs 28:9.

4 The Greek word for *stupid* arguments in 2:23 is *apaideutos*, which means *uninstructed* or *undiscipled*. Paul reminds us that the greatest safeguard against false teaching is to disciple people well in the truth.

unhelpful airtime to theological quarrels.[5] Patton told his men that *"Our mortars and our artillery are superb weapons when they are firing. When silent they are junk – see that they keep firing!"* Too many Christians spend all of their best energies fighting perceived errors inside the Church, when we have been called to fill the whole earth with the sound of the Gospel. *"Wars are not won by defensive tactics",* Patton reminds us. There comes a time when Christians simply have to say to false teachers the words of Nehemiah 6:3: *"I am carrying on a great project and cannot go down. Why should the work stop while I leave it and go down to you?"*

Paul warns Timothy in 2:24 that he must not be tricked into viewing the false teachers as his enemies. He warns Timothy that, in dealing with troublemakers in the church, it is very easy to become so belligerent, unkind and resentful that we lose the ability to teach them. Perhaps it is significant that the name Philetus means *Beloved* and that the name Hymenaeus means *Ready for the Wedding*. We must not forget that God loves troublemakers and sent his Son to die for them. Jesus still wants them to become part of the Church, his holy Bride.

Paul therefore keeps encouraging Timothy in 2:25–26 to launch a rear attack of his own upon the Devil. He must gently instruct his opponents in the hope that God will grant them repentance by bringing them to their senses. He tells Timothy that they are like rats caught in a trap because they succumbed to the temptation to nibble on the Devil's bait of financial greed or intellectual pride. He needs to treat them as the victims of deceptive demons instead of as his enemies. He needs to help them to *"escape from the trap of the devil, who has taken them captive to do his will."*[6]

When most people think of General Patton, they think of

---

[5] Paul tells us literally that they *give birth to* quarrels, whereas our calling is to help people get born again.

[6] Paul uses the same Greek word for *trap* in 2:26 as he used in 1 Timothy 3:7 and 6:9.

destruction. He rained down more firepower on his opponents than any commander before him in the whole of history. But he was also the greatest bridge-builder in history, crossing rivers and reaching places his advisers told him were unreachable. Third Army engineers built over 2,500 bridges, which together stretched over eight and a half miles, and they reconstructed over 2,000 miles of railway track and well over 2,000 miles of road. He recalls in his memoirs that *"All the historical studies we had ever read on the crossing asserted that, between Bingen and Coblentz, the Rhine was impassable. Here again we took advantage of a theory of our own, that the impossible place is usually the least well defended."*

We do not know from Church history whether Timothy was able to win back to the Lord the false teachers at Ephesus, but we do know from the book of Acts that the Holy Spirit loves to work in the hearts of the Church's biggest opponents for the sake of God's glory. Paul himself had been a persecutor and so had Sosthenes, the greatest enemy of the church at Corinth, who later co-authored a letter to the church in that city with Paul.[7] In dealing with false teachers, we should always have the words of General Patton ringing in our ears: *"Fire from the rear is more deadly and three times more effective than fire from the front."* Let's beware of the Devil's subtle plans to tempt us to sin even as we deal with sin in others, and let's be ready to launch a rear attack of our own. If we do so, we won't just save the Church. We will also save some very unlikely individuals.

---

[7] Compare Acts 18:12–17 with 1 Corinthians 1:1. Never write off anyone.

Jannes and Jambres (3:1–9)

Just as Jannes and Jambres opposed Moses, so also these teachers oppose the truth.

(2 Timothy 3:8)

Timothy must have felt a bit like Moses when he stood before the burning bush. Replacing some of the elders at Ephesus had been difficult. Putting the false teachers out of the Church had been difficult too. But now Paul was giving him a far larger task. He was telling him that it was not enough to put the false teachers out into the world. The Church's job is to go after them into the world and to save thousands of unbelievers from their clutches. We can tell that Timothy was intimidated by this task, because Paul talks to him about Jannes and Jambres.

Moses had protested at the burning bush that preaching about Israel's God would be too difficult in Pharaoh's palace. Pharaoh had many powerful magicians who would not allow the Egyptians to respond to the Gospel.[1] Jewish tradition named the two leading magicians as Jannes and Jambres, so Paul mentions them in order to help Timothy to see that nothing can stand in the way of the Gospel. Jannes and Jambres could not stop Moses from saving thousands of Egyptians. Exodus 12:38 tells us that many of them chose to suffer in the desert with the People of God rather than continue to live as part of pagan Egypt.

Paul tells Timothy in 3:1–5 that Christians need to get

---

[1] I am not being anachronistic by referring to the Gospel centuries before the birth of Jesus. Galatians 3:8 tells us that God announced the Gospel in advance to people through pictures such as the Passover Lamb.

used to advancing the Gospel under a barrage of hostile fire. He chooses Jannes and Jambres as examples because he wants to make it ambiguous where the problem lies. The problem includes false teachers inside the Church, which is why Paul tells Timothy to *"have nothing to do with such people."* But it also includes the thought leaders of the non-Christian world, because Jannes and Jambres were leading Egyptians and not leading Hebrews. These verses describe the values of the non-Christian world throughout AD history, seeping into the Church from outside.[2] Paul tells us not to let it stop us from advancing under hostile fire. There will never be an easier generation in which to preach the Gospel.

Paul tells Timothy that people will be characterized throughout AD history by *their intense selfishness.* They will love themselves instead of God, and they will chase money and pleasure as the currency of their self-worship. They will be characterized by *their arrogance,* thinking they know better than their parents and drowning out the wisdom of the old with their own proud and abusive boasting.[3] They will be characterized by *their sense of entitlement,* ungrateful for the good and holy things that God has entrusted to them and using them as if they were the real owners. They will be characterized by *their self-assertiveness,* attacking one another physically and verbally, bearing grudges, and turning so recklessly on their friends and family that in the end they destroy themselves.[4] The portrait Paul paints is not a pretty picture.

Yet, far from being intimidated by the thought leaders of a world that has turned its back on God, Paul sees that they are

[2] Acts 2:17 and Hebrews 1:2 make it clear that the *"the last days"* is shorthand for the period between Jesus' ascension to heaven and Jesus' return. Paul is describing Timothy's generation as well as ours.

[3] We have grown so used to children talking back to their parents that we tend not to treat it as the massive sin it is. Paul tells us that it is one of the major foundational sins of our generation.

[4] The word which Paul uses for *without love* in 3:3 is *astorgos*, which means literally *without love for family*.

no better than Jannes and Jambres. They may look impressive – these men turned staffs into snakes and turned water into blood – but we have nothing to fear from people *"having a form of godliness but denying its power."* The boasting of so-called Christian false teachers is exposed as a lie the moment we demonstrate God's true power. Clever atheists and religious leaders can be silenced just as easily as Pharaoh's magicians.

All we need to do is perform miracles like Moses. That may sound difficult, but it isn't. It's impossible, which is entirely different. It means that this is something only God can do through us, which is precisely what he has promised to do. Moses did not turn his staff into a snake because he was cleverer than us, but because God empowered him to expose the lies which dominated Egyptian culture. Moses did not free the Hebrews by performing ten plagues because he knew secrets that are hidden from us, but because he believed the Lord enough to obey him. Paul talks in 3:5 about the importance of God's power because he has not lost sight of the basic strategy which Jesus gave to his followers when he sent them out into the world: *"As you go, proclaim this message: 'The kingdom of heaven has come near.' Heal those who are ill, raise the dead, cleanse those who have leprosy, drive out demons... I am sending you out like sheep among wolves."*[5]

Ramsay MacMullen, professor of history at Yale University, concludes that this is precisely how the Gospel advanced in the early generations of Church history:

> *Driving all competition from the field head-on was crucial. The world, after all, held many dozens and hundreds of gods. Choice was open to everybody. It could thus be only a most exceptional force that would actually displace alternatives and compel allegiance; it could*

[5] Matthew 10:7–8, 16. If this was necessary in first-century Israel, it is certainly necessary in pagan lands.

be only the most probative demonstrations that would work. We should therefore assign as much weight to this, the chief instrument of conversion, as the best, earliest reporters do.[6]

The Gospel is not advancing quite so quickly in our generation. Many churches look no different from mosques and synagogues and yoga classes. They have a form of godliness, but they deny its power. They are ever teaching and learning about the Bible, but they never come to a full knowledge of the truth. They never grasp that God wants us to do more than learn about him; he wants us to experience him daily. They never grasp that God wants us to demonstrate that his Kingdom has come through mighty miracles, not just to proclaim it through solid sermons. They long to see Paul's success with the Gospel, but they forget that he explains in Romans 15:19 that he only achieved it *"by the power of signs and wonders, through the power of the Spirit of God."*

Peter Brown, professor of history at Princeton University, tells us that this has got to change: *"However many sound social and cultural reasons the historian may find for the expansion of the Christian church, the fact remains that in all Christian literature from the New Testament onwards, the Christian missionaries advanced principally by revealing the bankruptcy of men's invisible enemies, the demons, through exorcisms and miracles of healing."*[7]

So let's believe God for miracles in our generation, attempting to demonstrate as well as preach about his power. Let's expect him to unmask this world's thought leaders for their manipulation (3:6), their ignorance (3:7),[8] their corruption

[6] Ramsay MacMullen in *Christianizing the Roman Empire*, AD *100–400* (1984).

[7] Peter Brown in *The World of Late Antiquity* (1971). Compare this with Exodus 8:18–19.

[8] The subject of 3:7 is the women who are led astray by false teachers, but Paul also intends us to grasp that the false teachers are ignorant too. For all

(3:8) and their folly (3:9). Let's expect him to make them just like Jannes and Jambres: exposed as liars by the power of the true God.

their academic prowess, they have completely missed the truth.

Sword and Shield (3:10–17)

All Scripture is God-breathed and is useful for teaching, rebuking, correcting and training in righteousness.

(2 Timothy 3:16)

Peter Cartwright was just about to begin his sermon to a crowded church when he looked up and saw General Andrew Jackson walking in. The year was 1818, and nobody in America had a tougher reputation than the man who had defeated the British at the Battle of New Orleans three years earlier. They called him "Old Hickory" because he was tough and aggressive. He had killed men in duels for offending him. One of the church leaders whispered to him that he had better not be too offensive, but he began: *"What shall it profit a man if he gain the whole world and lose his own soul? Who is General Jackson? If he don't get his soul converted, God will damn him as quick as any of the slaves he has seen fit to buy for a guinea."*

The church leaders were horrified. Speaking out against the evils of slavery in Tennessee was taboo. Doing so by offending a great national hero who was tipped to become president was unforgiveable. They apologized to the general, but Old Hickory sought out Peter Cartwright to tell him: *"I highly approved of your independence; a minister of Jesus Christ ought to love everybody and fear no mortal man... If I had a few thousand such independent, fearless officers as you were, and a well-drilled army, I could take old England."*[1]

Paul knew that time was running out for him. He had to

[1] He recalls this incident in his *Autobiography of Peter Cartwright* (1856).

prepare Timothy to lead a new generation of Christian leaders forward with the Gospel. Having told him that he needs to use miracles as his artillery, he therefore tells him that he needs to follow up with a good old-fashioned sword and shield.

Paul tells Timothy in 3:10–13 that he is going to have to learn to use the shield of faith. That's the picture Paul used to describe faith when he wrote to the church a few years earlier in Ephesians 6:16. *"Everyone who wants to live a godly life in Christ Jesus will be persecuted,"* he warns Timothy. Everyone. Not just some people, but everyone. It might look very different in North Korea and North Dakota, but the difference is simply one of degree. Paul warns Timothy that as AD history progresses, *"evildoers and impostors will go from bad to worse, deceiving and being deceived."*[2] If we want to see the Gospel advance in our generation, we need to have the courage of Peter Cartwright. We need to be prepared for people to misunderstand us, laugh at us, hate us and try to harm us because they resent our message. We need to arm ourselves with the shield of faith.

Paul tells Timothy that he needs to take a lead in this courageous advance because he has had a ringside seat on Paul's eventful ministry. He knows Paul's teaching better than any man alive. He knows Paul's lifestyle and his driving ambition for Christ's glory.[3] He has seen Paul's faith and patience and love and endurance under a constant barrage of enemy fire. He knows how much persecution Paul willingly suffered in order to reach his region with the Gospel. In Timothy's hometown of Lystra, after a mob threw rocks at him and left him for dead, Timothy knows that *"he got up and went back into the city"* (Acts 14:20). Timothy has watched Paul go into battle every day

---

[2] The Greek word *goēs* means more than just an *impostor*. It means a *magician* like Jannes and Jambres.

[3] Paul warns us that we will not inspire new leaders simply by letting them see our teaching and our character. We also need to share with them our burning sense of vision if they are to catch fire too.

carrying the shield of faith. Now he is ready to take the shield from Paul's dying hands.

It is easier to admire a man like Peter Cartwright than it is to copy him. Most of us would love to baptize 12,000 converts, just as he did, but very few of us are willing to pay the price which he did as a horseback preacher.

> *He went through storms of wind, hail, snow, and rain; climbed hills and mountains, traversed valleys, plunged through swamps, swam swollen streams, lay out all night, wet, weary, and hungry, held his horse by the bridle all night, or tied him to a limb, slept with his saddle blanket for a bed, his saddle or saddle-bags for his pillow, and his old big coat or blanket, if he had any, for a covering.*

In addition to these physical hardships, he and his friends were *"not only opposed and denounced by the Catholics, but by all Protestant Churches; we were everywhere spoken against, caricatured, and misrepresented."*[4] Paul tells us that Christ's call means renouncing this world's comforts. If we want to see God's Kingdom come, we must have faith to suffer with the King.

In addition to the shield of faith, Paul tells Timothy in 3:14–17 that he is going to need a sword. Hebrews 4:12 tells us that *"The word of God is alive and active. Sharper than any double-edged sword, it penetrates even to dividing soul and spirit, joints and marrow; it judges the thoughts and attitudes of the heart."* Peter Cartwright was courageous enough to confront Andrew Jackson because he believed that the Bible is the Word of God and that it demands an urgent verdict. The battle with false teachers, past and present, has always been a battle over Scripture: can we trust that everything the Bible says is true? Paul tells Timothy that he is his perfect successor in this battle

4 Both of these quotations are from Peter Cartwright's autobiography.

because he was suckled on the Word of God along with his mother's milk from a very early age.[5] He knows the outcome of their Bible-believing lives. Nobody knows better than he does that the Scriptures *"are able to make you wise for salvation through faith in Christ Jesus."*

This battle still rages in our generation. The Bible is still under attack from those who hate the way it challenges their thinking and their sinful desires. But Paul is adamant. *"All Scripture is God-breathed and is useful for teaching, rebuking, correcting and training in righteousness, so that the servant of God may be thoroughly equipped for every good work."*[6] Paul told us in Titus 1:2 that the Lord is *The God Who Does Not Lie,* so every word he inspired the authors of the Bible to write is comprehensively true. Complete submission to the Bible is true submission to God, and selective submission to the Bible is disobedience. Paul tells Timothy that, if he preaches Scripture as the inspired Word of God, he will slice his way through the defences of unbelievers until they come to believe it too. But if he doubts Scripture, so will they.

Jim Packer writes that *"One cannot doubt the Bible without far-reaching loss, both of fullness of truth and of fullness of life. If therefore we have at heart spiritual renewal for society, for churches and for our own lives, we shall make much of the entire trustworthiness – that is, the inerrancy – of Holy Scripture as the inspired and liberating Word of God."*[7]

So pick up the sword of Scripture and the shield of faith. Having launched the artillery of miracles on the unbelieving

---

[5] If you are a parent, Paul encourages you to do the same thing. Parents who love their children should disciple them in the Bible and convince them that God inspired it.

[6] Paul sees faith that the Bible is *theopneustos*, or *God-breathed*, as the major battleground in the fight against false teaching. Since Scripture is breathed by God's Spirit, it is more than simply information. It lives inside us and has power to change us from the inside out (2 Timothy 1:5; John 1:1; 2 Peter 1:20–21).

[7] J. I. Packer in *Truth and Power: The Place of Scripture in the Christian Life* (1996).

world, follow up with the Word of God. Don't let subtle or overt persecution stop you. God's truth will always overcome the Enemy's lies.

The Main Thing (4:1–5)

I give you this charge: preach the word; be prepared in season and out of season; correct, rebuke and encourage.

(2 Timothy 4:1–2)

During the English Civil War, the future founder of the Quakers decided it was time for him to get right with God. George Fox wandered from town to town looking for a church leader who would help him to find peace and friendship with his Maker.

In the first town he visited, the minister was fascinated by his questions and confessed that he too had many more questions like them. Disappointed, he went to a second town where the minister told him that his spiritual anguish might be eased if he just smoked a little tobacco. Frustrated, he went to a third town but instead of helping him the minister flew into a rage because he had accidentally stepped on his flowerbed. In a fourth town, the minister suggested that bleeding himself with leeches might soothe his unsettled soul. George Fox lamented in his journal that *"they were all as nothing to me, for they could not reach my condition."*[1]

Shocking as George Fox's experience may have been, it was not unique. Christians throughout history have struggled to remain focused on their essential calling. Stephen Covey argues that *"The main thing is to keep the main thing the main thing"*[2], but Christians have never found this easy. We are far too easily

---

[1] George Fox recounts these encounters in his journal, which was published in 1694.

[2] Stephen Covey wrote this in his book *First Things First* (1994).

distracted by what Paul refers to in 2:4 as "civilian affairs" – by our work and our chores and our hobbies. We far too easily lose sight of what God has put us on the earth to do. Even full-time church leaders, who have been set apart to focus on what really matters, are just as easily distracted. Days are filled with emails, paperwork, meetings and projects – mostly good, yet none of them the main thing. That's why Paul charges Timothy very strongly as he starts the final chapter of his letter. He is ready to hand over his ministry to Timothy, but before he does so he makes a final plea for him to keep the main thing the main thing.

Paul tells Timothy *to preach the Word*. This is the main thing. Paul is not just talking about the Word of God in general, but the Gospel in particular.[3] Paul uses the Greek word *kērussō*, or *to herald*, because the main thing is proclaiming to the world that Jesus Christ has won the victory over sin and death and Satan.[4] Paul urged Timothy to guard the Gospel in chapter 1, to suffer for the Gospel in chapter 2 and to persevere in the Gospel in chapter 3. Now he urges Timothy, with a very solemn charge in the presence of God the Father and of Jesus the Messiah who is King and Judge, to preach the Gospel.[5]

Paul tells Timothy to preach the Gospel *even when it feels awkward*. He knows that he will often feel too tired, too scared, too distracted or too discouraged to proclaim that Jesus is Lord, so he insists that he *"be prepared in season and out of season."*[6] As George Fox lay dying, his final words were, *"I am clear! I am*

---

[3] A few examples of *the Word* being used to refer to the Gospel in particular can be found in Acts 4:29, 31; 6:7; 8:4, 14, 25; 11:1; 12:24; 13:5, 7, 46, 49; 14:25; 16:6, 32; 17:13; 19:10, 20; 20:32.

[4] *Kērussō* is the verb of the noun *kērux*, or *herald*. It was used to describe the announcement of good news, and especially good news about the birth of a king or about victory on the battlefield.

[5] This solemn charge goes alongside two other similar charges in 1 Timothy 5:21 and 6:13–14.

[6] Paul uses the word *epiphaneia* in 4:1 and 4:8 to emphasize that Jesus will make the only royal visit that really matters. The Gospel is not just the promise of Jesus as Saviour. It is his proclamation as Lord and King.

clear!" He was convinced that he was innocent of any person's blood because he had never failed to proclaim that Jesus is Lord. Paul said something similar to the Ephesian elders in Acts 20:26–27. Before he dies, he wants to prepare his successors to be able to say the same.

Paul tells Timothy to preach the Gospel *even when people do not want to hear it.* He prophesies that there will be many periods throughout AD history when people will refuse to listen to Bible preaching in general and to Gospel preaching in particular. Sometimes they will resist and persecute Christian preachers, but at other times they will flatter them into delivering messages that are about something other than Jesus crucified, raised to life, glorified and coming back again to judge the world. Paul warns Timothy that Christians will be tempted to talk about *"myths"* instead of biblical truth.[7] They will be tempted to say what people want to hear instead of confronting them with their sin and with the holy God who wants to lead them to salvation.[8]

Don Carson writes: *"I fear that the cross, without ever being disowned, is constantly in danger of being dismissed from the central place it must enjoy, by relatively peripheral insights that take on far too much weight. Whenever the periphery is in danger of displacing the centre, we are not far removed from idolatry."*[9]

Paul tells Timothy to preach the Gospel *even when it leads to persecution.* He tells him literally to *"be sober"* in all situations, because Christians need to keep a calm head when they are threatened with reprisals unless they water down

[7] The Greek word *mythos* refers to a fictional story with a spiritual meaning. It is not used at all until the later New Testament letters, but it is used five times in 1 Timothy 1:4, 4:7, 2 Timothy 4:4, Titus 1:14 and 2 Peter 1:16. Nobody is offended by spiritual stories. It is the call to surrender to Jesus that offends.

[8] Paul emphasizes in 4:2 that we must instruct people carefully if we want them to be saved. Gospel preaching is about information impartation as much as it is about fiery exhortation. 4:2 links back to 3:16.

[9] D. A. Carson in his book *The Cross and Christian Ministry* (2004).

their message.[10] I had the privilege of preaching recently at the British Houses of Parliament, which was built to intimidate visitors with its amazing pageantry and history. I knew that the message that God had given me to preach was confrontational and was unlikely to win me many friends, so I had to fight hard to resist the intoxicating influence of my surroundings and of the subtle pressure put on me by the Christians who had invited me to speak. For Paul and Timothy, persecution meant imprisonment and the threat of death. For you and me, it more often means being willing to risk not being invited back.

Paul tells Timothy to preach the Gospel *even when it is not our primary gifting*. Nowhere in the New Testament are we ever told that Timothy was an evangelist, so Paul is not telling him in 4:5 to use his primary gifting.[11] Nor is he telling him to pretend that he is an evangelist. He is telling him to do the work of an evangelist even though he knows he isn't one! Paul tells Timothy to *"discharge all the duties of your ministry,"* because the duty of any Christian minister is to proclaim the Gospel and to help other Christians do the same. Our other gifts must not distract us from keeping the main thing the main thing.

Instead, we must proclaim the Gospel in season and out of season, when people want to listen and when they don't, when people praise us for it and when people persecute us for it, even when we know it is not our primary gifting. Somebody once took a risk to tell you that Jesus is Lord, so Paul charges you very solemnly to take the same risk to tell others: *"I give you this charge: Preach the Word."*

---

[10] The Greek verb *nēphō* is the root of the adjective that Paul uses to say that church leaders must be *sober* in 1 Timothy 3:2, 11 and in Titus 2:2.

[11] Philip is the only person named in the New Testament as an evangelist (Acts 21:8; Ephesians 4:11).

You Only Die Once (4:6–8)

I am already being poured out like a drink offering, and the time for my departure is near.

(2 Timothy 4:6)

Many things are uncertain in life but at least one thing is guaranteed. Unless Jesus returns first, every single one of us will die. We don't get to decide whether or not to die. We only get to decide how we will do so when the moment comes.

Some people die kicking and screaming against death, but not Paul. He is not like Vladimir Lenin or Mao Zedong, whose embalmed bodies are still on public display in Moscow and Beijing as a foolish parody of immortality. Paul refuses to treat his life in the way a miser does his money, as something to be hoarded for as long as possible. He sees it as something to be spent, like the drink offerings that were poured out by ancient priests as liquid sacrifices to their gods.[1] During his first imprisonment in Rome, he told the Philippians that *"If I am being poured out like a drink offering on the sacrifice and service coming from your faith, I am glad and rejoice with all of you."* Now, as he faces certain death, he repeats that he is happy to be *"poured out like a drink offering."*[2] He does not see death as a waste of his life. He sees it as the glorious culmination of a life that has been consumed with God.

Some people die clinging onto their positions of leadership,

---

[1] Libations were not just offered in pagan temples. The Hebrew word for *drink offering* is used 60 times in the Old Testament because it was also part of Jewish Temple worship. See Exodus 29:40–41.

[2] Philippians 2:17 and 2 Timothy 4:6 are the only New Testament uses of the Greek word *spendō*, or *to pour out a libation* or *drink offering*.

unwilling to relinquish them to the next generation. They destroy the achievements of their younger days by acting like the US National Rifle Association bumper sticker: *"I'll give you my gun when you pry it from my cold, dead hands."* The great missionary statesman Oswald Sanders lamented the way that *"Advance is held up for years by well-meaning but aging men who refuse to vacate office and insist on holding the reins in their failing hands."*[3] Whatever God has achieved through your life, you are going to have to hand it over to the next generation. The only question is whether you will do it willingly and full of faith, or whether you will do it in a way that proves it was all about you and not about God.

Paul knows that each of us only gets to die once, so he is determined to do it well. Despite his amazing fruitfulness in his own generation, he is perfectly content to pass on the baton to Timothy because he believes that God has turned the scrap metal of the younger man's life into gold. In 4:6, he refers to his imminent death as his *analusis*, the Greek word that was used for *unloosing* the moorings of a ship so it could set sail. Paul never moored his identity to his leadership position, so he is happy to be unmoored from it by death. He looks to the horizon like a sailor eager to set out to sea.

Some people die full of regret that they have not seen all their dreams fulfilled, but not Paul. He looks back positively on what he has managed to accomplish, instead of mourning the years that have been wasted. He has spent five of the final ten years of his life in a Roman jail, but he is not bitter. He tells Timothy that he is grateful to have completed the charge that he passed on to him in 1 Timothy 6:12: *"I have fought the good fight, I have finished the race, I have kept the faith."* He never had the chance to preach the Gospel in Germania or Britannia, but he is content to accept that those were not part of the race that God had laid out for him. He never saw the fulfilment of his

[3] Oswald Sanders in his book *Spiritual Leadership* (1967).

great longing to see the Jewish nation turn en masse to Jesus as their Messiah, but he trusts that he has played his part in that unfolding drama.[4] He knows that he is one of God's extras and his lines are over. He steps off the stage to allow many others to come on and play their role.

Death is the true test of our faith in God. It demonstrates whether we trust God to fulfil the dreams he has given us without us. Hebrews 11:13 tells us that Abraham, Sarah, Isaac and Jacob *"were still living by faith when they died. They did not receive the things promised; they only saw them and welcomed them from a distance."* The writer commends them for passing their prophetic promises on to their children, trusting God that he would accomplish their dreams without them. People who die with regrets over their dreams die without faith. The two simply cannot share the same heart together. Faith looks at God and believes that, by his grace, the next generation is ready to take over.

The British missionary Henry Martyn dreamed of reaching the whole of Persia, Arabia and India with the Gospel. When he landed in Calcutta in 1806, he was only twenty-five years old and had a whole lifetime ahead of him. Within four years, however, he had contracted tuberculosis and was dying. He wrote down his reaction in his diary: *"If I live to complete the Persian New Testament, my life after that will be of less importance. But whether life or death be mine, may Christ be magnified in me. If he has work for me to do, I cannot die."* Despite his failing health, he managed to finish his translation work and travelled from Calcutta to Persia in order to give a copy to the Shah. On his way back he succumbed to fever and died a lonely death, hundreds of miles away from any of his friends or family. Instead of complaining to God or regretting his unfulfilled dreams, the final entry in his diary simply reads: *"I sat in the orchard, and*

[4] Paul talks about this longing in Romans 9–11. A dream that is not surrendered to God is an idol.

thought with sweet comfort and peace, of my God; in solitude my company, my friend and comforter."[5]

Some people die afraid that God will not receive them into heaven, but not Paul. In 4:8, he mentions Judgment Day for the third time in this short letter because he is convinced that for him it will be a day of great reward.[6] He believes that Jesus is *"the righteous Judge"* who will not forget the sacrifices Paul has made. He is in no doubt that a *"victory crown of righteousness"* awaits him.[7] He ends these verses by telling us that similar victory crowns await us all if we let our lives burn out for Jesus, just as he did.

None of us gets to decide whether we will die. We only get to decide how we will do so. Paul models for us what it means to die without reluctance or resistance or regrets. He shows us how to trust in God's grace for the next generation. If we believe that God turns scrap metal into gold, we can trust him that those we leave behind are truly ready to carry on without us.

[5] Taken from the entries in Henry Martyn's journal on 8th January 1812 and 6th October 1812.

[6] Paul refers to *"that Day"* in 1:12, 18 and 4:8. Far from being fearful about Judgment Day as he ran towards the finishing tape of his life, he became more and more excited that it would vindicate him.

[7] The Greek word *stephanos* in 4:8 was used for the laurel crowns awarded to victorious Olympic athletes.

Never Alone (4:9–22)

Everyone deserted me... But the Lord stood at my side and gave me strength.

(2 Timothy 4:16–17)

In Coleridge's classic poem, *The Rime of the Ancient Mariner*, the tragic hero is driven mad by his intense loneliness and despair. As the sole survivor on an empty ship in an even emptier ocean, he cries out: *"Alone, alone, all, all alone, alone on a wide, wide sea! And never a saint took pity on my soul in agony."*[1] But the ancient mariner never knew loneliness as acutely as the apostle Paul. There is nothing lonelier than being deserted by everyone while you are at the heart of the world's largest city.

The Mamertine Prison in Rome was designed to make its inmates feel lonely. It was located in the north-west corner of the Roman Forum, the busiest shopping centre in the world, so that its prisoners could hear the shouts of a world that had forgotten them. Its entrance was so public that everyone could see who was visiting those condemned to die. As a result, most prisoners were abandoned by their friends for fear that they would be suspected and condemned of wrongdoing themselves. Even when friends came to visit, they were forced to descend into dungeons so putrid and foul that they prayed for the swift execution of their friends.[2] The Roman historian Sallust describes the Mamertine Prison: *"Sunk about twelve feet*

---

[1] Samuel Taylor Coleridge in *The Rime of the Ancient Mariner* (1798).

[2] Paul does not tell us explicitly that he was in the Mamertine Prison. We can deduce this from the fact that he was cold during summer (4:13, 21) and from the fact that this was Rome's death-row prison.

underground... its appearance is disgusting and horrible, due to the filth, darkness and stench."[3]

Sure enough, Paul's friends had abandoned him one by one. He tells us that Demas, the close friend and co-worker who is mentioned in Colossians 4:14 and Philemon 24, deserted him *"because he loved this world."* This comment suggests that Demas fled back home to Thessalonica so that the Roman authorities would not connect him with Paul. Alexander the metalworker was a former teammate who had abandoned his faith and who now took advantage of Paul's imprisonment to undermine his message.[4] These wounds from former friends must have hurt Paul far more than the chains placed on his wrists and ankles by his enemies. Paul experienced far greater loneliness than the ancient mariner ever knew.

Some of Paul's friends had left him for the best of reasons, but this did not make his loneliness any easier to bear. We are able to piece together what happened in the final months of Paul's life from these verses and from the rest of his letters. He had evidently been reunited with Titus at Nicopolis on the western coast of Greece and had sent him along the coast to plant churches in modern-day Croatia.[5] He had then been arrested at Troas and transported to Rome via the Asian port of Miletus and the Greek port of Corinth. He left his Ephesian co-worker Trophimus behind in Miletus because he was ill,[6] and he left Erastus behind in Corinth because he had served as

[3] Sallust writing in about 40 BC in his *Conspiracy of Catiline* (chapter 55). He calls the Mamertine Prison the Tullian Dungeon, naming it after the ancient Roman king who originally constructed it.

[4] Acts 19:33 probably goes alongside 1 Timothy 1:20. Paul lives out his teaching in Romans 12:17–21 and Colossians 3:25 by refusing to rail against Alexander. Instead, he leaves vengeance to the Lord.

[5] See Titus 3:12. Nicopolis was a Greek port which traded with the Balkans via the Adriatic Sea.

[6] See Acts 20:4 and 21:29. This verse reminds us that healing was not automatic in the Early Church and it reminds us God knows best. Because Trophimus was not healed, he was saved from execution in Rome.

a senior civil servant in the city and would therefore be able to help the church in Paul's absence.[7] Once at Rome, he sent Crescens to help the churches in Galatia and Tychicus to relieve Timothy at Ephesus so that he could come and join him.[8] He also sent Onesiphorus back to his family in Ephesus, along with Priscilla and Aquila.

The only people who were left to bring comfort to Paul in his hour of need were his old friend Luke the doctor[9] and four otherwise unknown friends named Eubulus, Pudens, Linus and Claudia.[10] Their visits were probably few and far between, because the Mamertine Prison was not designed with visitors in mind. Roman courts never sentenced criminals to imprisonment – they always fined or exiled or executed them – so Paul's dungeon was simply a short-term holding cell for those whose lives were as good as over. Paul's friends were not informed when he received his first judicial hearing, since he tells us, *"At my first defence, no one came to my support, but everyone deserted me."* He is so cold and lonely that he begs Timothy to come to him quickly, bringing his cloak to keep him warm in the dungeon and his scrolls and parchments to help him pass the long and lonely days.[11]

Coleridge's ancient mariner complains that *"This soul hath been alone on a wide, wide sea: So lonely 'twas, that God himself scarce seemed there to be."* Yet despite his loneliness, Paul tells

---

[7] See Acts 19:22 and Romans 16:23. The post of *aedile* was one of the most prestigious in Roman government.

[8] Tychicus was an Ephesian (Acts 20:4) who delivered Paul's letters to the Ephesians and Colossians several years earlier when Paul was under house arrest in Rome (Ephesians 6:21; Colossians 4:7).

[9] The prologue to a manuscript of Luke's gospel that dates back to 170 AD tells us that, despite the risks he took to comfort Paul, Luke was not arrested and executed. He died peacefully at the age of 84.

[10] We know nothing about these friends except that the first three were men and the last was a woman.

[11] Since nobody would leave on a journey in the ancient world without their *phailonēs*, or *travelling cloak*, Paul was evidently arrested unexpectedly at Troas and had no time to go back to his lodgings.

us that he has never been alone: *"The Lord stood at my side and gave me strength, so that through me the message might be fully proclaimed and all the Gentiles might hear it."*[12] The Emperor Nero might have dragged him back to Rome in chains in order to silence the Christian Gospel, but his plan has backfired. He has simply given Paul a platform to preach Jesus to the people of pagan Rome. Paul forgives his friends for failing him, praying in 4:16 that God might not hold their sin against them, because Jesus gives him all the strength he needs.[13] Christians may feel lonely, but they can never be alone.

Paul is about to make his final defence before a Roman judge. Nero has already spilled so much Christian blood that Paul knows his fate is sealed. Nevertheless, he rejoices that *"I was delivered from the lion's mouth"* and he is confident that *"the Lord will rescue me from every evil attack and will bring me safely to his heavenly kingdom."*[14] Paul was beheaded by the emperor's soldiers shortly after he wrote this letter, but the King he served delivered him from death by receiving him safely into heaven.[15] His final words ring in our ears as we finish these final sentences in Paul's discipleship training school.

They promise us that the Lord will be with us always, just as he was always with Paul. They promise us that God's grace will be sufficient for us and for all those we bring to faith in the Gospel.[16] They promise us that Jesus is a far greater King than

---

[12] The Greek word *endunamoō* in 4:17 means literally that Jesus *empowered* Paul. It comes from the word *dunamis*, a word commonly used in the New Testament to refer to the *power* of the Holy Spirit.

[13] Paul's prayer in 4:16 echoes Jesus' prayer in Luke 23:34 and Stephen's prayer in Acts 7:60.

[14] Paul writes literally that the Lord will save him *into* his heavenly Kingdom. He is not expecting to be saved from death, but through death (4:6–8).

[15] Eusebius tells us this, writing just after 300 AD in his *Church History* (2.25.5). As a Roman citizen, Paul was spared crucifixion or being thrown to wild beasts in the amphitheatre.

[16] The first half of 4:22 prays for Timothy (*you* singular). The second half prays for the Ephesians (*you* plural).

the Emperor Nero and any modern politician. He never fails in his promise to take weak and unimpressive men and women from the Devil's scrapheap and to turn the scrap metal of their lives into precious gold.

Conclusion: God Turns Scrap Metal into Gold

Get Mark and bring him with you, because he is helpful to me in my ministry.

(2 Timothy 4:11)

Paul was dead but his message was not. Nero could kill an apostle but he could not kill the Gospel. It is fitting that the closing words of Paul's final letter speak of the grace of God. This was the message for which he lived and died, and it is the message that he has handed down to us.

Paul has repeatedly told us in these five letters that God turns scrap metal into gold. He demonstrated this by trusting that the Thessalonians were true converts and that God would quickly turn them into true warriors. He took it to a new level by trusting Titus to be able to turn Cretan liars into fruitful church leaders who would reach their entire island with the Gospel. He continued to demonstrate it by trusting Timothy to be mature enough to handle the false teachers who were threatening the church in Ephesus, and by telling him that he was truly ready to carry on the work without him. Now, as a final reminder of the theme of these letters, Paul says something very startling. He tells us that John Mark *"is helpful to me in my ministry."*

Few people had disappointed Paul as much as John Mark. Paul had trusted him by making him part of the team for his first missionary journey in 48 AD. Paul believed the best for him because his mother was a prominent member of the church in Jerusalem and because his cousin was Barnabas. But John Mark had rewarded Paul's trust by deserting the team and rushing back to his mother in Jerusalem. Paul had been so disappointed that he personally threw John Mark back onto the scrapheap. He even had a major falling out with Barnabas for wanting to give his cousin a second chance. Paul believed that God turns scrap metal into gold, but for John Mark he made an exception.[1]

That's why it is so significant that Paul finishes these five letters by requesting in 2 Timothy 4:11: *"Get Mark and bring him with you, because he is helpful to me in my ministry."* As he exits the stage of Church history, Paul reminds us that nobody is beyond the reach of God's grace. No Christian is too weak or too disqualified for God to take them and to turn the scrap metal of their life into gold.

John Mark had connected with Peter when he arrived back in Jerusalem. He refused to let his future be shaped by the failures of his past, and he soon set about making a book out of Peter's sermons on what it was like to travel around with Jesus. He wrote what we now know as Mark's gospel and it spurred Matthew, Luke and John into producing similar gospels of their own.[2] As a result, Paul was forced to revise his opinion about John Mark and to confess that God can turn anyone – absolutely *anyone* – into a fruitful Christian. He commended him and his freshly-written gospel to the Corinthians in 55 AD and he received him back onto his team in around 60 AD.[3] Paul wants us to understand that, whenever we give up on people and consign them to the scrapheap, God does not. He never stops turning scrap metal into gold.

This is of vital importance to your own life as we end this commentary. Far too many Christians write themselves off and

---

[1] See Acts 12:12, 25; 13:5, 13; 15:36–41. *John* was his Hebrew name and *Mark* was his Roman name.

[2] Papias of Hierapolis taught this in c.140 AD, as recorded by Eusebius in *Church History* (3.39.14–15).

[3] Colossians 4:10; Philemon 24. I believe Paul is referring to Mark's newly written gospel in 2 Corinthians 8:18 when he speaks about *"the brother who is praised by all the churches for his service to the gospel."*

settle for a life that is nothing like the one Jesus died and rose again to give them. If you are tempted to think you could never be a true warrior like the Thessalonians or truly fruitful like Titus and the Cretans, think again. If you doubt that you will ever be truly mature and truly ready to follow in Paul's footsteps, you haven't grasped the message of these five letters. Time and time again, they remind us that God does what the ancient alchemists dreamed in vain of doing. He takes base and worthless metal and he turns it into gold.

God raised up Timothy to become part of a new generation of church leaders. Although he was imprisoned (Hebrews 13:23), he survived the Emperor Nero's persecution and helped the Church to spread the Gospel right across the Roman Empire. It didn't matter that the Jews threw him on the scrapheap because he was too Greek. It didn't matter that the Greeks threw him on the scrapheap because he was too Jewish. It didn't matter that older people threw him on the scrapheap because he was too young. He helped lead the charge that saw the Gospel triumph in nation after nation. Shortly after Timothy's death, the Roman governor Pliny complained to the emperor that the Christian faith was everywhere: *"The contagion of this superstition has spread not only to the cities but also to the villages and countryside."*[4] As we end these five letters, God wants you to be like Timothy in your own generation. He wants you to believe that he will turn the scrap metal of your own life into gold too.

God wants you to believe that he can use you as much as an immoral drunkard named Augustine, who was converted and led a Christian revival in the fifth century. He wants you to believe that he can use you as much as a young slave named Patrick who was converted and spent his life preaching the Gospel to his Irish former masters. He wants you to believe that he can use you as much as an obscure German monk named

---

4 Pliny the Younger wrote this in a letter to the Emperor Trajan in c.112 AD. See his *Letters* (10.96). According to Church tradition, Timothy was martyred in Ephesus in c.97 AD.

Martin Luther who rescued the Gospel from false teachers, or as much as a university student named William Tyndale who sacrificed his life to translate the Bible into such simple English that even a common ploughboy could read it and believe. He wants you to believe that he can use you like a shoemaker named William Carey, a shop assistant named D. L. Moody, a pawnbroker's apprentice named William Booth, a plumber named Smith Wigglesworth, an Albanian nun named Mother Teresa or a farm boy named Billy Graham. God has not stopped turning scrap metal into gold. As you finish this commentary, he wants you to believe that he will do it in your life too.

How you respond to this message says more about what you believe about God than it does about what you believe about yourself. God makes true converts and turns them into true warriors who are truly fruitful, truly mature and truly ready to lead his People. As you put down this commentary, therefore, tell God that you believe it. Tell him that you believe he can do in your life what he did in the lives of John Mark and Paul and Timothy and Titus and the Thessalonians. Tell him that you will devote your life to him, just as they did. Tell him that you are ready to serve his purposes in your own generation.

Tell him that you believe he will turn the scrap metal of your own life into purest, purest gold.

STRAIGHT TO THE HEART SERIES

TITLES AVAILABLE: OLD TESTAMENT

ISBN 978 0 85721 001 2

ISBN 978 0 85721 056 2

ISBN 978 0 85721 252 8

ISBN 978 0 85721 428 7

ISBN 978 0 85721 426 3

TITLES AVAILABLE: NEW TESTAMENT

ISBN 978 1 85424 988 3

ISBN 978 0 85721 253 5

ISBN 978 1 85424 989 0

ISBN 978 0 85721 057 9

ISBN 978 0 85721 002 9

ISBN 978 0 85721 546 8

ISBN 978 0 85721 548 2

ISBN 978 1 85424 990 6

GAGGING JESUS
Things Jesus Said We Wish He Hadn't

Phil Moore

"Whether you are a believer or merely a curious sceptic, this book will help you to discover Jesus as he really is."
Sandy Millar – co-founder of The Alpha Course and former vicar of Holy Trinity Brompton

If you ever suspected that Jesus wasn't crucified for acting like a polite vicar in a pair of socks and sandals, then this book is for you. Fasten your seatbelt and get ready to discover the real Jesus in all his outrageous, ungagged glory.

THE BIBLE IN 100 PAGES
Seeing the Big Picture in God's Great Story

Phil Moore

15 short chapters on the Bible's main narratives and the central teachings, showing how the whole relates to Christ.

Written in a punchy and engaging style, this crisp, clear summary provides a handy reference tool enabling the reader to see how the Bible fits together. Despite its many authors and vast time frame, there is a core narrative that runs throughout the text.